THE SOUTHERN CRITICS:
AN ANTHOLOGY

THE SOUTHERN CRITICS

AN ANTHOLOGY

Editor

Glenn C. Arbery

Wilmington, Delaware

The Southern critics : an anthology / edited by Glenn C. Arbery.
    p. cm.
    ISBN 1-935191-80-2
    1. American literature—Southern States—History and criticism—Theory, etc. I. Arbery, Glenn C. (Glenn Cannon), 1951–

PS261.S519 2010
810.9'975—dc22   2009052662

The editor would like to thank the following publishers and copyright holders for permission to reprint their material: "The Heresy of Paraphrase" from *The Well Wrought Urn*, copyright 1947 and renewed 1975 by Cleanth Brooks, reprinted by permission of Houghton Mifflin Harcourt Publishing Company. Davidson, Donald. "Why the Modern South Has a Great Literature" and "Poetry as Tradition," from *Still Rebels, Still Yankees* (Baton Rouge: Louisiana State University Press, 1957); reprinted by permission of Louisiana State University Press. Lytle, Andrew, "The Hind Tit," from Twelve Southerners, *I'll Take My Stand and the Agrarian Tradition* (Baton Rouge: Louisiana State University Press, 1977) reprinted by permission of Louisiana State University Press. "The Catholic Novelist in the Protestant South" from *Mystery and Manners* by Flannery O'Connor, edited by Sally and Robert Fitzgerald. Copyright © 1969 by the Estate of Mary Flannery O'Connor. Reprinted by permission of Farrar, Straus and Giroux, LLC. Ransom, John Crowe, "Introduction: A Statement of Principles" from Twelve Southerners, *I'll Take My Stand and the Agrarian Tradition* (Baton Rouge: Louisiana State University Press, 1977); reprinted by permission of Louisiana State University Press. Ransom, John Crowe, "Criticism as Pure Speculation," from *The Intent of the Critic*. © 1941 Princeton University Press, 1969 renewed PUP Reprinted by permission of Princeton University Press. Ransom, John Crowe. "Forms and Citizens" and "Poetry: A Note in Ontology." Reprinted with the permission of Scribner, a Division of Simon & Schuster, Inc. from *The World's Body*, by John Crowe Ransom. Copyright © 1938 by Charles Scribner's Sons; copyright renewed 1966 by John Crowe Ransom. All rights reserved. Tate, Allen. "What is a Traditional Society," "Three Types of Poetry," "Our Cousin, Mr. Poe," and "The Symbolic Imagination" from *Essays of Four Decades*, © 1999, ISI Books. Reprinted by permission of ISI Books. Every effort was made to obtain permission to reprint all excerpts that appear in this volume.

ISI Books
Intercollegiate Studies Institute
3901 Centerville Road
Wilmington, DE 19807-1938
www.isibooks.org
Manufactured in the United States of America

To Louise S. Cowan

Contents

🖉

The Sacramental South

The image of the South, in all its complexity, is so powerful in us that it is a force which has to be encountered and engaged. The writer must wrestle with it, like Jacob with the angel, until he has extracted a blessing.

—Flannery O'Connor

INTRODUCTION

For several decades now, the Southern critics who exerted a great influence on American letters in the twentieth century have been neglected. When they have been noticed, they have usually been faulted for not having the sensibilities that are now *de rigueur*, or they have been located politically in a strain of American conservatism that Eugene Genovese calls "the Southern tradition." When their literary criticism has been discussed as such, it has often been misrepresented as the work of men unconcerned with biographical or historical contexts. The aim of this anthology of essays is to bring their writing before a new generation of readers who can see them afresh and judge for themselves.

The principal authors in this collection—John Crowe Ransom, Allen Tate, Donald Davidson, and Robert Penn Warren—were members of a group of poets in Nashville who first attracted international attention for their poetry in the early 1920s with their small journal, the *Fugitive*. By 1930, they understood themselves as part of a larger cultural conflict, and they turned their talents to a defense of their region. Like many others before them, the Southern critics saw the destructive force of industrialism on traditional forms of society, but they were unique in seeing it from the perspective of what was happening in the American South in the first decades of the twentieth century. The book to which they contributed, *I'll Take My Stand: The South and the Agrarian Tradition*, articulated a defiant critique of mod-

1

ernization. One hundred and fifty years after the Civil War, with an African-American in the White House, it is easy now to point out the contradictions and ironies of some positions the Southerners espoused eighty years ago. But it is truer and more generous to recognize their courage in countering the major ideologies of their time—a widely fashionable Marxism, an endemic belief that positivistic science would rid the world of its miseries, and a faith that progress would increasingly make the past irrelevant. Against these ideologies they posed what was essentially an act of the imagination: the possibility of a coherent, integrated life in which the economic reality of man was not separated from the concerns of his intellectual and spiritual nature. Was it only rich plantation owners with their slaves who participated in something good in the Southern way of life, or was there a good in the agrarian way of life per se—a good therefore potentially universal? The nature of that good would include such things as attachment to place from generation to generation, the traditions and communities that sprang up around such attachments, attunement to the rhythms of nature and its contingencies, strong bonds of kinship, a sense of the sacred, and indifference to an abstract idea of wealth understood in terms of monetary values. These writers understood place itself, the particular character of a region and its history, as intrinsic to the forms of life, and they understood in poetry a profound analogy to such forms.

In other words, the natural ways of knowing in such a traditional life, which these critics knew might already be irrecoverable, had always been poetry and storytelling, not abstract argument. As Louise S. Cowan writes in *The Southern Critics*, poetry "cannot by itself produce myth, or symbol, or a sound moral and political order. What it can do—when fully understood and articulated—is to restore human feeling."[1] The *restoration* of feeling, of course, implies that something has happened to it, that somehow feeling has been lost. And indeed, one of the central crises of modernity, according to its most profound analysts (such as Dostoevsky and T. S. Eliot), was the division in man that led to what Eliot famously called the "dissociation of sensibility,"

---

1. Louise S. Cowan, *The Southern Tradition* (Irving, Texas: University of Dallas Press, 1972), vii.

a separation of intellect from the life of feeling. Poetry, as Cowan goes on to explain, has the power of redress:

> It can become a discipline for that ordering of the soul that the Greeks called *paideia*. It can open our eyes to the riches of the "world's body" (John Crowe Ransom); can place us in the midst of the "great vital continuum" of human culture (Donald Davidson); can enable us to find "the one lost truth that must be perpetually recovered"—the sense of community among men (Allen Tate). Poetry and criticism are two sides of the same creative act, both of them performed, as any act of love has always been performed, for all of mankind.[2]

Paradoxically, the creative act that these poets and critics performed could be for "all of mankind" because they did not begin by discarding their own particularity, which would be to separate intellectual understanding from place and time.

In his book on the place of the Agrarians in American conservative thought, Paul V. Murphy argues that there are two principal ways to understand what the Agrarians were doing. One is to follow Louis Rubin Jr., Louise S. Cowan, Lewis Simpson, and other scholars who see *I'll Take My Stand* as a great image or myth; the other is to follow its themes "as a tradition of social thought," which is what Murphy himself does.[3] He follows the path of M. E. Bradford, Eugene Genovese, and Richard Weaver, all of whom he discusses in his book, by focusing on the Southerners' enduring importance to conservatism. The selection of essays in this volume follows the path of image or myth. With one or two exceptions, the Southern Critics represented were men and women who served their geniuses most truly not in political arguments, but in the discipline of the imagination. Jacques Maritain would call it the *habitus* of art. Yet all of them share in what Fred Hobson has called "the Southern rage to explain."[4] To some, their explanations about the South appear disingenuous at best. Reviewing

---

2. Cowan, vii.

3. Paul V. Murphy, *The Rebuke of History: The Southern Agrarians and American Conservative Thought* (Chapel Hill, NC: University of North Carolina Press, 2001), 6.

4. Fred Hobson, *Tell About the South: The Southern Rage to Explain* (Baton Rouge: LSU Press, 1998).

several books about the principal Fugitive-Agrarians in 2002, Bruce Bawer wrote, "[M]ost of the contributors to *I'll Take My Stand* romanticized beyond recognition a region that was in fact scandalously overrun with poverty, disease, and illiteracy, and warned of the dire threat of industrialization, with its supposedly dehumanizing effects, even as they wrote about their darker-skinned neighbors as if they were some subhuman species on the level of dogs or horses."[5]

Louis Rubin Jr., anticipating such harsh criticisms, had tried to ward them off in his introduction to Louisiana State University's reissue of *I'll Take My Stand* in 1976, when Georgia's Jimmy Carter had just won the presidential election. Rubin could point to many changes, both in the region itself, which had handled racial integration with admirable civility, and in the nation as a whole, which showed a growing recognition that the heedless economic exploitation of nature could not go on, as the Agrarians had eloquently argued decades before. The Southern tradition worthy of preservation, Rubin argued, "was that of the good society, the community of individuals, the security and definition that come when men cease to wage an unrelenting war with nature and enjoy their leisure and their human dignity."[6]

The region's historical singularity in America—indeed, in the world—gives its story a complexity and power even today. For the literary world, at least, the defeat of the South was no calamity. A great Southern literature began to appear in the 1920s and continued through the following decades: the work of such poets as Allen Tate, Donald Davidson, Robert Penn Warren, and John Crowe Ransom; such novelists and masters of short fiction as William Faulkner, Eudora Welty, Katherine Anne Porter, Ralph Ellison, Andrew Lytle, Flannery O'Connor, Walker Percy, and William Styron. The South as a region with a history of defeat and violation emerges as unforgettably in their work as the Russia of Gogol, Turgenev, Tolstoy, and Dostoevsky, or the Ireland of Joyce, Yeats, and John Millington Synge.

In the 1920s and 1930s, Southerners found themselves in a milieu

5. Bruce Bawer, "Religious Atheist: The Case of Allen Tate," *Hudson Review*, Vol. 55, No. 1 (Spring 2002), 170.
6. Louis D. Rubin, Jr. Introduction. *I'll Take My Stand: The South and the Agrarian Tradition* (Baton Rouge: Louisiana State University Press, 1977), xxi.

that allowed them to engage the past—and what Robert Penn Warren called "the rebuke of history"—from a perspective that now
included such works as *The Waste Land* and *Ulysses*. The resources
of literary modernism also enabled them to counter modernity per
se. They were simultaneously flinging off a falsely romanticized history and trying to overcome a complacent contempt for the whole
region.[7] They bore witness to the erosion of a high tradition that
had existed with the fatal complexity of slavery at its heart. Tate
began delineating what he called the "true myth" of the South in an
essay on Faulkner written shortly after the novelist's death:

> [T]he South, afflicted with the curse of slavery—a curse, like that of
> Original Sin, for which no single person is responsible—had to be
> destroyed, the good along with the evil. The old order had a great
> deal of good, one of the "goods" being a result of the evil; for slav-
> ery itself entailed a certain moral responsibility which the capitalist
> employer in free societies did not need to exercise if it was not his
> will to do so. . . . The classical theocratic culture of New England
> merely declined; its decline could not be focused upon a great action
> in which the entire society was involved. But the Southern culture
> did not decline (so the myth goes); it was destroyed by outsiders in
> a Trojan war. The "older" culture of Troy-South was wiped out by
> the "upstart" culture of Greece-North. *Sunt lacrimae rerum*; and
> the Yankees were therefore to blame for everything—until, as I have
> pointed out, the time of World War I.[8]

The work of the Southern writers was to write from this myth. Quarreling with themselves over what had to be rejected in their own day
gave rise among the Southern writers to the greatest American poetry

---

7. H. L. Mencken later claimed partial credit for the Southern Renaissance because of his
essay, "The Sahara of the Bozart," originally published in 1917. He said of the South, "Down
there a poet is now almost as rare as an oboe-player, a dry-point etcher or a metaphysician.
It is, indeed, amazing to contemplate so vast a vacuity. One thinks of the interstellar spaces,
of the colossal reaches of the now mythical ether." Much later, Mencken wrote that "there
is reason to believe that my attack had something to do with that revival of Southern letters
which followed in the middle 1920s." in H. L. Mencken, *The American Scene: A Reader*. Ed.
Huntington Cairns (New York: Alfred A. Knopf, 1977), 157.
8. Allen Tate, *Memoirs and Opinions, 1926–1975* (Chicago: The Swallow Press, 1975),
151–52.

and fiction of the mid-twentieth century—and in Faulkner's case, perhaps the greatest in the world.[9]

It is no accident, in other words, that Southerners also revolutionized the practice of literary criticism in America. Ransom, Warren, Tate, and Davidson had been members of the group of poets in Nashville who first attracted international attention in the early 1920s with their small journal, the *Fugitive*. Cleanth Brooks Jr. and Robert Penn Warren helped start the *Southern Review* at Louisiana State University and coauthored the textbook *Understanding Poetry*. Ransom left the South to found the *Kenyon Review*, where he exercised wide influence in the heyday of the critical quarterly. Brooks and Warren fostered the practical spread of New Criticism when they published their famous poetry textbook, and at Kenyon, Ransom gave the movement a name—a "myth," as Tate put it—in *The New Criticism* (1941). Tate was instrumental in its success, according to Garrick Davis, who includes two of Tate's essays in his collection *Praising It New*, one of which—"Miss Emily and the Bibliographer"—makes a powerful case for concentrating on the actual poem rather than endlessly surrounding it with scholarship and scorning the critical act. Tate, already a prolific essayist, brought the *Sewanee Review* to prominence in the early 1940s, and Brooks's book on poetry, *The Well-Wrought Urn*, became nearly synonymous with the New Criticism.

But their range was always broader, and their concerns far deeper, than mere aesthetic formalism. In 1972, when most of the Fugitive-Agrarians were still alive, Louise Cowan pointed out that the broad term "New Critics" never fit most of them, at least if it meant "aestheticists who divorced the literary document from any sort of social

---

9. Ironically, or perhaps out of the instinctive self-defense of the artist, Faulkner had almost nothing to do with the Agrarians, regardless of how much they admired his work. Despite his greatness, Faulkner was, in Allen Tate's estimation, an intolerable poseur in person. "Years ago," Tate wrote in 1962, "I had some correspondence with him; his letters were signed 'Faulkner.' I wrote him that English nobility followed this practice and I never heard from him again. I suppose the main source of my annoyance with him was his affectation of not being a writer but a farmer; this would have been pretentious even had he been a farmer" (*Memoirs and Opinions*, 82–83). It seems an odd criticism from a former Agrarian, but Tate's real complaint was that Faulkner's pretensions cut him off from the friendship of writers who were his peers—perhaps not a tragedy for the writer, but a misfortune for Faulkner the man.

context."[10] Granted, their association with the New Criticism is hardly a random one. Nevertheless, it would be a mistake to regard the Southern Critics as practitioners, even as major theorists, merely of a technique of close reading. Tate commented in 1949, "I do not know what the New Criticism is. If the New Criticism differs radically from the best Old Criticism, it differs at its own peril. . . . The new thing may be the New Literature (how new it is I do not know), and a criticism sprang up to show us how to read it."[11] Cowan writes in *The Southern Critics* that "though [these critics] decry a current tendency to reduce poems to data serving other modes of cognition, they have nonetheless testified over the years to the existence of the poem in a total metaphysical and social (political, if you will) order outside itself."[12]

Today, their arguments for the deep traditions of culture speak to our situation as much as to their own, and perhaps with more urgency. When they published *I'll Take My Stand*, the Southern Critics argued—for those who had ears to hear—that the modern idea of the conquest of nature had become a human disaster. Industrialism overwhelmed regional economies; it standardized cultures, led to "world provincialism" (Tate's term for what is today called globalization), and held out false promises of endless growth. At stake was a way of life—never limited to the South—that combined spiritual ends with a gracious recognition of human limits. For generations, despite all its faults, the South retained many aspects of the medieval synthesis of Christianity and classicism whose remnants were largely destroyed in Europe by the French Revolution.

Nostalgia for a simpler (and more integral) life has become acute today, and such movements as the New Agrarianism reflect a growing interest in the practicality of small farms. But few in 1930 understood why these Southerners had raised an objection to what Ransom drily called "our incomparable modernity." Their quarrel was with a positivism that ignored place and particularity. The American public, swayed by stunning advances in the conquest of disease and distance, among other things, trusted technology and the science that informed it far more uncritically early in the twentieth century than it has since the

---

10. Cowan, 8.

11. Allen Tate, *Essays of Four Decades* (Wilmington, DE: ISI Books, 1999), 169.

12. Cowan, 8.

advent of the atomic bomb. Now virtually the whole scientific community, if the *New Yorker* and the *New York Times* are to be believed, has become Cassandra, warning the world of impending disasters that the abuse of technology has made inevitable. Their tone is catching. The Agrarians did not imagine in 1930 the apocalyptic scenarios that now dominate popular culture. Hollywood thrives on the anticipation of a cataclysm, indefinite in its details but sure to come, that will kill many millions of people, and writers with large followings expect a "die-off" after which small communities based on a return to agrarian principles might survive.[13]

Long before such forecasts began to gain credibility, the Southern critics decried any so-called "progress" that robbed life of access to the reality into which a traditional life might still sometimes touch— its slower pace, its homemade things and its customs, its rituals and manners. They tried to keep their hold on a traditional culture being steadily eroded by abstract market values. They started by reading poetry well, and as their interests broadened, they came to see the defense of poetry as a reactionary act almost indistinguishable from a revolutionary one. If their essays oppose the destructive effects of industrialization on traditional society, their opposition stems from the same ground as their understanding of what a poem does.

Against the dominant thinking of their day, these essays argued that poetry, the best use of language—not science and technology, as most of their contemporaries believed—is the way to the wholeness of the world and the good life. Modern scientific thought is not interested in the particular thing, except as a way to arrive at or instantiate concepts. Instead of concepts, Ransom argued for images: "The way to obtain the true *Dinglichkeit* of a formal dinner or a landscape or a beloved person is to approach the object as such, and in humility; then it unfolds a nature which we are unprepared for if we have put our trust in the simple idea which attempted to represent it."[14] Poetry like Shakespeare's has the power to give a "focus of repose" to the "will-driven intellect that constantly shakes the equilibrium of persons

---

13. See James Howard Kunstler, *The Long Emergency: Surviving the Converging Catastrophes of the Twenty-First Century* (New York: Grove Press, 2005).

14. John Crowe Ransom, *The World's Body* (Baton Rouge: Louisiana State University Press, 1968), 124.

and societies with its unremitting imposition of partial formulas," as Allen Tate wrote.[15] Literature is an indispensable mode of knowledge because only contact with the reality of "the world's body" can nourish the whole man and give rise to hale institutions.

Since the 1950s, the influence of the Southern Critics has steadily declined, partly for political reasons, partly because of inevitable shifts in academic fashion. Yet the loss cannot help but strike one as ironic. Students might have been shaped by the moderation and discipline of these critics and their deep respect for poetry as a mode of knowledge. Instead, there was violent recoil from the New Criticism, which most of the Southern Critics never practiced as a method. Stephen Greenblatt, the founder of the New Historicism, might be representative of the reaction in the generation of the '60s. He studied at Yale under William K. Wimsatt, from whom he learned the nature of the "concrete universal." Greenblatt writes that he believed that there was something "mysterious and special" about the poetic work, "but I wasn't sure I wanted to enlist myself for life as a celebrant of the mystery."[16] But what began perhaps as a move to take the poem out of its monstrance quickly became scorn of the place given to literature when more urgent issues of inequality in race, class, and gender remained to be addressed. As soon as the poem no longer stood apart as "privileged"—a word already charged with social implications—the line between literature and propaganda began to disappear. Admiring poetry was like admiring the South: the more one felt for a great work, the more "greatness" became a synonym for oppression and admiration for it an uncritical submission to the mystifications cast over power.

For two generations, those who love great literature have had to hide the silver when the armies of theory drew near. Perhaps a change is coming, and perhaps these essays will help spur it, not only by returning anew to the question of what poetry is in its relation to a

15. Tate, *Essays*, 196.
16. Stephen Greenblatt, *Learning to Curse* (New York: Routledge, 1992), 1.

traditional society, but also by offering a contemporary version of conservatism unfamiliar to those Americans who hear the word "conservative" and think of Rush Limbaugh. What the Southern Critics say has a complex, sometimes markedly polemical intention, and the book as a whole, I very much hope, will demonstrate the range of the Southerners' arguments with each other and with the prevailing culture. On the essential points, they agreed.[17]

This book falls into three parts, corresponding to the three major phases of Southern writing in the critical vein, which took place roughly in the decades between 1930 and 1960. The essays do not follow a strictly chronological pattern from the beginning of the book to the end, though they do so within each section to follow the thread of an ongoing conversation. For example, in the first section, the defense of Southern agrarianism includes two pieces from *I'll Take My Stand*, Ransom's statement of Agrarian principles and Lytle's forcefully vernacular "The Hind Tit"; Allen Tate's 1936 essay on traditional societies; and Davidson's return to a defense of the South in 1950, five years after Ransom publicly repudiated agrarianism in the *Kenyon Review*. That opening section is followed in the second by an extensive look at poetry as the form of knowledge best suited to the whole human being. The selection of essays is representative, and again, the criterion of selection has been the developing conversation. (Some crucial essays, such as Warren's "Pure and Impure Poetry" or Ransom's "Poets Without Laurels" have recently become available in Garrick Davis's *Praising It New* and are therefore not included here.) And finally, in a few writers comes the explicit reconnection in the third section of the Southern vision with Christendom—that is, with the sacramental

---

17. As Eugene Genovese writes,

> Southern conservatism has always traced the evils of the modern world to the ascendancy of the profit motive and material acquisitiveness; to the conversion of small property based on individual labor into accumulated capital manifested as financial assets; to the centralization and bureaucratization of management; to the extreme specialization of labor and the rise of consumerism; to an idolatrous cult of economic growth and scientific and technological progress; and to the destructive exploitation of nature.

Eugene Genovese, *The Southern Tradition: The Achievements and Limitations of an American Conservatism* (Cambridge: Harvard University Press, 1994), 34.

vision of order out of which the South's deepest assumptions implicitly arose.

These men and women concerned themselves with the place of literature as a mode of knowledge in a world that has lost its forms and its bearings, a tragic loss they felt more deeply than others of their time because they found themselves closer to it. These writings serve to revive the sense of "knowledge carried to the heart," in Tate's famous phrase, despite those who have busied themselves with looting the smokehouses and burning the mansions.

Glenn C. Arbery
Assumption College

IN DIXIELAND

The artist as man invariably has the same relation to the society of his time as everybody else has: his misfortune and his great value is his superior awareness of that relation. The "message" of modern art at present is that social man is living, without religion, morality, or art (without the high form that concentrates all three in an organic whole) in a mere system of money references through which neither artist nor plutocrat can perform as an entire person.

—Allen Tate, 1935

In Dixieland
Introduction

"Whatever else may be said of *I'll Take My Stand*," Donald
Davidson wrote in 1943, "it has this unique distinction: it
has been refuted by more people who have never read it—or even seen
a copy—than any other book in American history."[1] Not only was the
book ridiculed by critics, but it was also the cause of hot controversies
even among the Southerners who wrote it. Allen Tate hated the idea
of its being called *I'll Take My Stand*. He, Andrew Lytle, and Robert
Penn Warren all wanted the book to be called "Tracts against Communism." "The title, 'I'll Take My Stand,'" Warren wrote to Tate, "is
the god-damnedest thing I ever heard of; for the love of God block it
if you can. [John Donald] Wade [who suggested the title] must be an
idiot, and certainly all the rest are if they submit to it."[2] Tate reported
Warren's views to Lytle and followed them with an "amen."[3] Tate and
Warren tried to get the title changed even after the book went to press,
and even in admitting defeat to Davidson and John Crowe Ransom,
complained: "Our objection to the phrase from 'Dixie' is not based
on a disrespect for the song as such; we yield to none in our admira-

1. Donald Davidson, "The 'Mystery' of the Agrarians," *Saturday Review of Books* (January
23, 1943): 6–7.
2. Robert Penn Warren, *Selected Letters of Robert Penn Warren*, William Bedford Clark, ed.,
4 vols. (Baton Rouge: Louisiana State University Press, 2000), 185.
3. Andrew Lytle and Allen Tate, *The Lytle-Tate Letters*, Thomas Daniel Young and Elizabeth
Sarcone, eds. (Oxford, MS: University of Mississippi Press, 1987), 40.

tion for it. The objection, rather, is based on the inaccuracy of the phrase, taken either without or in connection with its context."[4] Tate objected so much that he insisted on appending a note to his own essay, "Remarks on the Southern Religion," registering his disagreement with the general title because of its "exclusivity." The title "points to a particular house but omits to say that it was the home of a spirit that may also have lived elsewhere and that this mansion, in short, was incidentally built with hands," he wrote.[5] In other words, the agrarian South being celebrated was far from being unique in history, and he recognized an idol when he saw one.

Still, their disclaimers aside, it was the phrase from "Dixie" that obviously bothered all three men. Their objections are visceral, as Ralph Ellison's in 1950s New York might have been had one of his essays on jazz been included in a volume that a lover of spirituals wanted to call *Dese Bones Gwine Rise Again*. Tate, Lytle, and Warren had all lived in the North, and they cringed at the idea of associating themselves and their growing intellectual reputations with the regional jingoism of the South's iconic song. They did not mind controversy, but they did not want to subject themselves to the mockery of men such as H. L. Mencken, already critical of the South's anti-intellectualism, not to mention their literary friends and acquaintances—in Tate's case, Edmund Wilson, Malcolm Cowley, Ernest Hemingway, and T. S. Eliot. But their objections to the title alarmed Ransom and hurt Davidson, who had already been so provoked by Warren's essay, "The Briar Patch," with its views on blacks in the South, that he had unsuccessfully urged Tate to help him get it removed from the book.

Nevertheless, all twelve of the contentious Southerners in the volume actually agreed on basic ideas. All of them subscribed to "A Statement of Principles," Ransom's introduction to the volume, which articulated a cogent opposition to industrial capitalism from a position not sympathetic to communism. *I'll Take My Stand* appeared in 1930, and caused a great stir with its opposition to the progressivism of the New South. And John Donald Wade was no idiot after all: The title,

4. Warren, *Selected Letters*, 189.
5. Allen Tate, "Remarks on the Southern Religion." From Twelve Southerners, *I'll Take My Stand: The South and the Agrarian Tradition* (Baton Rouge: Louisiana State University Press, 1977), 155–75.

and its distant echoes of Martin Luther, some-how struck just the right note, as "Tracts against Communism" almost certainly would not have done. To those contributors who continued to want real political and economic effects to come from their mani-festo—Donald Davidson stands out in this regard—the book did not match expectations. But in an impatient letter to Davidson in 1942, Tate wrote,

> You evidently believe that agrarianism was a failure; I think it was and is a very great success; but then I never expected it to have any political influence. It is a reaffirmation of the humane tradi-tion, and to reaffirm that is an end in itself. Never fear: we shall be remembered when our snipers are forgotten. I have had a certain disagreement with you from the beginning; you have always seemed to me to hold to a kind of mystical secularism, which has made you impatient and angry at the lack of results. We live in a bad age in which we cannot give our best; but no age is good.[6]

Davidson might have conceded the point, at least in part, when he wrote a piece called "The 'Mystery' of the Southern Agrarians" for the *Saturday Review* early in 1943. Against their critics, he held up once again the central principle: "If people are to lead a really human life, and enjoy the liberties to which rational consideration would entitle them, the pattern of their social, economic, and political being must not be antagonistic to the pattern and end of human life itself, as life. Agrarianism, as a basic pursuit, does not set up this antagonism; but industrialism does."[7] The great success of *I'll Take My Stand* in the long run is surely what Tate said it is, and his words have long since proven prophetic: These Southerners are remembered when their "snipers" are forgotten.

Not that the snipers are gone. One of the great mysteries of recent years is why Louisiana State University Press chose Susan V. Donald-son to write the introduction to the seventy-fifth anniversary reissue

6. Donald Davidson and Allen Tate, *The Literary Correspondence of Donald Davidson and Allen Tate*, John Tyree Fain and Thomas Daniel Young, eds. (Athens, GA: University of Georgia Press, 1974), 328–29.
7. Davidson, "Mystery," 7.

of *I'll Take My Stand* in 2005. Suffice to say that she loves it not. The source of the book's enduring appeal in a bad age, however, owes in no small measure to the work of its central contributors as artists. Without ever having explicitly intended it (as Faulkner *did* intend Yoknapatawpha County, for example), they fashioned a single imaginative world—the South—that largely holds its form from one writer to the next, despite their many different styles and emphases. As Allen Tate has suggested, they were born into a myth. The first essays in this section are discursive attempts to articulate the myth of the South in ways that engage the discourse of economics and (indirectly) of politics. To economists at the time of *I'll Take My Stand*, John Crowe Ransom and Andrew Lytle—the authors of the two selections included in Part I—must have seemed a Depression-era Don Quixote (in dustcoat) and Sancho Panza (in overalls) charging the dark Satanic mills of the New South. Like Anse Bundren in Faulkner's *As I Lay Dying*, Lytle even criticized good roads.

Richard Hofstadter writes that all believers in the "agrarian myth" share the idea that they are victims of a distant conspiracy.[8] Ransom and Lytle could and did underscore that idea with considerable credibility. They could point to Southerners as a people conquered in the Civil War and still suffering from restrictive tariffs that favored northern industry; they could call attention to the ways that the "cash nexus" fostered by northern industrialism had affected traditional life in the South. The question for us eighty years later, long after the specific issues of the time have faded, is why their writings continue to seem so cogent and contemporary. Is it because of the stubborn romantic survival of an "agrarian myth"? Or is it because their insights into what is morally corrosive about modern commercial life have been increasingly borne out? Much of the appeal might lie in the classical insistence of these essays that outside economic forces are not ultimately irresistible, as modern economics might give one to believe. A student of Aristotle's *Nicomachean Ethics*, Ransom recognized that virtue must be made, as art is made, in a different sense than the making or destroying carried out by modern industrialism. As he writes in the introduction to *I'll Take My Stand*, "Proper living is a matter of the

8. Richard Hofstadter, *The Age of Reform: From Bryan to FDR* (New York: Vintage, 1955).

intelligence and the will, does not depend on the local climate or geography, and is capable of a definition which is general and not Southern at all." Allen Tate picks up the point in his essay on traditional societies, stressing the necessity of an integral relation between one's "moral nature" and one's "livelihood." In Tate's view, "Traditional men are never quite making their living, and they never quite cease to make it. Or put otherwise: they are making their living all the time, and affirming their humanity all the time."

Was it possible, however, that far more than the Civil War had already been lost beyond recovery? In 1937, when John Crowe Ransom left Vanderbilt for Kenyon College, his fellow Southerners were distressed, not least because it seemed that Vanderbilt did not know Ransom's worth. But they soon realized, with some hurt, that he had also abandoned agrarianism. Just to make matters clear, he published an explicit renunciation of agrarianism in 1945 that effectively severed his friendship of three decades with Donald Davidson, as Tate later lamented. It is difficult not to read Davidson's essay "Why the Modern South Has a Great Literature" as a reassertion of the principles of the South and a rebuke to Ransom. Taking up earlier hints by Tate, the essay makes a powerful case for the high poetic understanding that emerges in certain conservative cultures at moments of shift from traditional forms toward "enlightenment." Not least among the distinctions of the essay is the analogy between Shakespeare's Warwickshire and Faulkner's Mississippi. Davidson recasts Southern literature in terms of a whole traditional culture becoming aware of its myth and realizing it most fully in the moment of its passing away.

1

INTRODUCTION:
A STATEMENT OF PRINCIPLES

JOHN CROWE RANSOM

In the statement which Ransom wrote and to which all twelve of the contributors to I'll Take My Stand *subscribed, the Agrarians questioned the ideology of progress and exposed the destructive tendencies of industrialism. But—unlike their Marxist contemporaries—they did so without proposing some alteration of human nature to be brought about by changing traditional structures of life. Widely ridiculed by progressives at the time, their principles retain an unmistakable freshness. As Russell Kirk put it in 1990, perhaps that's because we're "further down the road to Avernus."*

From *I'll Take My Stand*

The authors contributing to this book are Southerners, well acquainted with one another and of similar tastes, though not necessarily living in the same physical community, and perhaps only at this moment aware of themselves as a single group of men. By conversation and exchange of letters over a number of years it had developed that they entertained many convictions in common, and it was decided to make a volume in which each one should furnish his views upon a chosen topic. This was the general background. But background and consultation as to the various topics were enough; there was to be no further collaboration. And so no single author is responsible for any view outside his own article. It was through the good fortune of some deeper agreement that the book was expected to achieve its unity. All the articles bear in the same sense upon the book's title-subject: all tend to support a Southern way of life against what may be called the American or prevailing way; and all as much as agree that the best terms in which to represent the distinction are contained in the phrase, Agrarian *versus* Industrial.

But after the book was under way it seemed a pity if the contributors, limited as they were within their special subjects, should stop short of showing how close their agreements really were. On the contrary, it seemed that they ought to go on and make themselves known as a group already consolidated by a set of principles which could be stated with a good deal of particularity. This might prove useful for the sake of future reference, if they should undertake any further joint publication. It was then decided to prepare a general introduction for the book which would state briefly the common convictions of the group. This is the statement. To it every one of the contributors in this book has subscribed.

Nobody now proposes for the South, or for any other community in this country, an independent, political destiny. That idea is thought to have been finished in 1865. But how far shall the South surrender its moral, social, and economic autonomy to the victorious principle of Union? That question remains open. The South is a minority section that has hitherto been jealous of its minority right to live its own kind of life. The South scarcely hopes to determine the other sections, but it does propose to determine itself, within the utmost limits of legal action. Of late, however, there is the melancholy fact that the South itself has wavered a little and shown signs of wanting to join up behind the common or American industrial ideal. It is against that tendency that this book is written. The younger Southerners, who are being converted frequently to the industrial gospel, must come back to the support of the Southern tradition. They must be persuaded to look very critically at the advantages of becoming a "new South" which will be only an undistinguished replica of the usual industrial community.

But there are many other minority communities opposed to industrialism, and wanting a much simpler economy to live by. The communities and private persons sharing the agrarian tastes are to be found widely within the Union. Proper living is a matter of the intelligence and the will, does not depend on the local climate or geography, and is capable of a definition which is general and not Southern at all. Southerners have a filial duty to discharge to their own section. But their cause is precarious and they must seek alliances with sympathetic communities everywhere. The members of the present group would be happy to be counted as members of a national agrarian movement.

Industrialism is the economic organization of the collective American society. It means the decision of society to invest its economic resources in the applied sciences. But the word science has acquired a certain sanctitude. It is out of order to quarrel with science in the abstract, or even with the applied sciences when their applications are made subject to criticism and intelligence. The capitalization of the applied sciences has now become extravagant and uncritical; it has enslaved our human energies to a degree now clearly felt to be burdensome. The apologists of industrialism do not like to meet this charge directly; so they often take refuge in saying that they are devoted simply to science! They are really devoted to the applied sciences and to practical production. Therefore it is necessary to employ a certain skepticism even at the expense of the Cult of Science, and to say, It is an Americanism, which looks innocent and disinterested, but really is not either.

The contribution that science can make to a labor is to render it easier by the help of a tool or a process, and to assure the laborer of his perfect economic security while he is engaged upon it. Then it can be performed with leisure and enjoyment. But the modern laborer has not exactly received this benefit under the industrial regime. His labor is hard, its tempo is fierce, and his employment is insecure. The first principle of a good labor is that it must be effective, but the second principle is that it must be enjoyed. Labor is one of the largest items in the human career; it is a modest demand to ask that it may partake of happiness.

The regular act of applied science is to introduce into labor a labor-saving device or a machine. Whether this is a benefit depends on how far it is advisable to save the labor. The philosophy of applied science is generally quite sure that the saving of labor is a pure gain, and that the more of it the better. This is to assume that labor is an evil, that only the end of labor or the material product is good. On this assumption labor becomes mercenary and servile, and it is no wonder if many forms of modern labor are accepted without resentment though they are evidently brutalizing. The act of labor as one of the happy functions of human life has been in effect abandoned, and is practiced solely for its rewards.

Even the apologists of industrialism have been obliged to admit that some economic evils follow in the wake of the machines. These are such as overproduction, unemployment, and a growing inequality in the distribution of wealth. But the remedies proposed by the apologists are always homeopathic. They expect the evils to disappear when we have bigger and better machines, and more of them. Their remedial programs, therefore, look forward to more industrialism. Sometimes they see the system righting itself spontaneously and without direction: they are Optimists. Sometimes they rely on the benevolence of capital, or the militancy of labor, to bring about a fairer division of the spoils: they are Cooperationists or Socialists. And sometimes they expect to find super-engineers, in the shape of Boards of Control, who will adapt production to consumption and regulate prices and guarantee business against fluctuations: they are Sovietists. With respect to these last it must be insisted that the true Sovietists or Communists—if the term may be used here in the European sense—are the Industrialists themselves. They would have the government set up an economic super-organization, which in turn would become the government. We therefore look upon the Communist menace as a menace indeed, but not as a Red one; because it is simply according to the blind drift of our industrial development to expect in America at last much the same economic system as that imposed by violence upon Russia in 1917.

Turning to consumption, as the grand end which justifies the evil of modern labor, we find that we have been deceived. We have more time in which to consume, and many more products to be consumed. But the tempo of our labors communicates itself to our satisfactions, and these also become brutal and hurried. The constitution of the natural man probably does not permit him to shorten his labor-time and enlarge his consuming-time indefinitely. He has to pay the penalty in satiety and aimlessness. The modern man has lost his sense of vocation.

Religion can hardly expect to flourish in an industrial society. Religion is our submission to the general intention of a nature that is fairly inscrutable; it is the sense of our role as creatures within it. But nature industrialized, transformed into cities and artificial habitations, manufactured into commodities, is no longer nature but a highly simplified picture of nature. We receive the illusion of having power over nature, and lose the sense of nature as something mysterious and contingent. The God of nature under these conditions is merely an amiable expression, a superfluity, and the philosophical understanding ordinarily carried in the religious experience is not there for us to have.

Nor do the arts have a proper life under industrialism, with the general decay of sensibility which attends it. Art depends, in general, like religion, on a right attitude to nature; and in particular on a free and disinterested observation of nature that occurs only in leisure. Neither the creation nor the understanding of works of art is possible in an industrial age except by some local and unlikely suspension of the industrial drive.

The amenities of life also suffer under the curse of a strictly-business or industrial civilization. They consist in such practices as manners, conversation, hospitality, sympathy, family life, romantic love—in the social exchanges which reveal and develop sensibility in human affairs. If religion and the arts are founded on right relations of man-to-nature, these are founded on right relations of man-to-man.

Apologists of industrialism are even inclined to admit that its actual processes may have upon its victims the spiritual effects just described. But they think that all can be made right by extraordinary educational efforts, by all sorts of cultural institutions and endowments. They would cure the poverty of the contemporary spirit by hiring experts to instruct it in spite of itself in the historic culture. But salvation is hardly to be encountered on that road. The trouble with the life-pattern is to be located at its economic base, and we cannot rebuild it by pouring in soft materials from the top. The young men and women in colleges, for example, if they are already placed in a false way of life, cannot make more than an inconsequential acquaintance with the arts and humanities transmitted to them. Or else the understanding of these arts and humanities will but make them the more wretched in their own destitution.

The "Humanists" are too abstract. Humanism, properly speaking, is not an abstract system, but a culture, the whole way in which we live, act, think, and feel. It is a kind of imaginatively balanced life lived out in a definite social tradition. And, in the concrete, we believe that this, the genuine humanism, was rooted in the agrarian life of the older South and of other parts of the country that shared in such a tradition. It was not an abstract moral "check" derived from the classics—it was not soft material poured in from the top. It was deeply founded in the way of life itself—in its tables, chairs, portraits, festivals, laws, marriage customs. We cannot recover our native humanism by adopting some standard of taste that is critical enough to question the contemporary arts but not critical enough to question the social and economic life which is their ground.

The tempo of the industrial life is fast, but that is not the worst of it; it is accelerating. The ideal is not merely some set form of industrialism, with so many stable industries, but industrial progress, or an incessant extension of industrialization. It never proposes a specific goal; it initiates the infinite series. We have not merely capitalized certain industries; we have capitalized the laboratories and inventors, and undertaken to employ all the labor-saving devices that come out of them. But a fresh labor-saving device introduced into an industry does not emancipate the laborers in that industry so much as it evicts them. Applied at the expense of agriculture, for example, the new processes have reduced the part of the population supporting itself upon the soil to a smaller and smaller fraction. Of course no single labor-saving process is fatal; it brings on a period of unemployed labor and unemployed capital, but soon a new industry is devised which will put them both to work again, and a new commodity is thrown upon the market. The laborers were sufficiently embarrassed in the meantime, but, according to the theory, they will eventually be taken care of. It is now the public which is embarrassed; it feels obligated to purchase a commodity for which it had expressed no desire, but it is invited to make its budget equal to the strain. All might yet be well, and stability and comfort might again obtain, but for this: partly because of industrial ambitions and partly because the repressed creative impulse must break out somewhere, there will be a stream of further labor-saving devices in all industries, and the cycle will have to be repeated over and over. The result is an increasing disadjustment and instability.

It is an inevitable consequence of industrial progress that production greatly outruns the rate of natural consumption. To overcome the disparity, the producers, disguised as the pure idealists of progress, must coerce and wheedle the public into being loyal and steady consumers in order to keep the machines running. So the rise of modern advertising—along with its twin, personal salesmanship—is the most significant development of our industrialism. Advertising means to persuade the consumers to want exactly what the applied sciences are able to furnish them. It consults the happiness of the consumer no more than it consulted the happiness of the laborer. It is the great effort of a false economy of life to approve itself. But its task grows more difficult every day.

It is strange, of course, that a majority of men anywhere could ever as with one mind become enamored of industrialism: a system that has so little regard for individual wants. There is evidently a kind of thinking that rejoices in setting up a social objective which has no relation to the individual. Men are prepared to sacrifice their private dignity and happiness to an abstract social ideal, and without asking whether the social ideal produces the welfare of any individual man whatsoever. But this is absurd. The responsibility of men is for their own welfare and that of their neighbors; not for the hypothetical welfare of some fabulous creature called society.

Opposed to the industrial society is the agrarian, which does not stand in particular need of definition. An agrarian society is hardly one that has no use at all for industries, for professional vocations, for scholars and artists, and for the life of cities. Technically, perhaps, an agrarian society is one in which agriculture is the leading vocation, whether for wealth, for pleasure, or for prestige—a form of labor that is pursued with intelligence and leisure, and that becomes the model to which the other forms approach as well as they may. But an agrarian regime will be secured readily enough where the superfluous industries are not allowed to rise against it. The theory of agrarianism is that the culture of the soil is the best and most sensitive of vocations, and that therefore it should have the economic preference and enlist the maximum number of workers.

These principles do not intend to be very specific in proposing any practical measures. How may the little agrarian community resist the Chamber of Commerce of its county seat, which is always trying to import some foreign industry that cannot be assimilated to the life-pattern of the community? Just what must the Southern leaders do to defend the traditional Southern life? How may the Southern and the Western agrarians unite for effective action? Should the agrarian forces try to capture the Democratic party, which historically is so closely affiliated with the defense of individualism, the small community, the state, the South ? Or must the agrarians—even the Southern ones—abandon the Democratic party to its fate and try a new one? What legislation could most profitably be championed by the powerful agrarians in the Senate of the United States? What anti-industrial measures might promise to stop the advances of industrialism, or even undo some of them, with the least harm to those concerned? What policy should be pursued by the educators who have a tradition at heart? These and many other questions are of the greatest importance, but they cannot be answered here.

For, in conclusion, this much is clear: If a community or a section, or race, or an age, is groaning under industrialism, and well aware that it is an evil dispensation, it must find the way to throw it off. To think that this cannot be done is pusillanimous. And if the whole community, section, race, or age thinks it cannot be done, then it has simply lost its political genius and doomed itself to impotence.

2

THE HIND TIT

ANDREW LYTLE

*Andrew Lytle's memorable description of a self-sufficient farm imag-
ines a life that precedes even the "city of utmost necessity" in Plato's
Republic. When the farm enters the money economy, the falling off
might be put beside Plato's account in Book VIII of degeneration
from the best regime. Lytle is giving his readers a paradigm, a fable.
He reveals both the slowly developed, organically coherent good life
and the fact that people will jettison it, if not for the couches and rel-
ishes of the Republic, then for radios and movies in town. As for the
teasing title, Lytle's metaphor comes out of the experience of the farm
life he describes—the runt of the litter struggling to get some nourishment when all the best places have already been taken. It describes
what the Southerner will get from the great sow of consumer culture
once he leaves behind "his natural economy and his inherited life."*

When we remember the high expectations held universally by the
founders of the American Union for a more perfect order of
society, and then consider the state of life in this country today, it is
bound to appear to reasonable people that somehow the experiment
has proved abortive, and that in some way a great commonwealth has
gone wrong.

There are those among us who defend and rejoice in this miscarriage, saying we are more prosperous. They tell us—and we are ready to believe—that collectively we are possessed of enormous wealth and that this in itself is compensation for whatever has been lost. But when we, as individuals, set out to find and enjoy this wealth, it becomes elusive and its goods escape us. We then reflect, no matter how great it may be collectively, if individually we do not profit by it, we have lost by the exchange. This becomes more apparent with the realization that, as its benefits elude us, the labors and pains of its acquisition multiply.

To be caught unwittingly in this unhappy condition is calamitous; but to make obeisance before it, after learning how barren is its rule, is to be eunuched. For those who are Southern farmers this is a particularly bitter fact to consider. We have been taught by Jefferson's struggles with Hamilton, by Calhoun's with Webster, and in the woods at Shiloh or along the ravines of Fort Donelson where the long hunter's rifle spoke defiance to the more accelerated Springfields, that the triumph of industry, commerce, trade, brings misfortune to those who live on the land.

Since 1865 an agrarian Union has been changed into an industrial empire bent on conquest of the earth's goods and ports to sell them in. This means warfare, a struggle over markets, leading, in the end, to actual military conflict between nations. But, in the meantime, the terrific effort to manufacture ammunition—that is, wealth—so that imperialism may prevail, has brought upon the social body a more deadly conflict, one which promises to deprive it, not of life, but of living; take the concept of liberty from the political consciousness; and turn the pursuit of happiness into a nervous running-around which is without the logic, even, of a dog chasing its tail.

This conflict is between the unnatural progeny of inventive genius and men. It is a war to the death between technology and the ordinary human functions of living. The rights to these human functions are the natural rights of man, and they are threatened now, in the twentieth, not in the eighteenth, century for the first time. Unless man asserts and defends them he is doomed, to use a chemical analogy, to hop about like sodium on water, burning up in his own energy.

But since a power machine is ultimately dependent upon human control, the issue presents an awful spectacle: men, run mad by their inventions, supplanting themselves with inanimate objects. That is, follow the matter to its conclusion, a moral and spiritual suicide, foretelling an actual physical destruction.

The escape is not in socialism, in communism, or in sovietism—the three final stages industrialism must take. These change merely the manner and speed of the suicide; they do not alter its nature. Indeed, even now the Republican government and the Russian Soviet Council pursue identical policies toward the farmer. The Council arbitrarily raises the value of its currency and forces the peasant to take it in exchange for his wheat. This is a slightly legalized confiscation, and the peasants have met it by refusing to grow surplus wheat. The Republicans take a more indirect way—they raise the tariff. Of the two policies, that of the Russian Soviet is the more admirable. It frankly proposes to make of its farmers a race of helots.

We have been slobbered upon by those who have chewed the mad root's poison, a poison which penetrates to the spirit and rots the soul. And the time is not far off when the citizens of this one-time Republic will be crying, "What can I do to be saved?" If the farmers have been completely enslaved by that time, the echo to their question will be their only answer. If they have managed to remain independent, the answer lies in a return to a society where agriculture is practiced by most of the people. It is in fact impossible for any culture to be sound and healthy without a proper respect and proper regard for the soil, no matter how many urban dwellers think that their victuals come from groceries and delicatessens and their milk from tin cans. This ignorance does not release them from a final dependence upon the farm and that most incorrigible of beings, the farmer. Nor is this ignorance made any more secure by Mr. Haldane's prognostication that the farm's ancient life will become extinct as soon as science rubs the bottle a few more times. The trouble is that already science has rubbed the bottle too many times. Forgetting in its hasty greed to put the stopper in, it has let the genius out.

But the resumption by the farmer of his place of power in the present order is considered remote. Just what political pressure he will be able to bring upon the Republicans to better his lot is, at the moment, unknown. Accepting the most pessimistic view, the continued supremacy of this imperialism and his continued dependency upon it, his natural enemy, the wealth-warrior who stands upon the bridge of high tariff and demands tribute, he is left to decide upon immediate private tactics. How is the man who is still living on the land, and who lives there because he prefers its life to any other, going to defend himself against this industrial imperialism and its destructive technology ?

One common answer is heard on every hand: industrialize the farm; be progressive; drop old-fashioned ways and adopt scientific methods. These slogans are powerfully persuasive and should be, but are not, regarded with the most deliberate circumspection, for under the guise of strengthening the farmer in his way of life they are advising him to abandon it and become absorbed. Such admonition coming from the quarters of the enemy is encouraging to the landowner in one sense only: it assures him he has something left to steal. Through its philosophy of Progress it is committing a mortal sin to persuade farmers that they can grow wealthy by adopting its methods. A farm is not a place to grow wealthy; it is a place to grow corn.

It is telling him that he can bring the city way of living to the country and that he will like it when it gets there. His sons and daughters, thoroughly indoctrinated with these ideas at state normals, return and further upset his equilibrium by demanding the things they grew to like in town. They urge him to make the experiment, with threats of an early departure from his hearth and board. Under such pressure it is no wonder that the distraught countryman, pulled at from all sides, contemplates a thing he by nature is loath to attempt . . . experimentation.

If it were an idle experiment, there would be no harm in such an indulgence; but it is not idle. It has a price and, like everything else in the industrial world, the price is too dear. In exchange for the bric-à-brac culture of progress he stands to lose his land, and losing that, his independence, for the vagaries of its idealism assume concrete form in urging him to over-produce his money crop, mortgage his land, and send his daughters to town to clerk in ten-cent stores, that he may buy the products of the Power Age and keep its machines turning. That is the nigger in the woodpile . . . keep the machines turning!

How impossible it is for him to keep pace with the procession is seen in the mounting mortgages taken by banks, insurance companies, and the hydra-headed loan companies which have sprung up since the World War. In spite of these acknowledged facts, the Bureau of Agriculture, the State Experimental Stations, farm papers, and county agents, all with the best possible intentions, advise him to get a little more progressive, that is, a little more productive. After advising this, they turn around and tell him he must curtail his planting. They also tell him that he (meaning his family) deserves motor-cars, picture shows, chain-store dresses for the women-folks, and all the articles in Sears-Roebuck catalogues. By telling him how great is his deserving, they prepare the way to deprive him of his natural deserts.

He must close his ears to these heresies that accumulate about his head, for they roll from the tongues of false prophets. He should know that prophets do not come from cities, promising riches and store clothes. They have always come from the wilderness, stinking of goats and running with lice and telling of the different sort of treasure, one a corporation head would not understand. Until such a one comes, it is best for him to keep to his ancient ways and leave the homilies of the tumble-bellied prophets to the city man who understands such things, for on the day when he attempts to follow the whitewash metaphysics of Progress, he will be worse off than the craftsman got to be when he threw his tools away. If that day ever comes, and there are strong indications that it may, the world will see a new Lazarus, but one so miserable that no dog will lend sympathy enough to lick the fly dung from his sores. Lazarus at least groveled at the foot of the rich man's table, but the new Lazarus will not have this distinction. One cannot sit at the board of an insurance company, nor hear the workings of its gargantuan appetite whetting itself on its own digestive processes.

He must close his ears because an agrarian culture and industrial warfare are sustained through the workings of two different economies. Nothing less than confusion can follow the attempt of one economy to react to the laws of another. The progressive-farmer ideal is a contradiction in terms. A stalk of cotton grows. It does not progress. In 50,000 years it may evolve into something different, but for us and our four score and ten, it grows.

This error is also seen in the works of those highly respectable historians who, pointing to the census returns and the mounting wealth of the industrial states during the early decades of the nineteenth century, declared that the Southern culture was then already doomed, and that the Civil War merely hastened its demise. This view holds that industrialism is manifest destiny, but it would have supplanted agriculture in the South even if the Confederacy had maintained its withdrawal from the already disrupted Union. It strangely argues that the victorious planter and the small yeoman farmer would have abandoned what they had waged a desperate war to preserve from others; and what, in spite of defeat, survived in its essential features until the second decade of the twentieth century; and what still possesses sufficient strength to make a desperate fight for its inherited way of life.

If an abundance of those things which a people considers the goods and the riches of the earth defines wealth, then it follows that that particular culture is wealthy in proportion to the production and distribution of just those things and no others; and it does not depend upon what another people may consider the goods and riches, no matter how greatly those things have multiplied for them, nor how many individuals they have to possess them. What industrialism counts as the goods and riches of the earth the agrarian South does not, nor ever did. It is true that the planting aristocracy bought freely from England and the North. It is also true that the Cotton Kingdom was hastened into being by the invention of the cotton gin, an apparatus of the Machine Age; but because of this, it did not assume the habits and conduct of a factory town. Stocks and bonds and cities did not constitute wealth to the planter. Broad acres and increasing slaves, all tangible evidence of possession, were the great desiderata of his labors; and regardless of their price fluctuation on the world market, if they were paid for, their value remained constant in the planting states.

But the farming South, the yeoman South, that great body of free men, had hardly anything to do with the capitalists and their merchandise. In the upland country, the pine barrens, in the hills and mountains, and interspersed between the large plantations or lying on their fringe, and in the bad-road districts wherever they lay, communication with the main arteries of trade was so difficult that the plain people were forced into a state of self-sufficiency. And those who could reach the main turnpikes or the rivers and those who owned a few slaves in the planting districts, when they sold their cotton in New Orleans, were even less dependent than the planters, for they kept their looms going and fed their stock home-grown feed. Even the planters were beginning to say in the middle fifties that horses do not fatten on bought corn.

By 1860 these broad, as yet somewhat flexible, outlines marked the structural formation of the Confederacy: belonging to the planting body, in round numbers, 3,000,000; slaves and free negroes, 4,000,000; townsmen, 1,000,000; plain people, including those who owned a few slaves, 4,000,000. By 1830 the lower South, leavened by Tennessee and Kentucky, became dominant in the agrarian stronghold below the line; and the lower South at this time was largely the plain people. From them the planter class was made.

After 1860 there would have been no fundamental economic rivalry between the yeoman farmer and the great landowner. The struggle before that time had been to determine who would rule, and the planters who emerged had done so because they were the more vigorous, the more intelligent, the more fortunate—the strong men of their particular culture. Jackson, demanding for the talented obscure the chance to grow rich and distinguished, expressed their demands politically. Jacksonian Democracy was, therefore, no Democracy; and although it claimed to be sired by Jefferson, his self-sufficient republic of freeholders did not contemplate any such leadership. "Down here, men like me and Gineral Jackson and Colonel Davy Crockett always demands our rights; and if we don't git 'em, somebody else is mighty liable to git Hell" is not the assertion of one contented to live easily and at peace on a fifty-acre steading. Cotton had changed the connotation of the demand.

In a society which recognizes the supremacy of nature and man's frailty each individual enjoys or subdues nature according to his capacity and desires, and those who accumulate great estates deserve whatever reward attends them, for they have striven mightily. This is the common way a ruling class establishes itself. The South, and particularly the plain people, has never recovered from the embarrassment it suffered when this class was destroyed before the cultural lines became hard and fast.

The Whig party was evidence of the painful readjustment between the static East and the dynamic West, and it pointed to the metamorphosis of the two into Calhoun's Feudal Aristocracy. It is significant that when the Western states were changing their constitutions to deliver universal suffrage into the hands of the farmer and artisan, Dew from Virginia and Harper from South Carolina were publishing tracts defending the strictest sort of society.

The force of Jackson's character introduced tragedy into the drama. His fight with Calhoun divided the house with an internecine struggle and so confused the agrarian states that they were unable to stand united before the irrepressible conflict. Calhoun, a philosopher as well as a logician, could see beyond his times the conclusion to the premises; but Jackson and Clay, men of action, one a soldier, the other a politician, could only act the parts their periods gave them. It was impossible for them, living pleasantly on their country estates, to foresee the impending dominion of technology.

The story of these strong men and their negro slaves has been told and mistold; but the farming South has had few to tell of its virtues, and it has left fewer written records to tell its story. Oblivion has almost covered it in a generation. The planters whom it looked to in the days of its strength to defend their common life have busied themselves after the migration to the towns with a defense of their own part in the story, ignoring or referring to the yeomanry as the pore white trash.

Travelers have remembered the bedbugs, greasy food, rough cribs found in some places, and all those disagreeable elements which in the midst of the fatigues and worries of travel over-emphasize the virtue of clean sheets and native food. Fresh linen has too often been mistaken for culture by people who scrub all the oil from their skins in the articles of the plumbing industry.

The most unique example of a garbled interpretation is found in the journals of one Olmstead, who traveled through the South in the early fifties. In the hill country he called to a young ploughman to inquire the way, and when not one, but several, ambled over and seemed willing to talk as long as he cared to linger, his time-ordered attitude was shocked at their lazy indifference to their work. Others who were mixed in their geography, who thought, for example, that New York lay to the south of Tennessee, amazed him. Although he could never know it, it was the tragedy of these people that they ever learned where New York lay, for such knowledge has taken them from a place where they knew little geography but knew it well, to places where they see much and know nothing.

This will be the most difficult task industrialism has undertaken, and on this rock its effort to urbanize the farm will probably split—to convince the farmer that it is time, not space, which has value. It will be difficult because the farmer knows that he cannot control time, whereas he can wrestle with space, or at least with that particular part which is his orbit. He can stop, set, chaw, and talk, for, unable to subdue nature, it is no great matter whether he gets a little more or little less that year from her limitless store. He has the choice of pleasant conversation, the excitement of hunting, fishing, hearing the hounds run, or of the possibility of accumulating greater spoils. Olmstead's young ploughmen did well to stop and talk with the "quair strangy"; ask "whare he's bin"; "whare he's aimin' to go"; and "air he bin to see his kin in Texas?" for by so doing they exchanged an uncertain physical satisfaction for a certain mental pleasure.

But those records which have been left, some few in writing, some through the patronage of journalists like Olmstead, through folk-games, songs, and ballads, particularly in the bad-road districts, and scattered more generally than is supposed upon the farms of the South, make it clear just how Southern life, and that part of it which was the plain people, was crystallizing when the war came.

One of these records comes from C. C. Henderson's *Story of Murfreesboro*. Martin Van Buren, when he was Chief Executive, made a speech from the court-house balcony. Everybody who could travel was there, for no Southern man ever missed, or misunderstood, a speech. Among those who had come to town that day was one Abner L., a squatter living on a large farm near the town. The landowner had promised Abner that he would introduce him to the President. After the speaking the planter moved through the crowd to keep his promise. This gentleman understood thoroughly the honor he was about to receive. In a becoming, if somewhat nervous, manner he received the hand of the New-Yorker, squeezed it damply, then turned and presented Abner. Unlike the planter, Abner stepped up with perfect composure, pressed His Excellency's hand deliberately down, and said in a calm, even tone:

"Mr. Buren, the next time you come down here I want you to come out my way and ra'r around some with us boys."

This man worked a little truck patch on somebody else's land; hunted at night for pelts; fished in Stone's River; and ra'red around when he was a mind to. He possessed nature as little as possible, but he enjoyed it a great deal, so well that he felt the President might be satisfied with what hospitality he had to offer. Whenever a society has at its base people so contented with their lot, it may not be perfect ideally, but it is the best politicians will ever effect and maintain.

When Confederate defeat destroyed the planter as a class, it upset the balance of the whole. The yeomanry, who had had little to do with the money crop before, moved down from the hills and bought for a song the planter's dismembered plantations. As this was done, it only prepared the way to undermine the Southern culture, for the destruction of the rulers did not mean its destruction. The plain man brought from his isolation his ways and habits, and the impoverished state which had fallen upon the country after war and reconstruction forced him to rely upon home manufactures. In the great exodus to Texas in 1873 all the emigrants wore homespun. It looked as if conditions were preparing to produce another set of rulers.

Unfortunately, the plain man did a thing which prevented this. When he took over the planter's land, he took over the worst of his habits, the furnishing system. Whereas with the planter it had been the factor of the great ports, with him it became the merchant of the county towns, the villages, and even the crossroads. The high price of cotton was responsible for this. When the prices broke in 1870, the small farmer was faced with a new experience: his reliance upon a money economy and make him responsible to its laws. So long as they paid him well for his labors, it was profitable; but he learned that there was no assurance that this would continue. Something he could not understand was beginning to control his life. He could only hope for better days, and in the meantime mortgage next year's crop. Because it was the money crop, the merchant forced him to grow only cotton and buy the feed for his stock. This caused over-production, a drop in prices, more mortgages, and still greater over-production.

Such conditions broke many, and for the first time in the Cotton Kingdom, white tenantry developed. This was a definite social loss. With an entirely different race to serve the rich men as in slavery, the small white man could feel no very strong social inequality, and those who lived in isolation none at all. Now, economic dependence brought about social lines drawn, not upon a comparative use and enjoyment of nature, but upon a possession of cash.

This turned the plain man, for he had lost his independence, into something he had never been before, the pore white, the hookwormed illiterate. Formerly, no matter how wealthy or how powerful a neighbor might grow, or how many slaves he might own, the small farmer who lived next to his plantation was still a free man so long as he paid his taxes and provided his family with food, clothes, and shelter. He was economically and politically independent.

The uses of fertilizers, making for a quicker maturity, spread cotton culture northward and into Texas. Railroads ended the isolation of those places which bad roads had cut off from the markets, and the plain people who remained at home were brought into the money economy. The Cotton Kingdom before 1860 was supported by black backs. It now changed its nature. The small white farmer, from raising 12 percent gradually worked and picked the greatest part of the crop. This spread of cotton meant the spread of a false set of economics.

He had been misled, and he was to wander farther afield under false doctrine. His former leaders, the generals and colonels and lawyer-statesmen, moved into the towns and cities and entered the industrial world. This move deprived them of any right to lead or rule the farmer, for no longer would his problems and theirs be the same. Nevertheless, for a long time after the war, from habit and affection, and because of the menace of the free negro, they still followed the counsel of these men. The time came when they realized their betrayal, for railroad and corporation presidents as they spoke of chivalry and pure womanhood did not put sow-belly in the pantry, nor meal in the barrel. This protest expressed itself politically through Private John Allen from Mississippi, Tom Watson in Georgia, and Bob Taylor in Tennessee, and farmer candidates everywhere.

But he had listened too long. He himself began to think more and more of money, and his inability to take much of it from the industrial scheme produced a feeling of moral defeat. His ambitious sons, instead of becoming the leaders of the farm communities, went North and West and to the growing Southern cities to make their fortunes, and as they left he did not protest. Those who remained, caught by the furnishing system, could not rise to lead. They were bound hand and foot—so firmly bound that the high price of cotton during the World War led them deeper into the money economy instead of freeing them.

As a result, up to the entrance of the United States into this war the farmer was trying unconsciously to live by two antithetical economies. In spite of his dual existence he managed to secure many good things from the soil, for his life was still largely ordered after his agrarian inheritance. The next, the fatal step, is to become a progressive farmer, for then he must reverse this dualism and think first of a money economy, last of a farmer's life. The new emphasis puts him in a critical condition; the precedence of the money economy means the end of farming as a way of life.

II

On a certain Saturday, a group of countrymen squatted and lay about the Rutherford County court-house yard, three-quarters of a century after Abner L. extended his invitation to Van Buren. One remarked to the others that "as soon as a farmer begins to keep books, he'll go broke shore as hell."

Let us take him as a type and consider the life of his household before and after he made an effort to industrialize it. Let us set his holdings at two hundred acres, more or less—a hundred in cultivation, sixty in woods and pasture, and forty in waste land, too rocky for cultivation but offering some pasturage. A smaller acreage would scarcely justify a tractor. And that is a very grave consideration for a man who lives on thirty or fifty acres. If the pressure becomes too great, he will be forced to sell out and leave, or remain as a tenant or hand on the large farm made up of units such as his. This example is taken, of course, with the knowledge that the problem on any two hundred acres is never the same: the richness of the soil, its qualities, the neighborhood, the distance from market, the climate, water, and a thousand such things make the life on every farm distinctly individual.

The house is a dog-run with an ell running to the rear, the kitchen and dining-room being in the ell, if the family does not eat in the kitchen; and the sleeping-rooms in the main part of the house. The dog-run is a two- or four-crib construction with an open space between, the whole covered by one roof. The run or trot gets its name from the hounds passing through from the front to the rear. It may or may not have a floor, according to the taste or pride of the occupant. This farmer will have it floored, because his grandfather, as he prospered, closed in the dog-run with doors, making it into a hall; added porches front and rear, weather-boarded the logs, and ceiled the two half-story rooms. His grandfather belonged to that large number of sturdy freemen who owned from three to five hundred acres of land and perhaps a slave or two in better days. But owning a few slaves did not make him a planter. He and his sons worked alongside them in the fields. Of farmers so situated in the South there was one to every twelve and one-tenth of free population.

There is a brick walk running from the porch to a horse block, lined on either side with hardy buttercups. From the block a road marked off by tall cedars goes out to the pike gate, two hundred yards away. The yard is kept grazed down by sheep, and occasionally the stock is turned in, when the pastures are burned in a drought. The house needs paint, but the trees are whitewashed around the base of the trunks to keep insects off and to give a neat appearance to the yard.

Over the front doorway is a horseshoe, turned the right way to bring luck to all who may pass beneath its lintel. The hall is almost bare, but scrubbed clean. At the back is a small stairway leading to the half-story. This is where the boys sleep, in their bachelorhood definitely removed from the girls. To the left is the principal room of the house. The farmer and his wife sleep there in a four-poster, badly in need of doing over; and here the youngest chillurn sleep on pallets made up on the floor.

The large rock fireplace is the center of the room. The home-made hickory chairs are gathered in a semicircle about it, while on the extreme left of the arc is a rough hand-made rocker with a sheep-skin bottom, shiny from use, and its arms smooth from the polishing of flesh, reserved always for "mammy," the tough leather-skinned mother of the farmer. Here she sets and rocks and smokes near enough for the draught to draw the smoke up the chimney. On the mantel, at one end, is dry leaf tobacco, filling the room with its sharp, pungent odor. A pair of dog-irons rests on the hearth, pushed against the back log and holding up the ends of the sticks which have burnt in two and fallen among the hot ashes. The fire is kept burning through the month of May to insure good crops, no matter how mild and warm its days turn out to be. The top rock slab is smoked in the middle where for generations the wind has blown suddenly down the chimney, driving heavy gusts to flatten against the mantel and spread out into the room. A quilting-frame is drawn into the ceiling, ready to be lowered into the laps of the womenfolks when the occasion demands, although it is gradually falling into disuse. Beneath it, spreading out from the center of the floor, a rag rug covers the wide pine boards which, in turn, cover the rough-hewn puncheons that sufficed during the pioneer days. From this room, or rather, from the hearth of this room, the life of the dwelling moves.

If this is the heart of the house, the kitchen is its busiest part. The old, open fireplace has been closed in since the war, and an iron range has taken its place. This much machinery has added to the order of the establishment's life without disrupting it. Here all the food is prepared, and the canning and preserving necessary to sustain the family during the winter is done.

The cooking is a complicated art, requiring mastery over all its parts to burden the table with victuals that can be relished. Each meal is a victory over nature, a suitable union between the general principles of cookery and the accident of preparation. The fire must be kept at the right temperature (without a thermometer), or the bread won't rise; too much lard, or too little, will spoil the pastry; and since the test of all cooking is the seasoning, which can never be reduced to exact rules but is partly intuitive, too many pinches of salt may ruin the dish. The farmer's wife learns to satisfy the tastes of her particular family, but she can never set two meals on the table exactly alike. She never, overcomes nature; her victories are partial, but very satisfying, for she knows her limitations.

The kitchen leads out to back it ell-shaped porch. Upon its banister, or, if there is no banister, upon the wash-table, a bucket of water and its gourd, a tin pan, soap, and towel wait to serve the morning toilet. The towel will hang on a folding rack fixed to the wall. This rack may also serve long strings of red peppers drying in the air. A bell-post rises up near the kitchen to ring the boys in from the fields at dinner-time. In the back, behind the kitchen, is the smokehouse and several outhouses. Iron kettles for washing tilt to one side in the ashes of an old fire, some distance away. An ash-hopper made from a hollow log, no longer in use, lies up against the buggy-house, having gone the way of the kitchen fireplace. The lye for soap- and hominy-making is now bought in town.

Convenient to the kitchen is the woodpile, made of different-sized sticks, some for the stove, split and cut to the right length, and some for the fireplaces, back logs and front sticks. The wood has been cut in the early fall, just as the sap begins to go down, not too early and not too late, but just at the right time, so that the outer surface will be dry and will catch quick, while the inside remains sappy and hard, burning slowly, it takes a great deal of study and intelligence to keep the fires going steadily.

Before dawn the roosters and the farmer feel the tremendous silence, chilling and filling the gap between night and day. He gets up, makes the fires, and rings the rising bell. He could arouse the family with his voice, but it has been the custom to ring the bell; so every morning it sounds out, taking its place among the other bells in the neighborhood. Each, according to his nature, gets up and prepares for the day: the wife has long been in the kitchen when the boys go to the barn; some of the girls help her, while the farmer plans the morning work and calls out directions.

One or two of the girls set out with their milk-pails to the barn, where the cows have been kept overnight. There is a very elaborate process to go through within milking. First, the cow must be fed to occupy her attention; next, the milker kneels or sits on a bucket and washes the bag which will have gotten manure on it during the night (she kneels to the right, as this is the strategic side; the cow's foot is somehow freer on the left). After the bag is clean, the milking begins. There is always a variation to this ritual. When the calf is young, the cow holds back her milk for it; so the calf is allowed to suck a little at first, some from each teat, loosening the milk with uniformity, and then is pulled off and put in a stall until his time comes. There is one way to pull a calf off, and only one. He must be held by the ears and the tail at the same time, for only in this manner is he easily controlled. The ears alone, or the tail alone, is not enough.

This done, the milking begins. The left hand holds the pail, while the right does the work, or it may be the reverse. The hand hits the bag tenderly, grabs the teat, and closes the fingers about it, not altogether, but in echelon. The calf is then let out for his share. If he is young and there are several cows, it will be all that is left, for careful milkers do not strip the cow until the calf is weaned. The strippings are those short little squirts which announce the end, and they are all cream.

The milk is next brought back to the house, strained, and put in the well to cool. This requires a very careful hand, because if it happens to spill, the well is ruined. The next step is to pour up the old milk and let it turn—that is, sour—for churning. Some will be set aside to clabber for the mammy whose teeth are no longer equal to tougher nourishment. What she does not eat is given to the young chickens or to the pigs.

After breakfast the farmer's wife, or one of the girls, does the churning. This process takes a variable length of time. If the milk is kept a long time before it is poured up, the butter is long in coming. Sometimes witches get in the churn and throw a spell over it. In that case a nickel is dropped in to break the charm. The butter, when it does come, collects in small, yellow clods on top. These clods are separated from the butter-milk and put in a bowl where the rest of the water is worked out. It is then salted, molded, and stamped with some pretty little design. After this is done, it is set in the well or the spring to cool for the table. The process has been long, to some extent tedious, but profitable, because insomuch as it has taken time and care and intelligence, by that much does it have a meaning.

Industrialism gives an electric refrigerator, bottled milk, and dairy butter. It takes a few minutes to remove it from the ice to the table, while the agrarian process has taken several hours and is spread out over two or three days. Industrialism saves time, but what is to be done with this time? The milkmaid can't go to the movies, read the signboards, and go play bridge all the time. In the moderate circumstances of this family, deprived of her place in the home economy, she will be exiled to the town to clerk all day. If the income of the family can afford it, she remains idle, and therefore miserable.

The whole process has been given in detail as an example of what goes on in every part of an agrarian life. The boys, coming in to breakfast, have performed in the same way. Every morning the stock must be fed, but there is always variety. They never shuck the same ears of corn, nor do they find the mules in the small part of the stall, nor the hogs in the same attitudes, waiting to be slopped. The buckets of milk did not move regularly from cow to consumer as raw material moves through a factory. The routine was broken by other phenomena. Breakfast intervened. One morning the cow might kick the pail over, or the milkmaid might stumble over a dog, or the cow come up with a torn udder. It is not the only task she performs, just as feeding the stock is not the only task done by the boys. The day of each member of the family is filled with a mighty variety.

After the morning work is over, the family gathers about the breakfast table. Thanks are returned and the meal is served, one of the daughters or the mother waiting on the table; and then, without undue haste, the men go to the fields and the women about their dishes. If it is spring, the women can be of great help in the garden. Very likely the cut-worms will be after the young corn. The cut-worm does not like heat. If some one gets into the garden before the sun gets hot, the worm can be found under a clod near the top of the ground and mashed. In another hour he will have gone far below the surface. It is imperative to go at the right time, for of all the thousands of insects and varmints on the land, he has the distinction of his own habits. By learning these habits, and not those of some other pest, can he be overcome.

Before going to the fields the farmer consults the signs. If the smoke from the chimney is blown to the ground, there will be rain. Lightning in the north early in the night means rain before morning. If there is enough blue in the sky to make the Dutchman a pair of breeches, the weather will turn fair. Lightning in the south is a sign of drought. If the moon lies on its back, it is holding water; if it is tilted so that the water can run out, the season will be dry. Charms, signs, and omens are folk attempts to understand and predict natural phenomena. They are just as useful and necessary to an agrarian economy as the same attempts which come from the chemist's laboratory in an industrial society, and far wiser, because they understand their inadequacy, while the hypotheses of science do not.

According to these signs the work is hard or leisurely. If the fish are biting, the boys might knock off a day and go fishing, or hunting. Their father has not begun to keep books, so their time is their own.

At eleven o'clock the dinner bell rings. The ploughmen take out and come to the house. So regular is this ritual that a mule on the farm of Gen. Joseph E. Johnston's quartermaster used to square his feet in the furrow and answer the bell with a long, loud bray. Nor was anybody ever able to make him, by beating or pleading, plough a step farther. The teams are watered and put into their stalls, where so many ears of corn are shucked into the troughs, and a section of hay is thrown into the racks.

If the corn is low in the crib, the boys are likely to shuck carefully, keeping their eyes open for the king snake. This snake is worth ten cats as a ratter, and careful, economical farmers always throw one in their cribs if one is to be found. But not only as a ratter is he valuable. He makes war on all poisonous snakes and drives them from his presence. His invincibility is believed to be due to his knowledge of snake grass, an antidote for poison; for after bouts in which he has been bitten by venomous snakes, he has been seen to wiggle toward this grass and chew it. There is only one time of the year when he is to be avoided. He goes blind in August; and, feeling his defenseless condition, he will leg you—that is, charge and wrap his strong body about your leg, squeezing and bruising it.

The midday meal, like all the meals in the country, has a great deal of form. It is, in the first place, unhurried. Diners accustomed to the mad, bolting pace of cafeterias will grow nervous at the slow performance of a country table. To be late is a very grave matter, since it is not served until everybody is present. But only some accident, or unusual occurrence, will detain any member of the family, for dinner is a social event of the first importance. The family are together with their experiences of the morning to relate; and merriment rises up from the hot, steaming vegetables, all set about the table, small hills around the mountains of meat at the ends, a heaping plate of fried chicken, a turkey, a plate of guineas, or a one-year ham, spiced, and if company is there, baked in wine. A plate of bread is at each end of the table; a bowl of chitterlings has been set at the father's elbow; and pigs' feet for those that like them.

And they eat with eighteenth-century appetites. There is no puny piddling with the victuals, and fancy tin-can salads do not litter the table. The only salad to be seen on a country table is sallet, or turnip greens, or if further explanation is necessary, the tops of turnips cut off and cooked with a luscious piece of fat meat. It has the appearance of spinach; but, unlike this insipid slime, sallet has character, like the life of the farmer at the head of the table. The most important part of this dish is its juice, the pot licker, a rich green liquid, indescribable except as a pot-licker green. Mixed with corn bread, it has no equal. Particularly is it fine for teething babies. If the baby is weaned in the dark of the moon and fed a little pot licker, he will pass through the second summer without great trouble. This will not relieve the pain of cutting. To do that a young rabbit must be killed, its head skinned, and the raw flesh rubbed on the gums. If this fails, tie a spray of alderberries around its neck, or hang a mole's foot. But sallet will do everything but cut the pain. His table, if the seasons allow, is always bountiful. The abundance of nature, its heaping dishes, its bulging-breasted fowls, deep-yellow butter and creamy milk, fat beans and juicy corn, and its potatoes flavored like pecans, fill his dining-room with the satisfaction of well-being, because he has not yet come to look upon his produce at so many cents a pound, or his corn at so much a dozen. If nature gives bountifully to his labor, he may enjoy largely.

The dishes of food are peculiarly relished. Each dish has particular meaning to the consumer, for everybody has had something to do with the long and intricate procession from the ground to the table.

Somebody planted the beans and worked them. Somebody else staked them and watched them grow, felt anxious during the early spring drought, gave silent thanksgiving when a deep-beating rain soaked into the crusty soil, for the leaves would no longer take the yellow shrivel. A townsman can never understand the significance of rain, nor why an agrarian will study the signs with so much care and often with so much pain, for to him it has no immediate connection. The worst it can do him is to interrupt a picnic, and the best to beat from the asphalt of its streets and its tall buildings for a few moments the enervating heat peculiar to such places. The fullness of meaning that rain and the elements extend to the farmer is all contained in a mess of beans, a plate of potatoes, or a dish of sallet. When the garden first comes in, this meaning is explicit. If the yield has been large and rich, it will be openly and pridefully commented upon; if the garden has burned and it has lost its succulence to the sun, some will remark that sorrier beans have been seen, while others, more resentful of nature's invincible and inscrutable ways, will answer that better, also, have been seen. But aside from some such conservative expression, in its formal tone masking a violent passion, no other comment will be made. And as the enjoyment of the garden's produce becomes more regular, this particular meaning which the dishes at a country table has for its diners settles into the subconscious and becomes implicit in the conduct of the household.

The description of this particular board is by no means general. Just as no two farms are managed alike, so no two tables will be set alike. It is better than most, and slightly changed from antebellum days. It is more stable, as it has had a century in which to harden its form. But this form, troubled by the dualism, is less strict than it would have been if nothing had happened to disturb the direction of its growth. This farmer, being a Tennessean, perhaps has some advantage over other Southwesterners except Kentuckians of a tradition less shaken during the hard years. Tennessee has never been given over to any one money crop. It has looked upon its land to sustain its culture, and from the beginning has diversified according to its needs. Serving as a furnishing state to the cotton regions, when these regions were overturned, it naturally stood the shock better than they. In consequence the table will be more formal, its meals better, than in those places where the small upland farmer moved down upon the segments of the broken plantations. He can never have the same respect for the sow-belly and cornmeal furnished him by the merchant, and actually a large body of these farmers in Alabama, Mississippi, Georgia, South Carolina, and West Tennessee did not vary a great deal this diet, as he could for the vegetables and meat brought to the table by his own hand.

After the midday meal is over the family takes a rest; then the men go back to the fields and the women to those things yet to be done, mending clothes, darning, knitting, canning, preserving, washing or ironing or sewing. By sundown they are gathered about the supper table, and afterward set before the fire if it is winter, or upon the porch in warmer weather. One of the boys will get out his guitar and play "ballets" handed down from father to son, some which have originated in the new country, some which have been brought over from the Old World and changed to fit the new locale. Boys from the neighborhood drop in to court, and they will jine in, or drive away with the gals in hug-back buggies. If they are from another neighborhood, they are sure to be rocked or shot at on the way over or on the way home.

If the gathering is large enough, as it is likely to be when crops are laid by, it will turn into a play-party.[1] Most of these games practiced by the plain people have maintained the traditions brought from England and Scotland, while the townsmen lost their knowledge of them in a generation. For example, "The Hog Drovers" is a version of the English folk-game, "The Three Sailors." The Southern country, being largely inland, could only speculate upon the habits of sailors, but they knew all about the hog drovers. Every year droves of razorbacks, with their eyelids sewed together to hinder them from wandering off into the woods, were driven ten or eleven miles a day toward the Eastern markets. They would be stopped at private farms along the route, where pens had been put up to receive them, to feed. The drovers, nomadic and as careless as sailors, could not be made to keep promises. Parents, therefore, were careful of their daughters.

---

1. [Lytle] The play-parties were to be found in operation much later in Mississippi and Arkansas than in Tennessee.

The game comes from, and is a copy of, the life of the people. A boy seats himself upon a chair in the middle of the room with a gal in his lap. He is the head of the house, and she is his daughter. The other gals are seated around the walls, waiting their turns; while the boys, representing the hog drovers, enter two abreast in a sort of a jig, singing the first stanza:

> "Hog drovers, hog drovers, hog drovers we air,
> A-courtin yore darter so sweet and so fair,
> Can we git lodgin' here, oh, here,
> Can we git er-lodgin' here?"

They stop in front of the old man, and he answers:

> "Oh, this is my darter that sets by my lap,
> And none o' you pig-stealers can git her from pap,
> And you can't git lodgin' here, oh, here,
> And you can't git er-lodgin' here."

The boys then jig about the chair, singing:

> "A good-lookin' darter, but ugly yoreself—
> We'll travel on further and sit on the shelf,
> And we don't want lodgin' here, oh, here,
> And we don't want er-lodgin' here."

They jig around the room, then return. The old man relents. Possibly it has as its genesis a struggle between greed and the safety of his daughter's virtue:

> "Oh, this is my darter that sets by my lap,
> And Mr. *So-and-so* can git her from pap
> If he'll put another one here, oh, here,
> If he'll put another one here."

The boy who is named jigs to one of the gals, brings her to the old man, takes his darter to the rear of the line, and the game starts over. After every couple has been paired off, they promenade all and seek buggies or any quiet place suitable for courting.[2]

---

2. [Lytle] A complete version and account of the Hog-Drovers game song will be found in A. P. Hudson's *Specimens of Mississippi Folklore.*

This and other games, "Fly in the Buttermilk," "Shoot the Buffalo," "Under the Juniper Tree," will fill an evening and break the order of their lives often enough to dispel monotony, making holidays a pleasure; and not so frequent nor so organized that they become a business, which means that games have become self-conscious, thus defeating the purpose of all playing. As they play they do not constantly remind one another that they are having a good time. They have it.

Besides these play-parties people pleasured themselves in other ways. There were ice-cream socials, old-time singings, like the Sacred Harp gatherings, political picnics and barbecues, and barn dances. All of these gatherings which bring the neighborhood together in a social way are unlike the "society" of industrialism. Behind it some ulterior purpose always lurks. It becomes another province of Big Business and is invaded by hordes of people who, unable to sell themselves in the sterner marts, hope to catch their prey in his relaxed moments and over the tea tables make connections which properly belong to the office. This practice prostitutes society, for individuals can mingle socially from no motive except to enjoy one another's company.

The songs of the Sacred Harp, like negro spirituals, are without accompaniment. The tune is pitched by the leader in the neighborhood schoolhouse under the shadows of oil-lamps. There is a grand meeting at the county seat once a year, and here the neighborhoods sing against each other and in unison under one general leader, who always remembers to turn the meeting over to each district leader for one song. This is a privilege jealously looked after; and if anyone is by chance overlooked, he will rise and make himself known. These songs of the Sacred Harp are songs of an agrarian people, and they will bind the folkways which will everywhere else go down before canned music and canned pleasure.

At the square dances, unlike round dancing, the stage is set for each individual to show the particularity of his art. Each couple is "out" in turn, swinging every other couple separately, ending up at "home" when the whole line swings "partners," then "corners." In this way a very fine balance is reached between group and individual action. Everybody is a part of the dance all the time, but a very particular part some of the time. There are no wall-flowers, no duty dances, no agonizing over popularity, and the scores of such things which detract from free enjoyment at the round dancings. "First lady out" means that she must step, cheat, and swing and show her superiority over the ladies who will follow; and likewise with the gentlemen. And the prompter, the one who calls the "figgers" (which happens still to be the proper English pronunciation of figure), is an artist and wit whose disappearance will leave the world much the poorer. Such calls as

> "Swing the gal you love best;
> Now cheat and swing."

> "Partners to yore places
> Like mules to the traces."

and from Mississippi,

> "Women swing hard, men swing harder,
> Swing that gal with the buckskin garter."

are metaphors and imperatives with full connotation for the dancers, and in an agrarian society will be as applicable a hundred years hence. But so will the fiddlers' tunes, "Leather Breeches," "Rats in the Meal Barrel," "Frog Mouth," "Guinea in the Pea Patch," "Arkansas Traveler," "Cotton-eyed Joe," "No Supper Tonight," "Hell Amongst the Yearlings," "Got a Chaw of Tobaccy from a Nigger," "All My Candy's Gone," and "Katy, Bar the Door." With a list of such dances as a skeleton, if all other records were lost, some future scholar could reconstruct with a common historical accuracy the culture of this people.

Before the farmer decided to keep books, the structure of his neighborhood culture had not been moved, and his sons and daughters, and he and the old woman, were a part of these things. Even mammy, if the rheumaticks had not frozen her jints, would put on her hickory-staved bonnet, a fresh-starched apron, and mount the waggin with the rest and drive to the singing and lift her cracked voice as the leader "h'isted" the tune, or at the barbecue pat her feet in time with the whining fiddle and think of better days when she and her old man balanced to "Cairo ladies, show yoreself," or "Jenny, the Flower of Kildare," until the sweat poured from her strong back, gluing the gray linen dress to her shoulders and ballooning it in places with air caught in the swing.

III

The Agrarian South, therefore, whose culture was impoverished but not destroyed by the war and its aftermath, should dread industrialism like a pizen snake. For the South long since finished its pioneering. It can only do violence to its provincial life when it allows itself to be forced into the aggressive state of mind of an earlier period. To such an end does bookkeeping lead. It is the numbering of a farm's resources—its stacks of fodder, bushels of corn, bales of cotton, its stock and implements, and the hundreds of things which make up its economy. And as the only reason to number them is to turn them into cash—that is, into weapons for warfare—the agrarian South is bound to go when the first page is turned and the first mark crosses the ledger.

The good-road programs drive like a flying wedge and split the heart of this provincialism—which prefers religion to science, handcrafts to technology, the inertia of the fields to the acceleration of industry, and leisure to nervous prostration. Like most demagoguery, it has been advertised as a great benefit to the farmer. Let us see just what the roads have done and who they benefit? They certainly can be of no use to the farmer who cannot afford to buy a truck. He finds them a decided drawback. The heavy automobile traffic makes it hazardous for him even to appear on the main highways. But if he has the temerity to try them, they prove most unsatisfactory. Besides being a shock to his mules' feet, it is difficult for the team to stand up on the road's hard, slick surface.

The large farmers and planting corporations who can afford to buy trucks are able to carry their produce to market with less wear and tear than if they drove over rougher dirt pikes. But this is a dubious benefit, for the question is not between trucks on good or bad roads, but between teams on passable roads and trucks on arterial highways.

But in any case the farmer receives few direct profits. Asphalt companies, motor-car companies, oil and cement companies, engineers, contractors, bus lines, truck lines, and politicians—not the farmer— receive the great benefits and the profits from good roads. But the farmer pays the bills. The states and counties float bonds and attend to the upkeep on the highways and byways, and when these states are predominantly agricultural, it is the people living on the land who mortgage their labor and the security of their property so that these super-corporations may increase incomes which are now so large that they must organize foundations to give them away.

But the great drain comes after the roads are built. Automobile salesmen, radio salesmen, and every other kind of salesman descends to take away the farmer's money. The railroad had no such universal sweep into a family's privacy. It was confined to a certain track and was constrained by its organization within boundaries which were rigid enough to become absorbed, rather than absorb. But good roads brought the motor-car and made of every individual an engineer or conductor, requiring a constant, and in some instances a daily, need for cash. The psychological pressure of such things, and mounting taxes, induce the farmer to forsake old ways and buy a ledger.

The great drain continues. The first thing he does is to trade his mules for a tractor. He has had to add a cash payment to boot, but that seems reasonable. He forgets, however, that a piece of machinery, like his mules, must wear out and be replaced; but the tractor cannot reproduce itself. He must lay aside a large sum of money against the day of replacement, whereas formerly he had only to send his brood mare to some jack for service.

The next thing it does, it throws his boys out of a job, with the possible exception of one who will remain and run it. This begins the home-breaking. Time is money now, not property, and the boys can't hang about the place draining it of its substance, even if they are willing to. They must go out somewhere and get a job. If they are lucky, some filling station will let them sell gas, or some garage teach them a mechanic's job. But the time is coming when these places will have a surfeit of farmer boys.

He next buys a truck. The gals wanted a car, but he was obdurate on that point, so he lost them. They went to town to visit kin, then gradually drifted there to marry or get a job. The time comes when the old woman succumbs to high-pressure sales talk and forces him to buy a car on the installment plan. By that time he is so far gone that one thing more seems no great matter.

He then has three vehicles which must be fed from the oil companies, several notes at the bank bearing interest, and payments, as regular as clock strokes, to be made on the car. He finds his payment for gasoline, motor oil, and power for his tractor is tremendously higher than the few cents coal oil used to cost him. Formerly he bought it by the lampful; he now buys it by the barrelful. In fact, he no longer uses coal oil for lighting. He has installed a Delco-plant. Besides giving illumination it pumps his water, turns the churn, washes the clothes, heats the iron to press them, and cooks the victuals. If his daughters had not already moved away, he would have had to send them, for Delco has taken their place in the rural economy. The farmer's wife now becomes a drudge. As the mainstay of the structure she was content to bear the greatest burden, but now she grows restive. She has changed from a creator in a fixed culture to an assistant to machines. Her condition is miserable because her burdens are almost as great without the compensation of the highest place in the old scheme. Her services cannot be recompensed with gold, and gold has become the only currency.

Gradually the farmer becomes more careless of his garden. Each year he cuts down on the meat—the curing takes too much time. He may finally kill only a hog or two, and, under the necessity of paying interest, sell all his cows but one.

He has concentrated on the money crop, and as bought fertilizers and war-time prices have brought cotton to Tennessee, he chooses cotton. This sinks him deeper into the money economy. He must buy highly productive, and also highly priced, seed, and artificial fertilizers. He used to haul manure from the barns, but this is too slow and too unscientific now. But the outlay of money is not ended. There are fertilizer-distributors, cultivators, and improved ploughs of all kinds, with a value arbitrarily inflated by the tariff. He is now as completely on the money basis as a farmer can ever get, and each day he buys more and more from the town and makes less and less on the farm.

Being in the race for wealth, he begins to learn that a farmer can only make war successfully by beating his plowshare into a sharp-cutting weapon. He cannot match the plough against the wheel. When he bought the various machines which roll where the mules stood and shivered the flies from their backs, he was told that he might regulate, or get ahead of, nature. He finds to his sorrow that he is still unable to control the elements. When it fails to rain and his fields are burning, he has no God to pray to to make it rain. Science can put the crops in, but it can't bring them out of the ground. Hails may still cut them down in June; winds may damage them; and a rainy season can let the grass take them. Droughts still may freeze and crack the soil. Dry weather does not greatly injure cotton, but if this farmer had happened to become a dairyman, his withered pastures and dry springs would have made him suffer.

The pests and insects are still with him. He may partially control them by poison: the army worm—possible; the boll weevil—evade by putting in early; flea—impossible! Neither can he control the tariff, nor a complete crop failure, nor a drop in prices. Since he cannot control these variables, his crop is not predictable; therefore his income is uncertain. But debt, the price of machinery, repairs, merchandise are all certain and must be met, if not by his crops, then by his land.

It is true that labor-evicting machines will give a greater crop yield, but a greater yield does not necessarily mean a greater profit. It means over-production and its twin, price deflation. Those who insist on the progressive-farmer ideal realize this, and for a long time the Federal Bureau of Agriculture and other agencies have insisted that he diversify his crops. In many instances this has brought relief, but it is not permanent. The diversification is always the money crop. The farmer is no better off when he has two or three money crops, if they are all over-produced, than he is with one. He has three crops, instead of one, to worry with.

There are farmers who manage to remain in the race, but they are few who actually make fortunes. When the land is very rich, the direction good, and the economy frugal, this is possible. Those places situated close to cities and towns may be turned very profitably into dairy, or poultry, farms; or a few acres may be turned advantageously into trucking. But where there is one like these there are thousands of others, one-horse, two-horse, or four-horsemen, who suffer from these progressives who have made good.

Another way of growing rich on the land is to develop a new seed. Les Bedezer[3] is an example of this. A few make enormous returns on

3. [Lytle] A Japanese Clover, splendid as a land builder, excellent for pasture or hay.

their outlay; others hear of their success, study the methods, and slowly make the effort to do likewise. By the time their crop is ready for the market there is too great an abundance, a fall in price, and the distress it always brings with it. Such farmers are enemies to the agricultural body. The horse-cropper, in attempting to follow their ways, puts his entire acreage in this crop, buying his feed elsewhere on credit at exorbitant interest. In Alabama 20 percent is the usual demand. When the time comes to settle up, if he makes any money, it goes for luxuries instead of discharging his debt. He is always optimistic and hopes that next year will be as good, and on this wish he gives a lien on his land, which under such circumstances means a sale.

But even for those who succeed the disadvantage is too great, and for the less fortunate who enter the conflict without the advantages of science, it is overwhelming. At the outset there is the great burden of direct and indirect taxation. Because land cannot be hidden away in strong boxes it bears the greatest part of the national, state, and county expenses. According to Governor Lowden, a considered authority on taxation and the farmer's problems, real property, which is largely farmlands or property dependent upon farming produce, bears 90 percent of the taxation and receives 10 percent of the income. Since Wilson's administration gave way to Harding's normalcy, taxes have been increased on land four times and decreased on great wealth four times, making a ratio of sixteen to one against the farmer. The tariff, which he has borne a century, grows heavier rather than lighter, and apparently the Republicans have every intention of further increasing it. The factory can close down to meet over-production and feed the market with its stock on hand; but the farmer is unable to do this because of the perishable quality attached to everything but cotton, tobacco, and sugar; and when he sells these crops, he is an individual competing with large organizations.

Thanks to applied science, the factory can concentrate stupendous power in one place and fabricate its commodities serially; that is, a hundred yards of cloth can be reproduced exactly as a previous hundred yards, or a hundred Ford cars with the same uniform strokes, but the product of the farm cannot be so reproduced. There can be but approximate, and very general, organization to agriculture. Certain seasons require certain kinds of work: there is a breaking season, a planting season, a cultivating season, a laying-by time, and a marketing time. This very loose organization is determined by nature, not by man, and points to the fundamental difference between the factory and the soil. When the farmer doubles his crop, he doubles his seed, his fertilizer, his work, his anxiety . . . all his costs, while the industrial product reduces in inverse ratio its costs and labor as it multiplies. Industrialism is multiplication. Agrarianism is addition and subtraction. The one by attempting to reach infinity must become self-destructive; the other by fixing arbitrarily its limits upon nature will stand. An agrarian stepping across his limits will be lost.

When the farmer, realizing where all this is leading him, makes the attempt to find his ancient bearings, he discovers his provincialism rapidly disintegrating. The Sacred Harp gatherings, and to a less extent the political picnics and barbecues, have so far withstood the onslaught; but the country church languishes, the square dance disappears, and camp meetings are held, but they have lost their vitality. Self-consciousness has crept into the meetings, inhibiting the brothers and sisters and stifling in their bosoms the desire to shout. When shouting ceases and the mourner's bench is filled up by the curious from the rear, the camp meeting may count its days, for they are numbered.

He finds that there is a vast propaganda teaching him, but particularly his children, to despise the life he has led and would like to lead again. It has in its organization public schools, high schools, the normals, and even the most reputable universities, the press, salesmen, and all the agents of industrialism. It has set out to uplift him. It tells him that his ancestors were not cultured because they did not appreciate the fine arts; that they were illiterate because their speech was Old English; and that the South will now come to glory, to "cultural" glory, by a denial of its ancestry.

This is the biggest hoax that has ever been foisted upon a people. It is nothing but demoniacally clever high-pressure sales talk to unload the over-producing merchandize of industrialism on the South. New England began it with her carrying trade. The shrewd Yankee skippers realized that if they could persuade prospective buyers that the bric-a-brac which they had brought from the Orient and elsewhere was "culture," their cargoes would fetch a fancier price. This brought about the overthrow of their own theocracy by 1830; but so long as the South had the planters for defenders the peddlers made no great headway. But now, in the hands of the industrialists everywhere, it is making very great headway.

And unless the agricultural South, like this farmer, wakes up to the fact that he is swapping his culture for machine-made bric-a-brac, there will be an absentee-landlordism far worse than that which afflicted the continent at the breakdown of medieval society. When the nobility flocked to the court of Louis XIV, leaving the tenants the burden of land without the compensation of local government, conditions were bad enough, precipitating the French Revolution. But, even so, the French nobility retained certain ties to their estates. They were descendants of men who had ruled there. But what of this absentee-landlordism of capitalism? Mortgage companies, insurance companies, banks, and binding-houses that are forced to take over the land of free men . . . what will be the social relationship? What can an abstract corporation like an insurance company, whose occupation is statistics and whose faro-bank can never lose, know of a farmer's life? What can their calculations do before droughts, floods, the boll weevil, hails, and rainy seasons? What will be the relationship between tenants who formerly owned the land and their abstract selves?

To avoid the dire consequences and to maintain a farming life in an industrial imperialism, there seems to be only one thing left for the farmer to do, and particularly for the small farmer. Until he and the agrarian West and all the conservative communities throughout the United States can unite on some (common political action) he must deny himself the articles the industrialists offer for sale. It is not so impossible as it may seem at first, for, after all, the necessities they machine-facture were once manufactured on the land, and as for the bric-a-brac, let it rot on their hands. Do what we did after the war and the Reconstruction: return to our looms, our handcrafts, our reproducing stock. Throw out the radio and take down the fiddle from the wall. Forsake the movies for the play-parties and the square dances. And turn away from the liberal capons who filled the pulpits as preachers. Seek out a priesthood that may manifest the will and intelligence to renounce science and search out the Word in the authorities.

So long as the industrialist remains in the saddle there must be a money crop to pay him taxes, but let it occupy second place. Any man who grows his own food, kills his own meat, takes wool from his lambs and cotton from his stalks and makes them into clothes, plants corn and hay for his stock, shoes them at the crossroads blacksmith shop, draws milk and butter from his cows, eggs from his pullets, water from the ground, and fuel from the woodlot, can live in an industrial world without a great deal of cash. Let him diversify, but diversify so that he may live, rather than that he may grow rich. In this way he will escape by far the heaviest form of taxation, and if the direct levies grow too exorbitant, refuse to pay them. Make those who rule the country bear the burdens of government.

He will be told that this is not economical, that he can buy clothes for much less than he can weave them, and shoes for half the labor he will put into their creation. If the cash price paid for shoes were the only cost, it would be bad economy to make shoes at home. Unfortunately, the matter is not so simple: the fifteen-hundred-dollar tractor, the thousand-dollar truck, the cost of transportation to and from town, all the cost of indirect taxation, every part of the money economy, enters into the price of shoes. In comparison, the sum he hands over to the merchant is nothing more than a war tax.

So long as he lives in a divided world he is rendered impotent in the defense of his natural economy and inherited life. He has been turned into the runt pig in the sow's litter. Squeezed and tricked out of the best places at the side, he is forced to take the little hind tit for nourishment; and here, struggling between the sow's back legs, he has to work with every bit of his strength to keep it from being a dry hind one, and all because the suck of the others is so unreservedly gluttonous.

As for those countrymen who have not gone so deeply in the money economy, let them hold to their agrarian fragments and bind them together, for reconstructed fragments are better than a strange newness which does not belong. It is our own, and if we had to spit in the water-bucket to keep it our own, we had better do it.

3

WHAT IS A TRADITIONAL SOCIETY?[1]

ALLEN TATE

When he gave the Phi Beta Kappa address at the University of Virginia in 1936, Allen Tate (perhaps echoing Oswald Spengler's The Decline of the West*) described a movement in the West not progressively upward but downward—from religious myth, which could include the whole of reality; to historical myth, a kind of idealization of men and deeds; and finally to "the complete triumph of positivism," in which "we get just plain, everyday history," the result of the application of "the historical method." Tate argues that a traditional society such as the Old South still held at least the historical myth. Moreover, in a traditional society, "the whole economic basis of life is closely bound up with moral behavior, and it is possible to behave morally all the time." Not so in the modern business world: "[W]e cannot pretend to be landed gentlemen two days of the week if we are middle-class capitalists the five others." Finance capitalism, in fact, "is necessarily hostile to the development of a moral nature," argues Tate, because it is "a system that has removed men from the responsible control of the means of a livelihood." After the financial collapse of 2008, it would be hard to argue the point.*

---

1. The Phi Beta Kappa address at the University of Virginia, June 1936.

Not long ago, I hope with no sinister purpose, I used the word "tradition" before a group of Southern men who had met to discuss the problems of the South. A gentleman from North Carolina rose; he said that tradition was meaningless, and he moved that we drop the word. I have a certain sympathy with that view. Many features of our lives that we call traditions are meaningless; we confuse with tradition external qualities which are now, in the rich American middle class, mere stage properties of a way of life that can no longer be lived. For the stage set differs from the natural scene, I take it, in offering us a conventional surface without depth, and the additional facility of allowing us to stand before it on Saturday and Sunday and to resume, on Monday, the real business of life. Tradition as we see it today has little to do with the real business of life; at best it can make that grim reality two-sevenths less grim—if indeed the pretense of our weekend traditionalists is not actually grimmer than the reality they apologetically prefer but from which they desire, part of the time, to escape.

I do not understand this romanticism, and I bring it to your attention because, here within the walls of Mr. Jefferson's University, there is a special tradition of realism in thinking about the nature of tradition. The presiding spirit of that tradition was clear in his belief that the way of life and the livelihood of men must be the same; that the way we make our living must strongly affect the way of life; that our way of getting a living is not good enough if we are driven by it to pretend that it is something else; that we cannot pretend to be landed gentlemen two days of the week if we are middle-class capitalists the five others. You will remember Ruskin's objection to the Gothic factory-architecture of his age—the ornamentation he suggested for the cornices of a kind of building that was new in that time. Ruskin's stylized money bags set at the right rhythmic intervals around the cornices of the Bethlehem Steel Corporation might be symbolic of something going on inside, but I think the chairman of the board would rightly object that Ruskin was not a good satirist, but merely a sentimentalist; and the chairman would leave his cornices bare. Yet, while the chairman of the board might be committed on the one hand to an economic realism, he might on the other indulge himself in softer materials in another direction; he might buy or build a Georgian mansion somewhere near Middleburg, Virginia, and add to it—if they were not already there—the correct row of columns that Mr. Jefferson adapted to Virginia after a visit to the Maison Carré at Nîmes.

Mr. Jefferson could not know Ruskin, but he knew about medieval Europe, and he disliked it. He never visited Mr. Walpole at Strawberry Hill, but I wish he had. He would have rejoiced that Walpole's weekend Gothic—if you will allow the anachronism for the sake of the moral—meant the final destruction, in England, of the Middle Ages. He would have known that to revive something is to hasten its destruction—if it is only picturesquely and not sufficiently revived. For the moment the past becomes picturesque it is dead. I do not agree with Mr. Jefferson about the Middle Ages, but I surmise that he would have considered a revival of the past very much in this light. He himself was trying to revive the small freeholder who had been dispossessed by the rising capitalist of the eighteenth century.

Now one of the curious features of our mentality since the Renaissance is the historical imagination. No other civilization, I believe, has had this gift. I use the term not in a strict sense, but in a very general sense, and perhaps in a somewhat pejorative sense. I mean that with the revival of Greek studies men in Europe began to pose as Greeks. After a couple of centuries, when the pose, too heroic to last, grew tired, they posed as Romans of the Republic. There we have a nice historical dramatization of the common sense of the eighteenth century. We on this side of the Atlantic were not unaffected by it. There is evidence that our Revolutionary fathers were the noblest Romans of them all. There is certainly not a Virginian, nor a Southerner of Virginian ancestry, whose great-great-grandfather did not write letters to his son in the style of Addison, a vehicle nicely fitted to convey the matter of Cicero. *Libidinosa enim et intemperans adulescentia effetum corpus tradit senectuti*—it is not from the orations, but the rhythm and sentiment here were the model of the *ore orotundo* style that dominated society in the South and other parts of America for three generations. Those generations, if our records of their more elegant representatives do not lie, were not much impressed with the ravages of youthful license upon the body, which, as Cicero has just told us, passes wearily into old age. The young blade of Albemarle of 1770, sitting over a punch bowl in the tavern after a day of Cicero with the learned Parson Douglas, was not, at that moment, an exemplar of Cicero's morals, but I suspect that his conversation, even after the bottom of the bowl began to be visible, retained a few qualities of the Ciceronian style.

The style is the point of a digression that I hope you will not think frivolous. I hold no brief for Cicero—he is a dull mind in any language—but I do hold that the men of the early American Republic had a profound instinct for high style, a genius for dramatizing themselves at their own particular moment of history. They were so situated economically and politically that they were able to form a definite conception of their human role: They were not ants in an economic ant hill, nor were they investigating statistically the behavior of other ants. They knew what they wanted because they knew what they, themselves, were. They lived in a social and economic system that permitted them to develop a human character that functioned in every level of life, from the economic process to the county horse race.

The Virginian of the 1790s might have found a better part in the play than that of the Roman in *toga virilis*—as Mr. Custis, the first Southern dilettante, liked to paint him—but it was the easiest role to lay hold upon at that time, and it was distinctly better than no imaginative version of himself at all. A few years ago Mr. T. S. Eliot told an audience at this university that there are two kinds of mythology, a higher and a lower. The Roman *toga* of our early Republic was doubtless of a sort of lower mythology, inferior to the higher mythology of the Christian thirteenth century, and I suppose Mr. Eliot would prefer the higher vision, as I myself should were I allowed a preference. But we must remember that the rationalism of the eighteenth century had made myths of all ranks exceedingly scarce, as the romantic poets were beginning to testify; yet the Virginian did remarkably well with the minor myth that his age permitted him to cultivate. Mr. Custis's paintings may seem to us to be afflicted with a sort of aesthetic giantism, and his blank-verse dramas, in which every hero is an alabaster Washington named Marcus Tullius Scipio Americanus, are unreadable today. They must have been a kind of inexquisite torture even when they were written. But Mr. Custis built Arlington, and Arlington is something to have built. He could not have built it, of course, if Mr. Jefferson had not first built a house upon a place that I believe is locally called the Little Mountain; but then Mr. Jefferson could not have built Monticello had he not been dominated by the lower myth of the *toga virilis*.

Perhaps this lower myth, from whatever source it may come—Rome, Greece, the age of Cellini, the naturalism of the South Seas, or even the Old South—this little myth is a figment of the historical imagination, that curious faculty of Western men that I have already mentioned. The men of our early republic were powerfully endowed in this faculty. It is not the same as a religion, if by religion we mean Christianity in the Middle Ages; nor is it the same as the religious imagination under any conceivable culture, for the religious imagination is timeless and unhistoric. The minor myth is based upon ascertainable history.

There is a chart that we might look at for a moment, but only for a moment; I offer it not as history, but as a device to ease the strain of the idea of traditional society that I am trying to give in so short a space. First, there is the religious imagination, which can mythologize indiscriminately history, legend, trees, the sea, animals, all being humanly dramatized, somehow converted to the nature of man. Secondly, there is the historical imagination, which is the religious imagination *manqué*—an exercise of the myth-making propensity of man within the restricted realm of historical event. Men see themselves in the stern light of the character of Cato, but they can no longer see themselves under the control of a tutelary deity. Cato actually lived; Apollo was merely far-darting.

The third stage is the complete triumph of positivism. And with the complete triumph of positivism, in our own time, we get, in place of so workable a makeshift as the historical imagination, merely a truncation of that phrase in which the adjective has declared its independence. It has set up for a noun. Under positivism we get just plain, everyday history. If this is an obscure conception, I must hasten to say that although history cannot write itself, although it must be written by men whose minds are as little immune to prejudice as to the law of contradiction, it is true that any sort of creative imagination is, on principle, eliminated. Yet in recognition of history's impotence to bring itself into being, the historians give us a new word: method. We live in the age of the historical method. Method brings history into being.

I shall not labor the point here, but I do think it is fair to say that "history," although it has become attached to "method," is still a noun of agency, as the grammarians call it, trying to do its own work. I think this is true simply because on principle scientific "method" is itself not attached to anything. It is just abstract method—from which plain, abstract, inhuman history differs not by a hair. Of course, I am talking about the historian's ideal of physical law—his belief that history must conform to the ideal of a normative science, whether or not it can mean anything written that way. The historical method then may be briefly described—by one who does not believe in its use—as the way of discovering historical "truths" that are true in some other world than that inhabited by the historian and his fellow men: truths, in a word, that are true for the historical method.

Most of you have read *The Waste Land*, but I shall ask you to hear a passage from it again for the sake of those who have not read it:

> The Chair she sat in, like a burnished throne,
> Glowed on the marble, where the glass
> Held up by standards wrought with fruited vines
> From which a golden Cupidon peeped out
> (Another hid his eyes behind his wing)
> Doubled the flames of seven-branched candelabra
> Reflecting light upon the table as
> The glitter of her jewels rose to meet it,
> From satin cases poured in rich profusion;
> In vials of ivory and colored glass
> Unstoppered, lurked her strange synthetic perfumes, . . .

In this handsome décor the lady, I imagine, is about to dress for dinner. On the walls and ceilings are scenes from an heroic past:

> Huge sea-wood fed with copper
> Burned green and orange, framed by the colored stone,
> In which sad light a carved dolphin swam.
> Above the antique mantel was displayed

As though a window gave upon the sylvan scene
The change of Philomel, by the barbarous king
So rudely forced; yet there the nightingale
Filled all the desert with inviolable voice . . .

People living in such favorable influences, partaking of the best of our
history and of the arts of the great tradition, command our most interested attention: They will at least exhibit the benefits of a good lower
mythology. We may expect them to show us, if not the innocence of
the religious imagination, a high style that expresses, or is the expression of, the walls that we have just looked at. But no; the poet warns
us as follows:

And other withered stumps of time
Were told upon the walls; staring forms
Leaned out, leaning, hushing the room enclosed.
Footsteps shuffled on the stair.

I hope you will forgive me if I venture to think that the shuffling feet
are about to bring into the room the historical method. For, after some
desperately aimless conversation, in which both the woman and the
man seem to feel little but a bored exhaustion and vacuity of purpose,
the woman suddenly says:

"What shall I do now? What shall I do?
I shall rush out as I am, and walk the street
With my hair down, so. What shall we do tomorrow?
What shall we ever do"?

Her companion replies—and I ask you to place what he says against
the heroic background of Renaissance art on the ceiling and walls—
what he says does reduce it, I think, to withered stumps of time:

The hot water at ten.
And if it rains, a closed car at four.
And we shall play a game of chess,
Pressing lidless eyes and waiting for a knock upon the door.

Now fortunately upon this occasion I am neither poet nor literary critic. Here I am a moralist, and if I find more to my use in Mr. Eliot's poem than he would willingly allow, you will remember that moralists these days are desperate persons, and must in their weaker moments squeeze a moral even out of modern poetry. If the chess game seems trivial as a symbol of aimless intellectuality, its intention is nevertheless just. The rich experience from the great tradition depicted in the room receives a violent shock in contrast with a game that symbolizes the inhuman abstraction of the modern mind. In proposing the game of chess the man is proposing an exercise in a kind of truth that has no meaning for either of them. The woman in this remarkable scene has just said that she can think of nothing to do—the moralist would gloss that as lack of purpose—and she intends to rush out into the street with her hair down.

What does this mean? It means that in ages which suffer the decay of manners, religion, morals, codes, our indestructible vitality demands expression in violence and chaos; it means that men who have lost both the higher myth of religion and the lower myth of historical dramatization have lost the forms of human action; it means that they are no longer capable of defining a human objective, of forming a dramatic conception of human nature; it means that they capitulate from their human role to a series of pragmatic conquests which, taken alone, are true only in some other world than that inhabited by men.

The woman in Mr. Eliot's poem is, I believe, the symbol of man at the present time. He is surrounded by the grandeurs of the past, but he does not participate in them; they do not sustain him. To complete the allegory, the man represents a kind of truth that I have described in very general terms as the historical method: He offers us the exercise of intellect to no purpose, a game that we cannot relate to our conduct, an instrument of power over both past and present which we can neither control nor properly use.

Man in this plight lives in an untraditional society. For an untraditional society does not permit its members to pass to the next generation what it received from its immediate past. Why is this so? I have tried to describe in moral terms some of the defects of life in an untraditional society—and I expect merely to ask, and not to answer, whether there is not some kind of analysis that we may subject our situation to that will show us one way of understanding the fundamental difference between tradition and non-tradition?

I shall return to a question that I asked in the beginning. Why do many modern people live one kind of life five days a week and another the two other days? Why is it that a middle-class capitalist from Pittsburgh or Birmingham desires an antebellum Georgian house near Lexington, Kentucky, or Middleburg, Virginia? And why was it that the men who built those houses desired only those houses, and made serious objections in the 1860s to being forcibly removed from them? There are many answers to these questions, but I have space for only one. The middle-class capitalist does not believe in the dignity of the material basis of his life; his human nature demands a homogeneous pattern of behavior that his economic life will not give him. He doubtless sees in the remains of the Old South a symbol of the homogeneous life. But the antebellum man saw no difference between the Georgian house and the economic basis that supported it. It was all of one piece.

I am exaggerating, but permit me the exaggeration so that I may make this matter as clear as I can. Man has never achieved a perfect unity of his moral nature and his economics; yet he has never failed quite so dismally in that greatest of all human tasks as he is failing now. Antebellum man, insofar as he achieved a unity between his moral nature and his livelihood, was a traditional man. He dominated the means of life; he was not dominated by it. I think that the distinguishing feature of a traditional society is simply that. In order to make a livelihood men do not have to put aside their moral natures. Traditional men are never quite making their living, and they never quite cease to make it. Or put otherwise: they are making their living all the time, and affirming their humanity all the time. The whole economic basis of life is closely bound up with moral behavior, and it is possible to behave morally all the time. It is this principle that is the center of the philosophy of Jefferson.

Yet what is there traditional about this? The answer is that if such a society could come into being now, and had no past whatever, it would be traditional because it could hand something on. That something would be a moral conception of man in relation to the material of life. The material basis of life, in such a society, is not hostile to the perpetuation of a moral code, as our finance-capitalist economics unquestionably is. It is an old story by this time that our modern economic system can be operated efficiently regardless of the moral stature of the men who operate it.

The kind of property that sustains the traditional society is not only *not* hostile to a unified moral code; it is positively the basis of it. Moreover it is the medium, just as canvas is the medium of the painter, through which that code is passed to the next generation. For traditional property in land was the primary medium through which man expressed his moral nature; and our task is to restore it or to get its equivalent today. Finance-capitalism, a system that has removed men from the responsible control of the means of a livelihood, is necessarily hostile to the development of a moral nature. Morality is responsibility to a given set of conditions. The further the modern system develops in the direction that it has taken for two generations, the more anti-traditional our society will become, and the more difficult it will be to pass on the fragments of the traditions that we inherit.

The higher myth of religion, the lower myth of history, even ordinary codes of conduct, cannot preserve themselves; indeed they do not exist apart from our experience. Since the most significant feature of our experience is the way we make our living, the economic basis of life is the soil out of which all the forms, good or bad, of our experience must come.

4

WHY THE MODERN SOUTH HAS
A GREAT LITERATURE

DONALD DAVIDSON

Among the Agrarians, Donald Davidson resembled Coriolanus in his intransigent championing of the old order, and though he was more of a gentleman than the early Roman, he was as little able to hide his real opinions. As a result, he was sometimes trying to his friends—not least for outspokenness in matters that came to embarrass them. For example, at the end of this essay, Davidson praises Mississippi for supporting the Dixiecrat ticket of Strom Thurmond in 1948. Yet, none would deny that a high nobility shone through his life. Davidson eschewed what he called the "guarded style" in his prose as in his poetry. His argument in the present essay is one of the most important explanations of the Southern Renaissance. Central to it is the parallel between William Faulkner and William Shakespeare. But what sets up the argument is his careful description, building on Tate's earlier one, of what he means by traditional society. In exploring the difference between the Latin words felix *and* fortunatus, *he presents a vision of what makes communities possible, and he employs Tate's phrase "knowledge carried to the heart" (from* Ode to the Confederate Dead*) for the kind of understanding that he found the South in 1950 still to possess.*

For a thematic text I ask you to consider a famous passage from Vergil's second *Georgic*:

> Felix, qui potuit rerum cognoscere causas,
> Atque metus omnes et inexorabile fatum
> Subjecit pedibus strepitumque Acherontis avari.
> Fortunatus et ille, deos qui novit agrestes
> Panaque Silvanumque senem Nymphasque sorores.
> Illum non populi fasces, non purpura regum
> Flexit et infidos agitans discordia fratres,
> Aut conjurato descendens Dacus ab histro,
> Non res Romanae perituraque regna; neque ille
> Aut doluit miserans inopem aut invidit habenti.
> Quos rami fructus, quos ipsa volentia rura
> Sponte tulere sua, carpsit nec ferrea jura
> Insanumque forum aut populi tabularia vidit.

Vergil, like, us lived at a time when republican institutions had been undermined by those who were responsible for upholding them. Skepticism and materialism were destroying religion. A New Deal, headed by a dictator on the make, was pretending to restore the republic but was actually subverting it. Foreign and civil war had produced economic and administrative chaos. The urban proletariat was being bribed into complacency by a program of bread and circuses. Veterans of the Roman armies were being subsidized. Tax burdens were enormous. Armies of occupation had to be maintained in various parts of the world, yet the threat of war in the direction of what is now Germany, the Balkans, and the Near East remained continuous. Since these, Vergil's circumstances, were much like ours, I trust I may be pardoned if I offer a free modern paraphrase of Vergil's Latin rather than a literal translation:

> Happy (no doubt) is the man who believes that science has the answer to everything, and so thinks that he no longer need fear anything—such as hell, which must be a mere superstition, or even death itself.
>
> But blessed, too (if not happy), is the man who knows that the God of his fathers is still manifest in the fields, woods, and rivers.

That man does not have to cater to the urban masses of New York and Detroit. He does not need to beg favors from Roosevelt or Truman. He has nothing to do with the jealous and traitorous schemes that split our parties in fratricidal strife. He doesn't spend his time worrying over where the Russians will strike next, or about Washington politics, or over whether the French or British cabinet will again have to resign. He may be one of the "have not's," but he doesn't envy the "have's." He just knows that country ham and fried apples are mighty good eating, especially when they come off your own land; and that "parity prices" don't have anything to do with their essential goodness. Knowledge of such things is his safeguard against the tediousness of bureaucrats, the madness of Washington, and statistics.

My answer to the question, "Why does the modern South have a great literature?" could easily hinge upon Vergil's deliberate contrast between two words, *felix* and *fortunatus*. To understand that, we must understand the two kinds of knowledge that Vergil associates with the intellectually "happy man" (*felix*) and the "blessed man" (*fortunatus*). But we cannot understand Vergil's meaning until we have examined our own condition of knowledge.

The man of our time who "knows the causes of things" is of course the scientist. We generally turn to the scientist for explanations of physical or social phenomena. We do not any longer ask a philosopher for explanations, and least of all a novelist or a poet—that is, if a public policy that will cost us money and trouble is to be based upon the answer. We live under the rule of scientific expertism. The President does not dare send a message to Congress, nor does Congress dare pass a law, without at least going through the motions of consulting scientific experts and bolstering up the "program" with an array of statistical information that they have compiled.

The Church itself—especially the Protestant church—no longer relies exclusively upon Scriptures and church doctrine. It still reads "lessons" from the Holy Scriptures as a part of its ritual, but the commentary upon the Scriptures avoids the Church Fathers and draws heavily upon social science. The Cole Lectures at Vanderbilt University, for example, were founded as religious lectures, to be delivered by clergymen. But in this, the seventy-fifth year of Vanderbilt University, those Cole lectures, offered under the auspices of the Vanderbilt School of Religion, were given by the famous white Russian sociologist Pitirim Sorokin. He was assisted by two or three prominent ministers who, if they are not as good sociologists as Sorokin, are just as sociological-minded.

So the official, the really valid answer to my question, "Why does the modern South have a great literature?" ought to come from modern science, which is supposed to know the answer to everything. I do not expect the physicist or chemist to deal with it, since as yet there does not seem to be a physics or chemistry of literature. The answer must come from the social scientist. Since literature is somehow or other related to the cultural condition of a people, I turn hopefully to the sociologist, for he makes it his business to deal with all cultural matters whatsoever.

My question contains two assumptions, which are implied in the terms "modern South" and "great literature." I hasten to explain that by "modern" I mean "contemporary" and perhaps a little more—in point of time, the South of the past thirty years, but also the South which in various ways seems consciously striving to be "modern." By "great literature" I mean "great" in the sense of being generally accepted by distinguished critics as of highest quality and most serious import.

One of the Southern writers thus accepted is William Faulkner of Mississippi. Suppose, then, I turn to sociology and ask whether it can account for the appearance in Mississippi, of all places, of William Faulkner, in the three decades between 1920 and 1950. My question has a corollary which I believe I am entitled to state: Can sociology also explain why William Faulkner, or some novelist of comparable stature, did not appear, during this period, somewhere north of the Ohio—say, in Massachusetts or Wisconsin?

For convenience, I shall seek my answer in the statistical tables assembled from various sources and approvingly published by Howard W. Odum and his associate, Harry Estill Moore, in a compendious book entitled *American Regionalism: A Cultural-Historical Approach to National Integration*. The authors are sociologists of unchallenged eminence. Their book is a synthesis of information gathered from many fields of inquiry over a long period. I assume that it is authoritative and reliable.

The focal point of my inquiry is the decade from 1920 to 1930, for if any cultural factors determined the performance of William Faulkner, they must have been the factors prevalent at about this time, when the new Southern literature was beginning to emerge. No figures are available in this book for the previous decade, but I believe we may safely assume that the decade from 1920–1930 is good enough for our purpose, since that was William Faulkner's formative period.

Now in the formative period of William Faulkner—and, if you wish, of his contemporaries—what cultural factors, exactly, were at work in the Southern scene?

I am very sorry to have to report to you that during William Faulkner's formative period the cultural factors were extremely forbidding in the State of Mississippi. I can hardly see how Mr. Faulkner survived, much less wrote novels. On the evidence of Mr. Odum's tables, culture was at a very low ebb in Mississippi—so low that, if I had only these tables to depend upon, I would confidently assert, as a devoted follower of sociology, that a William Faulkner in Mississippi would be a theoretical impossibility; and that, if he emerged at all, he would have to originate in, say, Massachusetts, where the cultural factors were favorable to literary interests.

Here is the picture. In Mississippi, in 1920, the per capita wealth, as estimated by bank resources, was under $250, and Mississippi, in this respect, was in the lowest bracket in the nation. In Massachusetts, on the other hand, which was in the highest bracket, the per capita wealth by the same measurement was $1,000 and up.

In this decade, too, Mississippi had a very small urban population. In 1930 it was less than 20 percent despite a small recent increase. Mississippi was almost entirely rural, while Massachusetts was just the other way—90 percent urban. Most of the South was nearly as rural as Mississippi. The point is important. It has often been thought that cities foster the literary arts, while the country does not. Lack of cities has frequently been assigned as the reason for the lack of a flourishing Southern literature.

As to "plane of living" (Mr. Odum's term) Mississippi by 1930 was about as low as a state can get. "Plane of living" in Mr. Odum's terminology refers to a composite figure calculated from per capita income, tax returns, residence telephones, ownership of radios, and the like. Well, Mississippi by this standard was on a plane of living described as 15 to 40 percent of the national average—but much nearer to 15 than to 40 percent. It was in the low bracket. In comparison, Massachusetts was in the high bracket, 70 percent and above.

Mississippi was in the lowest bracket in nearly everything as compared with Massachusetts and most of the Northern, Midwestern, and Western states. In ownership of automobiles per farm, it was 26.5 percent as compared with Massachusetts' 61.9 percent. In average value of farms Mississippi was in the lowest bracket, except for the Delta, which was in the next to the lowest bracket. In "farms with water piped into the house" Mississippi offered a pitiful 5 percent in comparison with Massachusetts' grand 79 percent. Mississippi farmhouses were almost without plumbing fixtures. Mississippi spent only a lean seven and a fraction cents per capita for libraries, the lowest expenditure in the nation, while Massachusetts, home of the Pilgrim Fathers and of Harvard University, spent $1.18 per capita, the highest in the nation. Mississippi was in the lowest bracket, too, in expenditures for public education. Only Georgia was lower. And Massachusetts in this respect was of course very high, though not quite as high as New York.

Mr. Odum offers no tables in this book as to religious belief, but we all know that Mississippians in the 1920s were mostly conservative, true-believing Christians rather Fundamentalist in tendency. On the other hand Massachusetts, except for its Catholic population, would certainly be rather heavily liberal, progressive, skeptical, as to religion, and perhaps even atheistical. If liberalism in religion is an index of cultural welfare—and it is often so regarded—then Massachusetts during this period would again be in a very high bracket, despite its Catholic Irish and its Italians, and Mississippi would be rated very low by modern standards.

We need not continue with Mr. Odum's interesting tables. By every cultural standard that the sociologist knows how to devise, Mississippi rates low in the national scale during William Faulkner's formative period. The only bracket in which it would stand high would be in ratio of farm tenancy to population. Its proportion of farm tenants would be very high—but that fact would put it low in Mr. Odum's cultural ratings, for he would take it to indicate a bad economic condition and hence a bad cultural condition.

So it would go for all the Southern states at the time of the emergence of the new Southern literature. All would rank low by the sociologist's measurements. The highest-ranking one would be North Carolina, which has long been heavily industrialized and is reputed to be fanatically liberal, and which, interestingly enough, has not contributed nearly as profusely to the new Southern literature as have Mississippi and other Southern states.

But we are perfectly familiar with the picture of the South that has been built up during the past three decades. It has been dinned into us—and into the nation—through newspapers, magazines, books, moving pictures, radio broadcasts, political speeches, and quasi-religious preachments that we are a backward area in an otherwise progressive nation. We have lacked everything, it seems, that makes Massachusetts and Wisconsin great: educational facilities, factories, libraries, hospitals, laboratories, art museums, theaters, labor unions, publishing houses, accumulations of wealth, high dams, electric power, agricultural machinery, birth control. Some of these material deficiencies have been corrected during recent years, but the South is still "backward" in most of the categories named. "Backward," however, is one of the mildest terms used to describe us. In more common use are such terms as "bigoted," "intolerant," "reactionary," "ignorant," "uncivilized." We have been reproached for being lynchers and Ku-Kluxers; for living in the past rather than in the future; for passing anti-evolution laws and electing to office Huey Long, Bilbo, Talmadge.

Nevertheless, we have produced William Faulkner, and the literary intellectuals of Harvard University are reading Faulkner, studying Faulkner, writing essays and books about Faulkner. To find a novelist comparable to Faulkner in all the Northeast they have to go to more backward times and read Henry James.

Let us look at some of the queer conjunctions of events that ought to be illuminated by the sociologists.

In 1925 the Dayton trial took place in Tennessee. In the light of the famous Monkey Law, Tennessee was immediately judged to be one of the most notorious spots of cultural depravity in the whole world. But in those same years the Fugitive group of poets emerged in Tennessee and soon, broadening their activities, became the Southern Agrarians. The same cultural factors that produce the so-called Monkey Laws must surely have operated upon the Fugitive-Agrarian writers. Did this condition of cultural depravity produce them? At any rate, the influence of this group now seems to have become so pervasive, even in the civilized North, that the defenders of Northern civilization have been thrown into a virtual panic. A flood of articles, many of them denunciatory, has suddenly appeared in the literary magazines. The most hysterical of all, written by Robert Hillyer, former professor of poetry at Harvard, though primarily directed at Pound and Eliot, wildly accused Allen Tate, Robert Penn Warren, and others of this group of organizing a kind of conspiracy to use the prestige of the national government in order to advance their "idiom."[1] This foolish charge might be interpreted to mean that Mr. Hillyer belatedly waked up to the fact that his own folks in the North liked the writings of the uncivilized Southerners better than they liked the writings of Mr. Hillyer and his party. Naturally, that was upsetting to a Harvard man.

But we do not have to stay at the high level of symbolist fiction, modern poetry, and the new criticism to get comparative examples. How did it happen that the State of Georgia, a very backward state, which has distressed the liberals by steadfastly keeping the Talmadge regime in power, also produced Margaret Mitchell, whose *Gone With the Wind*, as a book and as a movie, has won and kept the attention of the whole world?

How does it happen that Kentucky, the home of feudists, night riders, and julep-sipping colonels, produced that marvelous phenomenon, Jesse Stuart? How does it happen that that same Kentucky, with cultural factors of very low grade by Mr. Odum's indexes, produced Robert Penn Warren, whose most recent novel has shaken the seats of the mighty and, incidentally, won just about every award that it is possible for a novel or a movie to win?

Examples might be multiplied indefinitely. I must now strive to

1. [Davidson] Robert Hillyer, "Treason's Strange Fruit," *Saturday Review of Literature*, June 11, 1949.

answer the original question—in scientific terms if possible; in other terms if science fails.

The cultural factors described by Mr. Odum either had a causal influence on William Faulkner or they did not.

If they did have a causal influence, we must, under the rigorous impulsion of sociology, reach an astonishing conclusion: namely, that the way for a society to produce a William Faulkner is to have him born in a thoroughly backward state like Mississippi, of a chivalrously inclined, feudal-minded, landed Southern family that was ruined by the Civil War and later dipped, not very successfully, into modern business. In other words, a prevalence of rural society, devoted to cotton-growing, afflicted by sharecropping, rather poverty-stricken, conservative in religion and politics, prone to love the past rather than the future, chockful of all the prejudices and customs of the South— that is what it takes to produce a William Faulkner.

Contrarily, a prevalence of material progress, great wealth, modern institutions such as libraries and art museums, factories, industrial gimcracks, liberalism, science, political radicalism—that is the way not to produce a William Faulkner. If it were otherwise, Massachusetts and Wisconsin by this time would have produced not one but a couple of dozen William Faulkners.

This conclusion may be discomforting to all who argue that material improvements, liberalism, industrialism, science, and so on are what Mississippi and the South need to attain a high culture. If the appearance of a master artist is an indication of a high culture, they are wrong. Our sociological study clearly indicates either that material improvements, liberalism, industrialism of the order and scale prevalent in Massachusetts are not necessary to produce a master artist; or else—horrible, thought—that these factors have a negative, blighting effect, and prevent his appearance. And without master artists, especially literary artists, how can you have a high culture? I am not the one who proposes that test of a high culture. Our friends of the North have insisted upon it. The British, the French, the Italians, the Germans for centuries have held that view. For a hundred years, too, it has been said, over and over, that that test, above all, was the test the South failed to pass.

The critics of the South might perhaps feel more comfortable if they could argue that Mr. Faulkner's writings are in some sense a reaction against the backwardness of his Southern origin and situation. But there is not a solitary hint of such a reaction against backwardness in his novels and stories. Whatever Mr. Faulkner may be against, he is not in his novels against the so-called backwardness of the South. In his novels he has not advocated or even implied an advocacy of any social reform. He does not rush around issuing pronouncements and indictments. He does not join propagandist movements.[2] He doesn't even write literary criticism.

All the same he is as completely Southern as Shakespeare is completely English. So, too, in their various ways are his Southern contemporaries whose works the nation has been reading. They, too, have emerged from backward Southern states in which the cultural factors, by Mr. Odum's ratings, were most forbidding. We must then conclude that the way to produce a John Ransom, an Allen Tate, a Robert Penn Warren, a Julia Peterkin, a Stark Young, a Eudora Welty, a Thomas Wolfe, a Jesse Stuart, an Elizabeth Roberts, is to have them be born and grow up in a backward Southern community that loves everything that Massachusetts condemns and lacks nearly everything that Massachusetts deems admirable and necessary. Let us concede that some of the Southern writers have been more openly sensitive to Northern criticism of the South than Mr. Faulkner has been and that the sensitivity has affected their writing. But the literature of social protest, represented in the North by such men as Theodore Dreiser, Sinclair Lewis, John Dos Passos, is so uncommon among the distinguished Southern writers of our day as to be hardly worth comment. At its substantial best—the new literature of the South is not a literature of protest but a literature of acceptance which renders its material as objectively and seriously as any great literature has ever done. It also displays a sense of form, a vitality, a grace, a power, and often a finality of treatment that are remarkably scarce in American literature elsewhere.

2. [Davidson] True in 1950. But not true of the post–Nobel Prize Faulkner. In this essay I am taking Faulkner at the current estimate of 1950 and the years just previous. I offer no estimate of my own but merely use Faulkner as an example. Here I will add that Faulkner the storyteller is a man to take seriously. As a commentator on public affairs Faulkner is ignorant, gullible, and sophomoric.

But suppose we take the other horn of the dilemma. Suppose the cultural factors described by Mr. Odum did not operate in a causal way upon Mr. William Faulkner and his contemporaries. Where are we, in that case?

In that case, I should say, we are nowhere as social scientists. The social scientist must necessarily hold that human phenomena result from causal factors which may be broadly described as heredity and environment. At present he tends to favor environment over heredity, because heredity inevitably gets you into matters of race, and under present circumstances the social scientist does not enjoy discussing race and heredity together. At any rate, unless the social scientist can prove that cultural factors, mostly environmental, do determine human phenomena, his statistics have no more value than crossword puzzles, and he is not entitled to give expert advice on our social arrangements. If the sociologist admits that, because of its very "backwardness," the South produced a William Faulkner, he is in an uncomfortable plight, because that is something he didn't intend to prove. If he admits, on the other hand, that William Faulkner developed regardless of the backwardness or even in spite of it, he is still in a painful plight, because he must then admit that the cultural factors affect some people but not others, especially not high-class literary artists like William Faulkner—which is a very damaging admission.

Or else he must break down and say that, perhaps, after all, he has not yet been inclusive enough. There must be some cultural factors that he left out; but if he can get a large financial subsidy from the Social Science Research Council, he will assign a squad of graduate students to the job, and start punching cards and running the calculating machines, and in a few more years he will have some more indexes to round out the picture.

But I believe we have reached the point where we can dispense with his services. Let us turn back to Vergil, who knew a lot about people and society, as all great artists must.

Vergil's "happy man" who "knows the causes of things" is really a philosopher, not in any way like our modern experimental scientist. His knowledge, which includes a knowledge of science, results from a very lofty intellectual effort that lifts him far above human passions and fears. This knowledge is a sublime, most admirable attainment, and in Vergil's day it was not in conflict with poetry. In fact, the passage under discussion is thought to be a tribute to the Roman poet Lucretius, whose *De Rerum Natura* is perhaps the only completely successful "scientific epic" ever written. The happiness associated with this knowledge, however, must be considered a state of intellectual being so very sublime and abstract that few could ever attain it. In our day, it would be almost impossible for a modern experimental scientist to attain it, since he is a specialist and cannot in one operation combine the functions of philosopher, scientist, and poet. Whatever happiness the modern scientist attains is a negative rather than a positive state. His knowledge does not so much exalt him as it dissociates him, because it is exclusive and special rather than inclusive and general. This characteristic has made modern science the enemy rather than the friend of poetry and other literary arts. And any literature that accepts modern scientific knowledge as being an ultimate and complete knowledge is certain to be an incomplete, distorted literature.

But there is another kind of knowledge, which makes men "blessed"—for so I translate Vergil's *fortunatus*. It is the knowledge enjoyed by Vergil's countryman. In the context of the passage I have read, Vergil says that if he cannot have the high philosophic knowledge that makes men "happy" (*felix*) he would next choose the knowledge that makes men "blessed" (*fortunatus*). This is a stage lower than the very highest knowledge, but it is very admirable and desirable, and it, too, is a high form of knowledge. It rests upon traditional religion—or, in Vergil's exact language, "the rustic gods, Pan and old Silvanus, and the sister Nymphs," which I have freely translated "the God of his fathers." It is a knowledge that possesses the heart rather than a knowledge achieved merely by the head—a knowledge that pervades the entire being, as the grace of God pervades the heart and soul. In the phrase of Allen Tate's famous poem *Ode to the Confederate Dead*, it is "knowledge carried to the heart." Negatively, it relieves the individual from the domination of the mob, the insolence of rulers, the strife of jealous factions, the horrible commotion of foreign wars and domestic politics, the vice of envy, the fear of poverty. Positively, it establishes the blessed man in a position where economic use, enjoyment, understanding, and religious reverence are not separated but are fused in one.

The picture in Vergil is idealized, of course. Nevertheless, that is the kind of knowledge that the South has faithfully cultivated throughout its history. Devotion to such knowledge, knowledge "carried to the heart," is the dominant characteristic of Southern society. Through the influence of Thomas Jefferson and his great contemporaries, it has been woven into our political institutions.

Devotion to this knowledge, I would contend, is the great, all-pervasive "cultural factor" for which the sociologists have neglected to provide data. Therefore they cannot account for William Faulkner and other writers, and their diagnosis of Southern society is untrustworthy.

Furthermore, in viewing Southern society as "backward," they make a false and misleading assumption. In number and size of cities, in number of factories, in number of farmhouses with modern plumbing, the South may be "backward" as compared with a national average calculated from such data. That does not mean that Mississippi or any other state is, for that reason, socially, culturally, intellectually backward. In terms of the standard I have proposed, I can easily argue the contrary and assert that Southern society in the 1920s and 1930s was the most "advanced" in the United States. If "indexed" according to the quality and consistency of its literary performance, it would be indeed very advanced.

But I prefer to describe the South of the past three decades as, on the whole, a traditional society which had arrived at a moment of self-consciousness favorable to the production of great literary works. A traditional society is a society that is stable, religious, more rural than urban, and politically conservative. Family, blood-kinship, clanship, folk-ways, custom, community, in such a society, supply the needs that in a non-traditional or progressive society are supplied at great cost by artificial devices like training schools and government agencies. A traditional society can absorb modern improvements up to a certain point without losing its character. If modernism enters to the point where the society is thrown a little out of balance but not yet completely off balance, the moment of self-consciousness arrives. Then a process begins that at first is enormously stimulating, but that, if it continues unchecked, may prove debilitating and destructive in the end.

Greece in the fifth century B.C., Rome of the late republic, Italy in
Dante's time, England in the sixteenth century, all give us examples
of traditional societies invaded by changes that threw them slightly
out of balance without at first achieving cultural destruction. The
invasion seems always to force certain individuals into an examination of their total inheritance that perhaps they would not otherwise
have undertaken. They begin to compose literary works in which the
whole metaphysic of the society suddenly takes dramatic or poetic or
fictional form. Their glance is always retrospective, but their point of
view is always thoroughly contemporary. Thus Sophocles, in his *Oedi-
pos Tyrannos*, looks back at an ancient Greek myth, but he dramatizes
it from the point of view of a fifth-century Athenian who may conceivably distrust the leadership of Pericles. This is what I mean by the
moment of self-consciousness. It is the moment when a writer awakes
to realize what he and his people truly are, in comparison with what
they are being urged to become.

Such a writer is William Faulkner, and such are many of his Southern contemporaries. In sixteenth-century England there was also a
kind of William Faulkner—a country boy from the insignificant village of Stratford, handicapped from the beginning by his ridiculous
countrified name, William Shakespeare. That he also had a country
accent, not unlike a Southern accent, seems apparent from what the
printers have left of his original spelling. He did not have a college
education. In the words of his rival and friend, Ben Jonson, he had
small Latin and less Greek. But whatever new learning he needed he
readily acquired, perhaps in the very process of composing poems and
plays. And all the time he had—as Ben Jonson never did—that second
kind of knowledge that Vergil praises, that knowledge "carried to the
heart," which London and university education could not give, but
which he inherited by natural right through Stratford. Ben Jonson, a
city boy, schooled by a famous master, William Camden, could never
get out from under the weight of his learning. Jonson was always more
the critic than the poet, more the adapter and copyist than the original
dramatist. But Will Shakespeare, the country boy from a backward
region, became one of the world's incomparable originals. London
alone could never have produced him.

Prior to the Civil War the entire United States, in greater or less degree, was a traditional society. But the decision of the North to force war upon the Confederacy and the subsequent victory of the Northern armies threw the traditional society of the North into a state of disequilibrium so profound and so rapid in its development that Northern society has never recovered from the shock. The moment of self-consciousness that I have described could therefore not be utilized except by scattered individuals like Henry James, who had to flee to Europe to get his bearings. The Northern writer had scant opportunity to consult the knowledge in the heart that was his original right. The Northern triumph over the South meant the unchallenged rule in the North of science, industrialism, progressivism, humanitarianism. For Northern writers this rule was disastrous, since it meant that the kind of knowledge chiefly recommended to them was the kind that accomplishes material results—the limited, special knowledge of the scientist and technologist. The result has been that the works of the great Northern writers tend to be all head and no heart. Or else they bear the marks of a lamentable conflict between head and heart. Out of the schism between head and heart arises the literature of realism, of protest, of social criticism. Or else a literature all too evidently determined to be artistic, no matter whether the art has any real subject matter to exhibit.

Among Northern writers, therefore, a rich subject matter and a sense of form rarely go together. Sinclair Lewis has an excellent subject matter, but as to form he is still a cub reporter with a good memory, hacking out copy to catch the two-o'clock edition. Dreiser impresses us with the mass of his enormous case histories, but they are written in laborious prose and have apparently been organized with a meat saw and a butcher knife. On the other hand, Thornton Wilder has a beautiful, though somewhat precious, prose style, but he has no subject matter for the prose to use. One notable instance of a contemporary Northern writer in whom subject and form support each other perfectly is the poet Robert Frost; but Robert Frost rejects the orthodox modern knowledge of the progressive North and adheres to rural New England, which preserves the remnants of its old, traditional society. Beyond these selected examples, the North shows a hodgepodge of experimentalists, propagandists, plausible but empty Book-of-the-

Month Club specials, a vast number of scholars and critics, but very few writers of first rank who are not injured by the fearful imbalance of Northern civilization. The Northern writer cannot trust the knowledge in his heart, even when he has it, because he has allowed his civilization to discredit that knowledge. There are too many people looking over his shoulder as he writes—too many college professors, social welfare workers, atomic scientists, pressure groups, librarians, editors of slick magazines, impatient publishers, and seductive subsidizers.

In the South this destructive process has been slow to take hold. Defeated and ravaged in war, the South put up fierce underground resistance to the Reconstruction and thus emerged at the turn of the century, poor in money and what money will buy, but rich in what money can never buy, in what no science can provide, for the South was still a traditional society, injured but very much alive, and by this time wise and experienced in ways of staying alive. The advocates of a New South of industrialism and mass education, though eloquent and powerful, and heavily backed by Northern money, were not able to alter the traditional South very much. So it was not until the latter part of the Roosevelt administration that the South began to receive the full shock of modernism.

What the future offers, I do not know. In the immediate past it seems obvious that Southern writers have not generally been confused by the division between head and heart that is the great problem of Northern writers. The case of Thomas Wolfe offers an interesting exception to the general rule. From traditional sources Thomas Wolfe inherited a remarkably rich subject matter, but he was utterly incapable of reducing it to coherent form and without the aid of his editor, Maxwell Perkins, might never have been able to publish even the somewhat formless books that he did publish. I suggest that his trouble was that he had been taught to misunderstand with his head what he understood with his heart. Thomas Wolfe had a divided sensibility which very likely resulted from his education at Mr. Howard Odum's citadel, the progressive University of North Carolina, and from his subsequent unfortunate experience at Harvard.

But most of our abler Southern writers, unlike Thomas Wolfe, seem to be born in possession of an endless store of subject matter and also a sense of the form that belongs to the subject matter. I do not know how to explain this except by saying that the person who is born of a traditional society, if he is not corrupted, will act as a whole person in all his acts, including his literary acts. The truth of experience that fills his emotional being is not at war with the truth of his intellectual judgments, but the two, as he writes, are one. His apprehension of his subject matter, which is intuitive and comes from "knowledge carried to the heart," moves hand in hand with his composition, which derives from his intellectual judgment, his sense of fitness and order. Thus an act as coldblooded as deliberate literary composition must be is redeemed and assisted by the warm-blooded knowledge of the heart. It is natural for a Southern writer to compose that way, as it is natural for him to ride a horse with his whole heart as well as with his controlling intelligence.

It is also natural for him to see men in their total capacity as persons and to see things in all their rich particularity as things and to understand that the relationships between persons and persons, and between persons and things are more complex and unpredictable than any scientific textbook invites one to think. He needs no literary critic to tell him that, for his traditional society has already taught him to look at the world in such a way. It has also impressed upon him that the world is both good and evil. Toward nature, toward his fellow creatures, toward the historic past, he has learned to exercise that piety which Mr. Richard Weaver, in his book *Ideas Have Consequences* has praised as the virtue most needed in the modern world.

Thus it is that in the moment of self-consciousness the Southern writer, not only his personal view, but also the total metaphysic of his society. He is therefore unlikely to indulge in the exaggerations and oversimplifications that are the mark of a divided sensibility. For him the people in the bend of the creek are not only sharecroppers representing a certain economic function. They are complete persons with significant personal histories. In fact, they are Joe and Emma, who used to work on old man Brown's place but left him for reasons well known. The banker is not merely a banker. He is Mr. Jim, whose wife's mother was somebody's grandmother's double first cousin.

The difference between Southern and Northern writers is the difference it would make if Sinclair Lewis instead of Robert Penn Warren had written *All the King's Men*. In Sinclair Lewis's hands that same material would take on the exaggeration and oversimplification that we are familiar with in Mr. Lewis's novels. Willie Stark would be the caricature of a demagogue—he would be Babbitt recast as a politician. Hunks of satirical realism would be relieved by chunks of humor in the style of the sports page. Mr. Lewis could not achieve the intricate complexity of Mr. Warren's design, in which every seeming elaboration proves in the end to be, not an elaboration after all, but a supporting element of the grand scheme. Nor could Mr. Lewis achieve the ethical meaning of Mr. Warren's narrative. Mr. Lewis cannot do such things because he cannot use the knowledge of the heart, if he has it. He cannot use it because he belongs to an antitraditional society which gives its allegiance to a different sort of knowledge. Perhaps Mr. Lewis is in rebellion against that society; but in his novel about Willie Stark we would never be able to discover just why Willie Stark misbehaves. Willie Stark would of course misbehave in Sinclair Lewis's novel, but it would be only misbehavior, not evil behavior, not sin. For Sinclair Lewis, as for most Northern writers, evil and sin were abolished by Grant's victory over Lee at Appomattox, since which time the North has proceeded on the assumption that there is no defect or irregularity in human nature and human affairs that cannot be remedied by the application of money, science, and socialistic legislation. Therefore, in reading Mr. Lewis's novel about Willie Stark we would inevitably feel that there was no defect in Willie Stark that could not be remedied by a visit to a psychoanalyst or an amendment to the United States Constitution. But it is quite different in the novel that Mr. Warren has written about Willie Stark. We are there confronted with the ancient problem of evil and its manifestations. We must contemplate the imperfection of man, for whatever it is worth of good and bad. For Willie Stark, for the Compsons of Faulkner's novels, for the characters bad or good of most serious Southern novels, there is no remedy in law or sociology, and no reward but the reward of virtue and the hope of heaven.

The point of this discourse is a difficult one. I hope, in seeking to bring it to your attention, that I have not overstated it. At any rate it is the point I would be most anxious to make at this time before any group of Southern writers.

In summation I would say: study your art, all you can. It is indispensable, and no opportunity should be lost to master it. But it is not really the gravest problem, since whatever can be studied can surely be learned. The gravest problem is how and where to apply the art, once it is learned. No textbook, no school, no writers' conference can solve that problem for you. You only can solve it. To solve it you must become aware of the difference between what you think you know, and what you really know. The latter, what you really know, in your bones as much as in your brain, is what I mean by "knowledge carried to the heart." Only that will lead you to your real subject and release you from the false knowledge that brings imitation, subservience, and distortion.

For you as Southern writers that great problem—the problem of discovering your real subject—is easier to solve than if you were Northern writers. But even for Southern writers it is more difficult than it was thirty years ago. The regime of false knowledge has invaded us and threatens still heavier invasions. Therefore, as writers, we have not only a private interest to defend but also a public duty to perform. What that duty is I surely do not need to say, this morning in the State of Mississippi, which in 1948 cast its electoral vote for Thurmond and Wright. I trust you will understand that I have been attempting to define not only a principle of literature but also a principle of life. Out of the knowledge carried to the heart let us defend it, as the true source of virtue and liberty.

THE CASE OF POETRY

The features which the object discloses [in art] are not those which have their meaning for a science, for a set of practical values. They are those which render the body of the object, and constitute a knowledge so radical that the scientist as a scientist can scarcely understand it, and puzzles to see it rendered, richly and wastefully, in the poem, or the painting. The knowledge attained there, and recorded, is a new kind of knowledge, the world in which is set is a new world.

—John Crowe Ransom, 1938

THE CASE OF POETRY
INTRODUCTION

In 1938, a year when world attention was focused on more obviously violent events—a hurricane that devastated New England, Hitler's brutal occupation of the Sudetenland—Henry Holt and Company published a textbook by two young professors at "The Louisiana State University." Cleanth Brooks Jr. and Robert Penn Warren began *Understanding Poetry* with a "Letter to the Teacher." Not exactly impolite, it nevertheless handled the usual classroom approaches to poetry the way Lee handled Burnside's advances toward the Army of Northern Virginia at Fredericksburg. Not even four sentences into the first paragraph, they had annihilated three "substitutes" for "the poem as the object of study":

1.   Paraphrase of logical and narrative content.
2.   Study of biographical and historical materials.
3.   Inspirational and didactic interpretation.[1]

By insisting on the integrity of "the poem as a literary construct," and then showing in detail what that meant, *Understanding Poetry* revolutionized what happened in the classroom.

With this book, more than any other, the "New Criticism" (as John Crowe Ransom named it three years later) registered its first major

---

1. Cleanth Brooks Jr. and Robert Penn Warren, *Understanding Poetry* (New York: Henry Holt and Company, 1938), iv.

impact. No other single book published in the twentieth century had more influence on the teaching of literature. Decades later, in a different context, Robert Penn Warren quoted Harold Rosenberg's comment that, when revolution is the fashion, the decision to be revolutionary "counts for very little. . . . [T]he most radical changes have come from personalities who were conservative."[2] Warren might have been thinking about *Understanding Poetry*. Certainly, a basic conservatism underlay the radical changes that this textbook brought about. Written by Southerners who studied at Vanderbilt with John Crowe Ransom, *Understanding Poetry* also contained significant poems by the same men who had written essays attacking industrialism in *I'll Take My Stand* earlier in the decade.

The question is where exactly the connection lies. How does a concern for "the poem as a literary construct" coincide with—or supplant, or modify—earlier concerns about the agrarian South in an age of industrial technology? Is the poem a set of self-sufficient holdings? There is no simple, discursive explanation, and certainly no automatic agreement among the essayists in this book, but the way toward an answer lies in Ransom's call for an attention to the difference between "economic forms" and such "aesthetic forms" as courtship, ritual, and poetry. A poem is made as machines are made; both have their roots in *technē*. But the poem serves no immediate, useful purpose. Ransom, like Aristotle in the *Nicomachean Ethics*, argues that the truly human level of action arises only through training in virtue, understood as a schooling in aesthetic forms. Habituation in what generosity or temperance feel like, for example, should eventually lead to the conscious embrace of these virtues. One might behave more "naturally" through recourse to one's untutored impulses, such as sheer greed or gluttony (Ransom calls these "economic" forms), but in doing so, one would reduce the object sought to the "indifferent instance of a universal," as Ransom puts it. Poetry, understood in this way, can be a central part of one's schooling in the restraint and indirection that constitute human excellence or *aretē*.

All poetry? Certainly not. In fact, the primary task of criticism lies in discrimination, which requires attention to the poem's subject mat-

2. Robert Penn Warren, *Democracy and Poetry* (Cambridge, MA: Harvard University Press, 1975), 15–16.

ter in relation to its form, and "subject-matter may be differentiated with respect to its ontology, or the reality of its being."[3] Behind Ransom's emphasis lies the conviction that the images of poetry, far more than ideas, bring one in touch with being, which science forgets. The image "cannot be dispossessed of its priority. It cannot be dispossessed of a primordial freshness, which idea can never claim."[4] The emphasis on poetry becomes a way back to the world's body, "back out of all this now too much for us," as Robert Frost puts it in "Directive"—surely one impulse behind the Agrarian movement as well.

Behind the New Critical concentration on the literary construct and "the heresy of paraphrase," as Brooks puts it, lies a conviction that poetry best approaches the irreducibility of what exists. Impatience with "platonism" runs consistently through the essays of Tate and Ransom, and both men mean by it any tendency to believe that the truth lies in abstraction from "things as they are in their rich and contingent materiality."[5] Their emphasis sometimes seems too focused on lyric poetry, but Brooks, Warren, and Tate had much to say on the novel as well. In "Poetry as Tradition," Donald Davidson—never even remotely a New Critic, but always a friend and correspondent of many fellow Southerners—broadens the perspective in a late essay to pull his brethren out of their books and remind them of the oral tradition. Part of the emphasis on poetry surely derives from the attempt to understand what these men as poets experience in the act of composition as well as in the act of reading. Seventy years later, the poems that Brooks and Warren included in *Understanding Poetry* by Donald Davidson (*Lee in the Mountains*), Allen Tate (*Ode to the Confederate Dead* and *Last Days of Alice*), and John Crowe Ransom (*Winter Remembered* and *The Equilibrists*) take their stand, not only beside those of such contemporaries in the book as T. S. Eliot, Ezra Pound, and Robert Frost, but also with those of the English tradition.

3. John Crowe Ransom, *The World's Body* (1968), 111.
4. Ibid., 115.
5. Ibid., 116.

5

FORMS AND CITIZENS

JOHN CROWE RANSOM

Although it can be read separately, "Forms and Citizens" belongs
with "A Poem Nearly Anonymous," the essay about Milton's Lycidas
that John Crowe Ransom placed first in The World's Body. *Louis*
D. Rubin Jr. has shown that these paired essays—centering on Mil-
ton, who left his career as a poet for some years to become a polemi-
cist in the Puritan cause—also explain why Ransom left the South
in 1937 and abandoned Agrarian polemics for literary criticism.[1]
Rubin's reading illuminates the importance of Milton to Ransom,
but "Forms and Citizens" also says a great deal about the place of
poetry in the early '30s, when (as in Milton's day) radical politics
were on the rise. With his trademark wryness, Ransom analyzes the
relation between "economic," or "work," forms and "aesthetic," or
"play," forms. Economic forms seek efficiency for "the natural man
. . . a predatory creature to whom every object is an object of prey
and the real or individual object cannot occur." Limited to nature,
such a predator can have no experience of "the real or individual
object"—which means that "naturalness" should by no means be
confused with greater reality. Aesthetic forms, on the other hand,
force "the social man" to submit to "the restraint of convention," a

---

1. Louis D. Rubin Jr., "A Critic Almost Anonymous: John Crowe Ransom Goes North"
in *The New Criticism and After*, ed. Thomas Daniel Young (Charlottesville: University of
Virginia Press, 1976), 1–21.

submission that allows him to "respect the object and to see it unfold at last its individuality."

    Ransom's teasing paradoxes ask his reader to consider how, from the economic perspective, the wealth of detail that makes something "real and individual" might come to look like "irrelevant sensibilia." He takes up the point again in his discussion of the "image" in "Poetry: A Note in Ontology." He eschews discussion of the implications for politics of the destruction of aesthetic forms—a point that he takes up briefly (precisely on the score of Puritanism) in "Poets without Laurels"—but he surely remembers that Milton's party beheaded a king.

A first-rate poet performs in *Lycidas*, it is plain. And this is plain too: he performs because the decencies of an occasion require it of him, but the occasion catches him at a moment when his faith in the tradition of his art is not too strong, and in the performance rebellion is mixed up with loyalty. The study of the poem leads into a broad field of discussion, and the topic is the general relation of the poet to his formal tradition.

By formal we are not to mean the metre only; but also, and it is probably even more important, the literary type, with its fictitious point of view from which the poet approaches his object, and its prescription of style and tone. And by tradition we should mean simply the source from which the form most easily comes. Tradition is the handing down of a thing by society, and the thing handed down is just a formula, a form.

Society hands down many forms which the individual is well advised to appropriate, but we are concerned here with those which may be called the aesthetic ones. They contrast themselves with the other and more common forms in the remarkable fact that they do not serve the principle of utility. This point has not been sufficiently remarked, so far as my reading indicates. There are economic forms; there are also aesthetic forms, which are not same thing. Or, there are work-forms and there are play-forms.

First, the economic forms. We inherit the traditional forms of such objects as plough, table, boot, biscuit, machine, and of such processes as shepherding the flock, building, baking, making war. These, forms are of intense practicality, and it is a good thing that they exist for the instruction of the successive generations, whose makeshifts, if they had to tutor themselves, would be blundering and ineffectual. Such forms write their own valuations, and very clearly. They are the recipes of maximum efficiency, short routes to "success," to welfare, to the attainments of natural satisfactions and comforts. They are the stock services which society confers upon its members, and the celebrated ones; doubtless in themselves alone a sufficient justification for; constituted societies; sometimes, and especially where it is the modern temper which passes on it, the one usefulness which we can imagine attaching to societies, and the whole purpose of the social contract. But that is almost demonstrably an error, proceeding from a blind spot on the organ of insight which we are scarcely in a position to detect. Men absorbed in business and affairs may be excused for making that error, but it would be an egregious one for those who spend of their time and love upon aesthetic effects. It is in the aesthetic effects, if secured in those experiences that record themselves publicly as "art," or for that matter as manners and religion, that the given forms are both more and less than they seem, and not, on the whole, of any conceivable economic advantage.

Chiefly the error is an eidolon of period, a matter of the age and generation. Societies of the old order seemed better aware of the extent of their responsibilities. Along with the work-forms went the play-forms, which were elaborate in detail, and great in number, fastening upon so many of the common and otherwise practical occasions of life and making them occasions of joy and reflection, even festivals and celebrations yet at the same time by no means a help but if anything a hindrance to direct action. The aesthetic forms are a technique of restraint, not of efficiency. They do not butter our bread, and they delay the eating of it. They stand between the individual and his natural object and impose a check upon his action; the reason must have been known to the governors of old societies, for they honored the forms with unanimity; it must even yet be recoverable, for the argument shapes itself readily. To the concept of direct action the old society—the directed and hierarchical one—opposed the concept of aesthetic experience, as a true opposite, and checked the one in order to induce the other. Perhaps, since a social psychology is subtle, they fancied that the indissolubility of societies might depend as much on the definition they gave to play as on the definition they gave to labor. If so, our modern societies, with their horror of "empty" forms and ceremonies, and their invitation to men to be themselves, and handle their objects as quickly and rudely as they please, are not only destroying old arts and customs which they might not mind doing, but exposing incidentally their own solidarity to the anarchy of too much greed. But that is an incident. The formal tradition in art has a validity more than political, and the latter I am content to waive. What I have in mind is an argument from aesthetics which will justify any formal art, even a formal literature.

II

When a consensus of taste lays down the ordinance that the artist shall express himself formally, the purpose is evidently to deter him from expressing himself immediately. Or, the formal tradition intends to preserve the artist from the direct approach to his object. Behind the tradition is probably the sense that the direct approach is perilous to the artist, and may be fatal. It is feared that the artist who disregards the instruction may discover at length that he has only been artless or, what is worse, that he will not make this important discovery, which will have to be made for him by the horrid way of autopsy. I suggest, therefore, that an art is usually, and probably of necessity, a kind of obliquity; that its fixed form proposes to guarantee the round-about of the artistic process, and the "aesthetic distance."

A code of manners also is capable of being taken in this fashion; it confers the same benefit, or the same handicap if we prefer, upon its adherent. Let us represent graphically, as in the figure I have entered below, the conduct of a man toward the woman he desires.

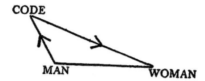

The event consists in his approach to the object. He may approach directly, and then his behavior is to seize her as quickly as possible. No inhibitions are supposed to have kept the cave-man or pirate, or any other of the admired figures of a great age when life was "in the raw," from taking this severely logical course. If our hero, however, does not propose for himself the character of the savage, or of animal, but the quaint one of "gentleman," then he has the fixed code of his *gens* to remember, and then is estopped from seizing her, he must approach her with ceremony, and pay her a fastidious courtship. We conclude not that the desire is abandoned, but that it will take a circuitous road and become a romance. The form actually denies him the privilege of going the straight line between two points, even though this line has an axiomatic logic in its favor and is the shortest possible line. But the woman, contemplated in this manner under restraint, becomes a person and an aesthetic object; therefore a richer object.

In fact the woman becomes nothing less than an individual object; for we stumble here upon a fruitful paradox. The natural man, who today sometimes seems to be becoming always a greater man in our midst, asserting his rights so insistently, causing us to hear so much about "individualism," is a predatory creature to whom every object is an object of prey and the real or individual object cannot occur; while the social man, who submits to the restraint of convention, comes to respect the object and to see it unfold at last its individuality; which, if we must define it, is its capacity to furnish us with an infinite variety of innocent experience; that is, it is a source, from which so many charming experiences have already flowed, and a promise, a possibility of future experiences beyond all prediction. There must then, really, be two kinds of individualism: one is greedy and bogus, amounting only to egoism; the other is contemplative, genuine, and philosophical. The function of a code of manners is to make us capable of something better than the stupidity of an appetitive or economic life. High comedy, for example, is technically art, but substantially it is manners, and it has the agreeable function of displaying our familiar life relieved of its fundamental animality, filled, and dignified, through a technique which has in it nothing more esoteric than ceremonious intercourse.

To return to the figure, and to change the denotation slightly. Let us have a parallel now from the field of religion. The man is bereaved, and this time the object of his attention is the dead body of his friend. Instead of having a code of manners for this case, let him owe allegiance to a religious society, one which is possessed preferably of an ancient standing, and at all events of a ritual. The new terms for our graph become: Man and Corpse at the base, and Rite at the top and back. The religious society exists in order to serve the man in this crisis. Freed from his desolation by its virtue, he is not obliged now to run and throw himself upon the body in an ecstasy of grief, nor to go apart and brood upon the riddle of mortality, which may be the way of madness. His action is through the form of a pageant of grief, which is lovingly staged and attended by the religious community. His own grief expands, is lightened, no longer has to be explosive or obsessive. A sort of by-product of this formal occasion, we need not deny, is his grateful sense that his community supports him in a dreadful hour. But what interests us rather is the fact that his preoccupation with the deadness of the body is broken by his participation in the pageantry, and his bleak situation elaborated with such rich detail that it becomes massive, substantial, and sufficient.

We may of course eliminate the pageantry of death from our public life, but only if we expect the widow and orphan not really to feel their loss; and, to this end we may inform them that they will not find it an economic loss, since they shall be maintained in their usual standards of living by the State. It is unfortunate for the economic calculus that they are likely to feel it anyway, since probably their relation to the one dead was not more economic than it was sentimental. Sentiments, those irrational psychic formations, do not consist very well with the indifference, machine-like, with which some modern social workers would have men fitting into the perfect economic organization. It is not as good animals that we are complicated with sentimental weakness. The fierce drives of the animals, whether human or otherwise, are only towards a kind of thing, the indifferent instance of a universal, and not some private and irreplaceable thing. All the nouns at this stage are common nouns. But we, for our curse or our pride, have sentiments; they are directed towards persons and things; and a sentiment is the totality of love and knowledge which we have of an object that is private and unique. This object might have been a simple economic object, yet we have elected to graft upon the economic relation a vast increment of diffuse and irrelevant sensibilia, and to keep it there forever, obstructing science and action. Sometimes we attach the major weight of our being, unreasonably, and to the point of absurdity, to a precious object. The adventitious interest, the sensibility that complicates and sometimes submerges the economic interest, does not seem to ask any odds of it, nor to think it necessary to theorize on behalf of its own existence. We may resent it, but eventually we have to accept it, as, simply, an "aesthetic" requirement, a piece of foolishness, which human nature will not forego. Wise societies legalize it and make much of it; for its sake they define the forms of manners, religions, arts; conferring a public right upon the sensibilia, especially when they organize themselves, or pile up notably, as they do, into the great fixed sentiments.

In Russia[2] we gather that there is a society bent seriously on "perfecting" the human constitution, that is, rationalizing or economizing it completely. The code of manners and the religious ritual are suspended, while the arts lead a half-privileged, censored, and furtive existence. Already a recent observer notes one result of the disappearance of the sex taboos: there is less sex-consciousness in Russia than anywhere in the Western world. That is to say, I suppose, that the loyal Russians approach the perfect state of animals, with sex reduced to its pure biological business. The above observer wonders painfully whether "love," of the sort that has been celebrated by so much history and so much literature, will vanish from Russia. It will vanish, if this society succeeds in assessing it by the standard of economic efficiency. The Russian leaders are repeating, at this late stage of history, with a people whose spirit is scored by all the traditional complications of human nature,

---

2. [Ransom] I am not sure at this time of second publication just how true of Russia this representation may be.

the experiment of the Garden of Eden; when the original experiment should be conclusive, and was recorded, we may imagine, with that purpose in view. The original human family was instructed not to take the life of the beast-couples as its model; and did not, exactly, mean to do so; occupied itself with a certain pretty project having to do with a Tree of Rationalization; and made the mortal discovery that it came to the very same thing. The question is whether the ideal of efficient animality is good enough for human beings; and whether the economic law, by taking precedence at every point over the imperative of manners, of religion, and of the arts, will not lead to perfect misery.

III

And now, specifically, as to art, and its form. The analogy of the above occasions to the occasion called art is strict. Our terms now are Artist, Object, and Form. Confronting his object, the artist is tempted to react at once by registering just that aspect of the object in which he is practically "interested." For he is originally, and at any moment may revert to, a natural man, having a predatory and acquisitive interest in the object, or at best looking at it with a "scientific" curiosity to see if he cannot discover one somewhere in it. Art has a canon to restrain this natural man. It puts the object out of his reach; or more accurately, removes him to where he cannot hurt the object, nor disrespect it by taking his practical attitude towards it, exchanging his actual station, where he is too determined by proximity to the object, and contemporaneity with it, for the more ideal station furnished by the literary form. For example: there is the position, seemingly the silly and ineffectual one, of the man who is required by some quixotic rule of art to think of his object in pentameter couplets, therefore with a good deal of lost motion; and there is the far-fetched "point of view," which will require him to adapt all his thought to the rule of drama. The motion is well lost, if that is what it costs to frustrate the natural man and induce the aesthetic one. Society may not after all be too mistaken in asking the artist to deal with his object somewhat artificially. There will be plenty of others glad to deal with it immediately. It is perfectly true that art, *a priori*, looks dubious; a project in which the artist has a splendid chance for being a fool. The bad artists in the world are cruelly judged, they are the good journeymen gone wrong; and the good artists may be humorously regarded, as persons strangely possessed. But the intention of art is one that is peculiarly hard to pursue steadily, because it goes against the grain of our dominant and carefully instructed instincts; it wants us to enjoy life, to taste and reflect as we drink; when we are always tending as abstract appetites to gulp it down; or as abstract intelligences to proceed, by a milder analogue, to the cold fury of "disinterested" science. A technique of art must, then, be unprepossessing, and look vain and affected, and in fact look just like the technique of fine manners, or of ritual. Heroic intentions call for heroic measures.

We should not be taken in for a moment when we hear critics talking as if the form were in no sense a discipline but a direct help to the "expressiveness"—meaning the forthrightness—of the poem. This view reflects upon the holders credit for a reach of piety which is prepared to claim everything for the true works of art, and also a suspicion of ingenuousness for their peculiar understanding of the art-process. Given an object, and a poet burning to utter himself upon it, he must take into account a third item, the form into which he must cast his utterance. (If we like, we may call it the body which he must give to his passion.) It delays and hinders him. In the process of "composition" the burning passion is submitted to cool and scarcely relevant considerations. When it appears finally it may be said to have been treated with an application of sensibility. The thing expressed there is not the hundred-percent passion at all.

If the passion burns too hot in the poet to endure the damping of the form, he might be advised that poetry can exercise no undue compulsion upon his spirit since, after all, there is prose. Milton may not always have let the form have its full effect upon the passion; some modern poets whom I admire do not; neither of which facts, however, disposes one to conclude that poetry is worse for the formal tradition. The formal tradition, as I have said, lays upon the poet evidently a double requirement. One metrical or mechanical; but the measured speech is part of the logical identity of the poem; it goes into that "character" which it possesses as an ideal creation, out of the order of the actual. The other requirement is the basic one of the make-believe, the drama, the specific anonymity or pseudonymity, which defines the poem as poem when that goes we may also say that the poem goes; so that there would seem to be taking place in the act of poetry a rather unprofitable labor if this anonymity is not dearly conceived when a poet is starting upon his poem, and a labor lost if the poet, who has once conceived it and established it, forgets to maintain it.

IV

We accept or refuse the arts, with their complex intention, according as we like or dislike the fruits, or it may be the flowers, they bring to us; but these arts, and their techniques, may be always reinforced by the example of manners, and the example of religion; the three institutions do not rest on three foundations but on one foundation. A natural affiliation binds together the gentleman, the religious man, and the artist—punctilious characters, all of them, in their formalism. We have seen one distinguished figure in our times pronouncing on behalf of all three in one breath. In politics, royalism; in religion, Anglo-Catholic; in literature, classical. I am astonished upon discovering how comprehensively this formula covers the kingdom of the aesthetic life as is organized by the social tradition. I am so grateful that it is with hesitation I pick a little quarrel with the terms. I would covet a program going something like this: In manners, aristocratic; in religion, ritualistic; in art, traditional. But I imagine the intent of Mr. Eliot's formula is about what I am representing; and on the other hand might be only the more effective to fight with for being so concrete. Unfortunately its terms are not suited to Americans; but possibly this is so of mine too. The word for our generation in these matters is "formal," and it might even bear the pointed qualification, "and reactionary." The phrase would carry the sense of our need: to make a return to amenities which the European communities labored to evolve, and defined as their "civilization." For the intention of none of those societies can have been simply to confirm the natural man as a natural man, or to improve him in cunning and effectiveness by furnishing him with its tried economic forms. It wanted to humanize him; which means, so far as his natural economy permitted, to complicate his natural functions with sensibility, and make them aesthetic. The object of a proper society is to instruct its members how to transform instinctive experience into aesthetic experience. Manners, rites, and arts are so close to each other that often their occasions must be confused, and it does not matter much if they are. The rule of manners is directed to those occasions when natural appetites and urges are concerned; when we hunger, or lust, or go into a rage, or encounter strange or possibly dangerous persons. The rites take place upon religious occasions; but I suppose this is tautology. It is my idea that religion is an institution existing for the sake of its ritual, rather than, as I have heard, for the sake of its doctrines, to which there attaches no cogency of magic, and for that matter a very precarious cogency of logic. The issues upon which the doctrines pronounce are really insoluble for human logic, and the higher religionists are aware of it. The only solution that is possible, since the economic solution is not possible, is the aesthetic one. When these issues press upon us, there is little that one man, with whatever benefit of doctrines, can do toward the understanding of the event which another man cannot do; and he had better not try too hard to understand the precise event, but enlarge its terms, and assimilate it into the form of an ornate public ritual through which the whole mind can discharge itself. This is a subtle technique, it has been a successful technique; in insisting upon it as the one thing I do not mean to subtract dignity from the world's great religions—which I revere. And what are the specific occasions for ritual? Those which are startling in our biological and economic history, and provoke reflection, and also, for fear we may forget to be startled when we are living for a long interval upon a dead level of routine, some arbitrary occasions, frequent and intercalated; therefore birth, marriage, death; war, peace, the undertaking of great enterprises, famine, storm; the seasons of the year, Sabbath, the holidays. But as for the artistic process, what are its occasions? What prompts the artist? For we remark at once that many works of art embody ritual, and art is often apparently content to be the handmaiden to religion, as Hegel desired, and as she conceivably is in a painting by Michelangelo, or a poem on the order of *Lycidas*. We know also that works of art have been dedicated to the ceremonious life of society, commemorating chivalry, or some much easier code; art serving manners.

The occasions of art are innumerable; very probably its "future is immense." Its field is wider than that of manners, or than that of religion; the field of literary art alone is that. In fact it is about as wide as the field of science itself; and there I think lies the hint for a definition. What is the occasion which will do for the artist and the scientist indifferently? It is the occasion when we propose to "study" our object; that is, when we are more than usually undesirous and free, and find the time to become curious about the object as, actually, something "objective" and independent. Out of the surplus of our energy—thanks to the efficiency of our modern economic forms we have that increasingly—we contemplate object as object, and are not forced by an instinctive necessity to take it and devour it immediately. This contemplation may take one of two routes; and first, that of science. I study the object to see how I may wring out of it my physical satisfaction the next time; even how I may discover for the sake of a next time the physical satisfaction which it contains, but not too transparently; analyzing and classifying, "experimenting," bringing it under the system of control which I intend as a scientist to have over the world objects. It is superfluous to observe that I, the modern scientist, am in this case spiritually just as poor as was my ancestor the caveman. My intention is simply to have bigger and quicker satisfactions than he had, my head still runs on satisfactions. But I may contemplate also, under another form entirely, the form of art. And that is when I am impelled neither to lay hands on the object immediately, nor to ticket it for tomorrow's outrage, but am in such a marvelous state of innocence that I would know it for its own sake, and conceive it as having its own existence; this is the knowledge, or it ought to be, which Schopenhauer praised as "knowledge without desire." The features which the object discloses then are not those which have their meaning for a science, for a set of practical values. They are those which render the body of the object, and constitute a knowledge so radical that the scientist as a scientist can scarcely understand it, and puzzles to see it rendered, richly and wastefully, in the poem, or the painting. The knowledge attained there, and recorded, is a new kind of knowledge, the world in which it is set is a new world.

V

Poetry is more complicated than an animal act, which is ordinarily a scientific sort of act; it is even more complicated than the play of an animal, though the complication of that act is one difficult for the psychologists to handle. The poetic act involves the general sensibility, with its diffusive ranging, hardly familiar to science. But it certainly involves at the same time a discipline, very like that of science. Perhaps the best way to construe a poetic labor briefly is to take it as the analogue to a scientific one (though this latter is the paragon of labors which are serious and important) and then to fill in the differences.

The poetic labors of John Milton will do for an example. He is never discovered except meditating an object which is formidable, with a scrutiny which is steady, like that of a scientist; infinitely more sensitive. Milton's poetry exceeds most poetry in its logical closeness and symmetry; the difference between his epics and Virgil's is that his are powerfully and visibly motivated at every moment, and he will not if he can recover the purity of narrative, the innocence, that marks the ancient epic. Milton is a strong man, and has intense economic persuasions, if we may bring under that term his personal, moral, and political principles. These are his precious objects; or the situations in which he finds them exercising are. But the situations in the poetry are not his actual ones; they are fancied ones which do not touch him so nearly, distant enough to inhibit the economic impulse, which would have inhibited the sensibility. The result is that Milton's poetry, broadly speaking, may be said always to deal with "important" or highly economic subjects. But the importance of the subject is not the importance of the poetry; that depends more on the sensitiveness and completeness of the experience. The subject will generally be found to have been treated more precisely or practically somewhere in his economic prose; that is, in the ethical, theological, political tracts. It pleases us to imagine, on the strength of Milton's example, that there is no prose which is incapable of becoming a poetry, no subject in his mind so urgent that he is intimidated by it, and cannot feel it, enjoy it, and spread it out; live it, in the way we might call upon some superior man to live it.

So we look briefly and definitely as we may, at the whole net accomplishment of John Milton; starting from a convenient point, which will be *Lycidas*. This poem looks backward upon a long period of minor or practice poetry, and forward to the career of the major poet; while, as I pointed out in my previous essay, it does not fail to betray the man behind the poet.

We do not find in *Lycidas* quite the proper occasion for a modern tract on communism, nor even for a contemporaneous tract on divorce; which makes it unnecessary either to regret or to be glad that Milton has not attempted a demonstration that literature is sociology, or literature is science. We do find in the death of the young clergyman the occasion for a contemporaneous tract on the degeneration of the clergy; and Milton, with some difficulty, perhaps, dismisses that temptation. For his difficulty, if we detect it, he is probably the less an artist. Yet Milton entertained strict views upon the function of the artist, and only upon strong compulsion was apostate. Milton felt the impact of modernity which is perennial in every generation; or, if it is not, of the rather handsome degree of modernity which was current in his day. He was exposed to specific temptation because he was a man of his times and held strong views upon the contemporary ecclesiastical and political situations, in a period when the church and the political order were undergoing revolution; he was of the party of revolution. He had a natural inclination to preach, and display his zeal; to preach upon such themes as the reform of the clergy, and the reform of the government; and he tended to preach intemperately when he preached. He knew of this tendency in himself and opposed it. He went so far as to abandon that career in the church which his father had intended for him and to which he seems at first to have consented. The career which he chose instead was one which we are wrong to consider vague and indefinite, for he hardly considered it so—the career of an artist. He has a good deal to say about this choice. If in the course of a public controversy much later he argued that he had given up the church because he could not endure its tyrannical overlords, he made no such plea in the affectionate Latin letter written to his father when the issue was hot. Here he is content to assert the superiority of the poet to other men. He is impressed with the elevation of the poet's mind, which gives him a sort of aristocracy, an attitude habitually aesthetic; and Milton has studied it, and had it, enough to know. (We must not suppose, as Milton did

not, that a man has to be born in some statistical manner to this elevation. He may bring himself up to it.)

This is not quite the same as saying that Milton renounced his position as a man in order to take a position as a poet he expected to occupy
both positions, but at different times. But he did not consent to define
himself as the man; that is, as the man with a profession, the economic
man. As a man he was too much like any of us; if not too appetitive in
the flesh, at least too zealous in intellectual action, which comes aesthetically to the same thing. He might have elected to become not an
artist but a man of science; a character that is just barely not a man of
action, or a professional. Science belongs to the economic impulse and
does not free the spirit; its celebrated virtue is due to its position on the
economic scale, well distanced from the maw and the mouth of actual
red appetite, while its technique is precisely the same.

Like many other people, he had a blind spot. He could scarcely
receive from ritual the aesthetic benefit which was intended for him
in that dispensation. Ritual turned him suspicious and truculent; a
great modernism. Yet the inhibitions lay upon the act of public participation, not so much upon his intuitive understanding of the matter, and we may easily overstate it. It is probably a common variety of
Protestantism. When he came under the milder influences of poetry,
he composed the kind of effects which he valued, which he constantly
received in the traditional poetry of Greeks, Romans, Italians, and
Englishmen—poetry nearly as ornate, mythological, religious, as a
ritual itself could be. But when he was faced by the ritual, the effective
thing itself, administered by priests whom he had determined to hold
as hypocritical, he was roused invariably to resistance. So inveterate
and passionate did this resistance become that it took him into the
extremist Protestant camp to write hard doctrine, and actually to set
up his own religion as a project in dialectic. All the time he "knew"
better; probably no European poet exceeds him much, either for consistency or for depths of insight, in mythological sense. The same Milton appealed in a Latin exercise to Plato not to banish the myth-makers
from the Republic, and some years later would have liked publicly to
chase out of England the Anglican ritualists, the adherents of the then
myth, as idolaters. That is the Milton paradox.

He was obstinate in his idea of what the church must have been for him as a calling. His Anglo-Catholic contemporaries could have told him—probably they told him—that the priest who is charged with the performance of the ritual, and on some occasions with creating ritual on his own responsibility, is eminently in the service of the cult of aesthetic experience. His noble Italian friends certainly told him, during that triumphal tour on which he received honors incredible for a professing Puritan in Rome, except that he may have been regarded as a man not yet too openly committed, and still reclaimable. Among these friends was Manso, to whom it must have seemed a pity that a poet so prodigious, and so true to the ancient traditions of his calling, was capable of not perceiving that these had anything to do with the majestic ceremonial of a high church. We may imagine that Manso had this anomaly in mind—and not merely the havoc which the young collegiate Milton had wrought with the Catholics, or tried to wreak, in his exuberant exercise on the Gunpowder Plot—when he presented Milton with a fine Latin compliment, to which there was attached all the same an impressive qualification: "If your piety were such as your mind, your form, charm, face, and manners, then you would not be an Angle, but in sober truth an Angel." Manso was cribbing of course from the sixth-century Gregory, who had observed the fair-haired Anglian slaves in Rome, and hoped they might one day take their own part in the ritual of a world-wide catholic church. Gregory's hope had been realized, but now in Milton's time it seemed on the point of being deceived; and here was one of the race in question, brilliantly endowed in his mind and person, but stubborn in his barbarism; for Manso could not fail to appreciate just what it meant for a society to cast off its religious forms.

But, as I have said, Milton did know better than he acted; he made his choice and became the artist; and exercised his *métier* with an aristocratic taste that almost never failed him; though he was no more able as layman than he had been as prospective priest to apply this taste to the forms of his worship. We do not regret his decision when we have to follow him during the ten or fifteen years after 1640, the period in which he felt obliged as a citizen to drop the poet and become the preacher, the tractarian, and the economic man. During that period we remember gratefully that he shares our own view of his intractable nature, in which so much of the sin of Adam resides; that he understands his predicament. The formality of poetry sustained him, induced in him his highest nobility, and his most delicate feeling. The ding-dong of contemporary controversy brought out of him something ugly and plebeian that was there all the time, waiting. He took care that the preacher should be the Miltonic role for but a period; the artist came back, and may have been the better artist for the ignominy which he had suffered; though I shall not try to argue that.

Art was his deliberate career. It is a career, precisely as science is a career. It is as serious, it has an attitude as official, it is as studied and consecutive, it is by all means as difficult, it is no less important. It may be less remunerative, it is further from offering the sort of values which are materially rewarded; today it may be so unrewarded that, if we agree to regard it like science as a career, we are not inclined to regard it like science as a profession; but so far from being at a disadvantage on that account, it may be better off, as having the more innocence because of it, and finding innocence a good condition for its peculiar process.

It would follow that Milton has been widely if not generally misunderstood, by people who define him primarily as a Puritan moralist, or a theologian, or a political thinker, or an early modern, or a scholar. Some ultra-modern critics, as was inevitable, now have turned upon him "as a man," and in that capacity as one of the damned, having an inherited disease, or a libido, or a crack in his mind—which seems at this distance unimportant if true. He was chiefly and preferably, and on a life-long scale, an artist. Those who will not undertake to gather what this involved for him will be finding themselves constantly rebuffed by the mountains of irrelevance raised against them in the body of his poetry. Milton is the poetry, and is lost to them if they do not know how to make acquaintance there. What on earth will they do with the cool flora that bloom so uselessly in the formal if somewhat tangled garden which is *Lycidas*?

6

THREE TYPES OF POETRY

ALLEN TATE

Allen Tate published "Three Types of Poetry" in three consecutive issues of the New Republic *in March and April of 1934. John Crowe Ransom's essay "Poetry: A Note in Ontology," which immediately follows Tate's in this volume, appeared in* American Review *in May of the same year. The two essays are closely related, both by coincidence and by mutual influence. Before either was published, Ransom was writing his essay while he circulated a copy of Tate's to his colleagues Walter Clyde Curry and Donald Davidson at Vanderbilt, both of whom admired it. "I have just reread it," Ransom wrote Tate, "after a week on an essay of my own, and will put down a few of my reflections. It is a very important essay, the best in the field. My own will not be contradictory—couldn't be, for I endorse about everything in yours. Just another set of terms, a slightly different angle of approach."[1]*

Both Ransom and Tate divide poetry into three types. Ransom categorizes poetry as physical, platonic, or metaphysical. Tate, whose focus lies on the modern world, treats three "attitudes"—the first an allegorical poetry, "motivated by the practical will;" the second a "revolt against the domination of science," characterized by romantic irony; and the third a nameless poetry—because complete—whose

---

1. John Crowe Ransom, *Selected Letters of John Crowe Ransom*, Thomas Daniel Young and George Core, eds. (Baton Rouge: Louisiana State University Press, 1985), 214.

representative is Shakespeare. More than Ransom, Tate explicitly centers his analysis on the problem of the will (rather than predatory appetite) in its relation to art. In the contemporary world, Tate argues, "all the arts are assumed to be necessarily assertions of the will"—that is, either didactic or propagandistic. On the contrary, says Tate, "the foundations of poetry, and possibly of the other creative arts, are somewhat different. We cannot understand them until we shall have eliminated from our thinking the demands of the category of will with its instrument, the practical intellect." The idea is not original to Tate or Ransom—it goes back to Kant and Schopenhauer—but it takes on a new resonance in the general context of a defense of Southern leisure. Tate's view of a work like Macbeth *is that its greatness lies precisely in not prompting one to do something: "It proves nothing; it creates the totality of experience in its quality; and it has no useful relation to the ordinary forms of action." For a generation of students trained to search out injustices in race, class, and gender, the absence of a directive toward action—or even political indignation—might be a bracing shock.*

I

In this essay I propose to discuss three kinds of poetry that bring to focus three attitudes of the modern world. I do not say all three attitudes, because there are more than three attitudes. And there are more than three kinds of poetry.

The first attitude is motivated by the practical will: in poetry until the seventeenth century it leaned upon moral abstractions and allegory; now, under the influence of the sciences, it has appealed to physical ideas. It looks from knowledge to action. The second attitude has been developed from the second phase of the first; it is a revolt against the domination of science, and in poetry it has given us the emotion known as "romantic irony." The third attitude is nameless because it is perfect, because it is complete and whole. Criticism may isolate the imperfect and formulate that which is already abstract; but it cannot formulate the concrete whole. There is no philosophical or historical name for the kind of poetry that Shakespeare wrote. I shall call it, in this essay, the creative spirit. I use the term for convenience, and ask the reader to forget its current uses by the followers of the Expressionist school.

We happen to be dominated at the moment by the scientific spirit of the practical will. A hundred and fifty years ago rose the thin cry of romantic irony—the poet's self-pity upon the rack of science, which he mistook for reality. Most notably in the sixteenth century we had the creative spirit.

The reader is asked to keep in mind two more general statements with some brief commentary:

First, the power of seizing the inward meaning of experience, the power of poetic creation that I shall call here the vision of the whole of life, is *a quality of the imagination*. The apologists of science speak as if this were the scientific attitude, but the aim of science is to produce a dynamic whole for the service of the practical will. Our experience of nuclear energy seems to be very different from our capacity to control it. For the imaginative whole of life is the wholeness of vision at a particular moment of experience; it yields us the quality of the experience.

It may be conveyed in a poem of four or six lines or in an epic of twelve books; or the twelve books may contain less of it than the four lines. Blake's *To the Accuser* is the total vision in eight lines; Darwin's *The Loves of the Plants* is the aimlessly statistical aggregation of fact—pseudo-botany or semi-science—in a number of lines that I have not counted.

Second, there is a surer grasp of the totality of experience in Wyatt's *To His Lute* than in Shelley's *Adonaïs* This is the center of my argument. We must understand that the lines

Life like a dome of many-colored glass
Stains the white radiance of eternity

are not poetry; they express the frustrated individual will trying to compete with science. The will asserts a rhetorical proposition about the whole of life, but the imagination has not seized upon the materials of the poem and made them into a whole. Shelley's simile is imposed upon the material from above; it does not grow out of the material.

It exists as explanation external to the subject: It is an explanation of "life" that seems laden with portent and high significance, but *as explanation* it necessarily looks towards possible action, and it is there that we know that the statement is meaningless. Practical experimental knowledge can alone fit means to ends.

If the simile of the dome were an integral part of a genuine poem, the question of its specific merit as truth or falsehood would not arise. Yet Shelley's dome, as an explanation of experience, is quite as good as Edgar's reflection on his father's downfall:

Ripeness is all.

But the figure rises from the depth of Gloucester's situation. It is a summation not only of Gloucester's tragedy but of the complex tensions of the plot before the catastrophe in the last scene. Possibly *King Lear* would be as good without Edgar's words; but it would be difficult to imagine the play without the passage ending in those words. They are implicit in the total structure, the concrete quality, of the whole experience that we have when we read *King Lear*. The specific merit of Edgar's statement as general truth or falsehood is irrelevant because it is an *experienced statement*, first from Edgar's, then from our own, point of view; and the statement remains experienced, and thus significant and comprehensible, whether it be true or false.

The truth or falsity of Shelley's figure is the only issue that it raises. This bit of Platonism must be accepted before we can accept the material of the poem *Adonaïs* for it must be a true idea to afford to the poet a true explanation. He must have an explanation for a material that he cannot experience. The idea of the dome is asserted to strengthen a subject that the poet has not implicitly imagined.

It was this quality of modern poetry that Arnold had in mind, or doubtless should have had in mind, when he remarked that the romantics "did not know enough." We have not known enough since their time. Arnold wrote later that the Victorian critics permitted the poet "to leave poetic sense ungratified, provided that he gratifies their rhetorical sense and their curiosity." If the term rhetoric must have an invidious meaning, I think we may understand Arnold somewhat in this manner: that rhetoric is a forcing of the subject, which is abstractly conceived, not implicitly seized upon. It is external and decorative in the early romantics of the mid-eighteenth century; it is hysterical, and evasive of the material, in the great romantics—and it excites the "curiosity" of the reader, who dwells on the external details of the poem or pities the sad poet. The reader is not given an integral work of art. How could criticism since Shelley and Wordsworth be anything but personal?—strive for anything but evaluation of personality? It has been given little else to evaluate. And why should not criticism fail in evaluating Shakespeare's personality? And is this not the glory of Shakespeare?

The reader's curiosity is motivated by his will. In the lowest terms, he seeks information (even from a poet); then, more purposefully, he seeks for the information an explanation that, if it is good, is some branch of science. But like the recent neohumanists he tries to get explanations from the poets.

"For what is rhetoric," wrote W. B. Yeats nearly fifty years ago, "but the will trying to do the work of the imagination?" Mr. Yeats, with insight as profound as it is rare in our time, went straight to the problem. Rhetoric is the pseudo-explanation of unimagined material. The "right" explanation—the exhibit of workable relations among different parts of any material—although always provisional, is the scientific explanation. When the will tries to do the work of the imagination, it fails, and only succeeds in doing badly the work of science. When the will supplants the imagination in poetry, the task of the poet, because his instrument is not adequate to his unconscious purpose, which is that of a science, is bound to be frustrated. We get the peculiar frustration of the poet known as romantic irony.

The pure scientific spirit I shall call here, without much regard for accuracy, a positive Platonism, a cheerful confidence in the limitless power of man to impose practical abstractions upon his experience. Romantic irony is a negative Platonism, a self-pitying disillusionment with the positive optimism of the other program: the romantic tries to build up a set of fictitious "explanations," by means of rhetoric, more congenial to his unscientific temper. The creative spirit occupies an aloof middle ground—it is in no sense a compromise, as the late Irving Babbitt conceived it to be—between these positions. Its function is the quality of experience, the total revelation—not explanation for the purpose of external control by the will.

II

Dante distinguished two kinds of allegory. Religious allegory is both literally and figuratively true: We are to believe that the events of the story happened. But poetical allegory is true only in the figurative sense. The derivative meanings, called by Dante the moral and the anagogical, are legitimate, indeed they are the highest meanings; but they lean upon no basis of fact. Although fictional allegory is not popular today, it is the only sort that we can conceive. When the medieval allegorist used the Bible, it never entered his head that he was not using historical fact; and he brought the same mentality to bear upon material that even we, who are sophisticated, recognize as historical.

But a modern poet, attempting allegory, undoes the history. We accept his figures and images as amiable make-believe, knowing that historical fact and poetic figure have no real connection, simply because there is nothing true but fact. About this fact science alone can instruct us, not with a fundamentally different kind of instruction from that of the allegorist, but with the same kind, more systematic and efficient. When the author of the popular poem *John Brown's Body* shows us the machine age growing out of Brown's body, we know that nothing of the sort happened, and we ask for the more enlightened view of the facts available in the scientific historians.

It is the kind of poetry that is primarily allegorical that seems to me to be inferior. It is inferior as science, and it is inferior as poetry. Mere allegory is a vague and futile kind of science. And because its primary direction is towards that oversimplification of life which is the mark of the scientific will, it is a one-sided poetry, ignoring the whole vision of experience. Although *The Divine Comedy* is allegorical, it would not be one of the great poems of all time if Dante had not believed its structure of action to be true. It came out of an age whose mentality held the allegorical view of experience as easily as we hold the causal and scientific; so, in Dante, allegory never rises to an insubordinate place, but consistently occupies an implicit place, from which we must derive it by analysis.

There is a general sense in which all literature may be apprehended as allegory, and that sense explains the popular level of literary appreciation. When certain moral ideas preponderate over others in any kind of literature, the crudely practical reader abstracts them, and contents himself with the illusion that they are the total meaning of the work. The naïve Roman Catholic may see only this phase of Dante, who for him might as well have written a tract. Now when the preponderance of meanings receives from the author himself the seal of his explicit approval, in face of the immense complication of our experience, then the work tends towards allegory. The work is written in the interest of social, moral, and religious ideas apart from which it has little existence or significance. It becomes aesthetic creation at a low level of intensity. If the intention is innocent, the result is didacticism. If it is deliberate and systematic, and calculated to move people into some definite course of action, we get what is called in our time propaganda.

Didactic and propagandist works frequently have great artistic merit and power. Fiction different as *The Pilgrim's Progress* and *An American Tragedy* is overwhelming evidence of this. The perception of merit in this kind of writing has become a pretext, in our age, for believing that its defects, chiefly the defect of "propaganda," are a primary motive of all literature in all times. When the deficiency or impurity of inspiration is not forthright, it is nevertheless assumed as present but concealed: This is the kind of propaganda that is supposedly written from the security of a ruling class.

Pure allegory differs from this kind of writing in that the preponderance of meaning is wholly revealed; the characters, images, symbols, ideas, are simple, and invite restatement in paraphrases that exhaust their meaning; they stand, not in themselves, but merely for something else. *The Faerie Queene* belongs to this class of allegory. The summary remarks that I shall make about that great poem by no means encompass it; for there is more to be said that would not be to my purpose.

The structural feature that first impresses the reader of the poem is the arbitrary length of each canto: There is no reason inherent in the narrative why a canto should not be longer or shorter than it is. The characters remain homogeneous throughout; that is to say, they suffer no dramatic alteration; an episode ends when they have acted out enough of the moral to please the poet. The action has no meaning apart from the preconceived abstractions, which we may call Renaissance Platonism or any other suitable name, so long as we remember that the ideas suffer no shock and receive no complication in contact with the narrative. The narrative lacks inner necessity; it is all illustration. The capacity of the poet to allegorize the "philosophy" was illimitable, and terminated only with his death, which prevented completion of the poem.

One must remember that this sort of allegory has predominated in our tradition. Anglo-American literature, with the possible exception, at his high moments, of Nathaniel Hawthorne, has not given us allegory of the Dantesque order. I allude here to Dante's ability to look into a specific experience and to recreate it in such a way that its meaning is nowhere distinct from its specific quality. The allegorical interpretation *is* secondary. We get a genuine creation of the imagination. We get, in the Spenserian allegory, a projection of the will.

The quality and intention of the allegorical will are the intention and quality of the will of science. With allegory the image is not a complete, qualitative whole; it is an abstraction calculated to force the situation upon which it is imposed toward a single direction. In the sixteenth century, science proper had achieved none of its triumphs. The allegorist had before him no standard by which he could measure the extent of his failure to find the right abstractions for the control of nature. He could spin out his tales endlessly in serene confidence of their "truth." But by the end of the eighteenth century his optimism had waned; it had passed to the more efficient allegorist of nature, the modern scientist.

Now in a poet like Dante we may say that there is an element of "science" in so far as the allegorical interpretation is possible: *The Divine Comedy* has something to say, not only to the naïve Roman Catholic, but to the ordinary man whose prepossessions are practical, and whose literary appreciation is limited by the needs of his own will. The poem has a moral, a set of derivative ideas that seem to the reader to be relevant to practical conduct. But to say this is not to say, with most schools of modern criticism, that it is the primary significance of the work. For Dante is a poet; the didactic element is in solution with the other elements, and may be said barely to exist in itself, since it must be isolated by the violence of the reader's own will.

There is therefore a distinction to be drawn between a kind of writing in which allegorical meanings are fused with the material, and pure and explicit allegory. It is the difference between works of the creative imagination and the inferior works of the practical will. The reader will recall my first proposition: The power of creating the inner meaning of experience is a quality of the imagination. It is not a construction of the will, that perpetual modernism through which, however vast may be the physical extent of the poet's range, the poet ignores the whole of experience for some special interest. This modern literature of Platonism—a descriptive term used to set apart a kind of work in which the meanings are forced—carries with it its own critical apparatus. It is known at present as the revolutionary or social point of view. Since the rise of science it has been also the "capitalist" point of view. For our whole culture seems to be obsessed by a kind of literature that is derivative of the allegorical mentality.

By the time of Dryden, allegory of the medieval variety had lost its prestige; we get the political fables of *The Hind and the Panther*, of *Absalom and Achitophel*, where the intention is pleasantly fictitious and local, with little pretense of universal truth. By the end of the next century the Platonic conquest of the world, the confident assertion of control over the forces of nature, had contrived a system of abstractions exact enough to assume the new name of science. So, in poetry, the allegorical mentality, which had hitherto used all the crude science available, lost confidence in its unexperimental ideas. The poetical assertion of the will took the form of revolt from its more successful counterpart, science. We find here two assertions of the same erring will, diverging for the first time: science *versus* romanticism.

III

With the decline then of pure allegory, we see the rise of a new systematic structure of entities called science, which makes good the primitive allegorist's futile claim to the control of nature. Between allegorist and scientist there exists the illusion of fundamental opposition. They are, however, of one origin and purpose.[2] For the apparent hostility of science to the allegorical entities is old age's preoccupation with the follies of its youth.

When this situation became fully developed, the poets, deprived of their magical fictions, and stripped of the means of affirming the will allegorically, proceeded to revolt, pitting the individual will against all forms of order, under the illusion that all order is scientific order. The order of the imagination became confused. Thus arose romanticism, not qualitatively different from the naturalism that it attacked, but identical with it, and committed in the arts to the same imperfect inspiration.

This summary will, I believe, be illuminated by a passage from Taine, who is discussing Byron:

> Such are the sentiments wherewith he surveyed nature and history, not to comprehend them and forget himself before them, but to seek in them and impress upon them the image of his own passions. He does not leave the objects to speak for themselves, but forces them to answer him.

We have the endless quest of the romantic, who ranges over nature in the effort to impose his volitional ego as an absolute upon the world. Compare Taine's analysis of Byron with a sentence from Schopenhauer:

> While science, following the unresting and inconstant stream of the fourfold forms of reason and consequent, with each end attained sees further, and can never reach a final goal nor attain full satisfaction any more than by running we can reach the place where the clouds touch the horizon; art, on the contrary, is everywhere at its goal.

For the will of science and the will of the romantic poet (the frustrated allegorist) are the same will. Romanticism is science without the systematic method of asserting the will. Because it cannot participate in the infinite series of natural conquests, the romantic spirit impresses upon nature the image of its own passions:

2. "Always science has grown up on religion . . . and always it signifies nothing more or less than an abstract melioration of these doctrines, considered as false because less abstract." Spengler, *The Decline of the West.*

Make me thy lyre, even as the forest is:
What if my leaves are falling like its own!
The tumult of thy mighty harmonies
Will take from both a deep autumnal tone,
Sweet though in sadness. Be thou, Spirit fierce,
My spirit! Be thou me, impetuous one!

It is the "will trying to do the work of the imagination." The style is inflated and emotive. The poet, instead of fixing his attention upon a single experience, instead of presenting dramatically the plight of human weakness—the subject of his poem—flies from his situation into a rhetorical escape that gives his will the illusion of power. (It may be observed that at the culmination of French romanticism in Rimbaud, the poet, still caught upon the dilemma of the will, carried this dilemma to its logical and most profound conclusion—the destruction of the will.)

The momentary illusion of individual power is a prime quality of the romantic movement. In the intervals when the illusion cannot be maintained, arise those moments of irony that create the subjective conflict of romantic poetry. In generalizing about such a quality one must take care; it differs with different poets. I have just pointed out incidentally how the individual will receives, in a late and perhaps the greatest romantic, a self-destructive motivation. Yet the dramatic effect is similar in poets as different as Rimbaud and Shelley. Throughout the nineteenth century, and in a few poets today, we get an intellectual situation like this: There is the assumption that Truth is indifferent or hostile to the desires of men; that these desires were formerly nurtured on legend, myth, all kinds of insufficient experiment; that, Truth being known at last in the form of experimental science, it is intellectually impossible to maintain illusion any longer, at the same time that it is morally impossible to assimilate the inhuman Truth.

The poet revolts from Truth; that is, he defies the cruel and naturalistic world to break him if it can; and he is broken. This moral situation, transferred to the plane of drama or the lyric, becomes romantic irony—that is, an irony of his position of which the poet himself is not aware:

I fall upon the thorns of life! I bleed!

His will being frustrated by inhospitable Truth, Shelley is broken; falls into disillusionment; and asks the west wind to take him away and make him its lyre. In a contemporary poet, whose death two years ago was probably the climax of the romantic movement in this country, we get the same quality of irony. Invoking a symbol of primitive simplicity, Pocahontas, Crane says:

Lie to us! Dance us back our tribal morn!

The poet confesses that he has no access to a means of satisfying his will, or to a kind of vision where the terms are not set by the demands of the practical will. He returns to a fictitious past. There he is able to maintain, for a moment, the illusion that he might realize the assertion of his will in a primitive world where scientific truth is not a fatal obstacle.

At this point we must notice a special property of the romantic imagination. It has no insight into the total meanings of actual moral situations; it is concerned with fictitious alternatives to them, because they invariably mean frustration of the will. This special property of escape is the Golden Age, used in a special fashion. The romantic poet attributes to it an historical reality. In a great poet like Shakespeare, notably in *The Tempest*, we get the implications of the poetic convention of the Golden Age; properly looked at, it is more than a poetic convention, it is a moral necessity of man. The use to which Shakespeare puts it is not involved in the needs of his personal will; it assists in defining the quality of his insight into the permanent flaws of human character. For the Golden Age is not a moral or social possibility; it is a way of understanding the problem of evil, being a picture of human nature with the problem removed. It is a qualitative fiction, not a material world, that permits the true imagination to recognize evil for what it is.

Now the romantic and allegorical poet, once he is torn with disbelief in the adequacy of the poetic will, sees before him two alternatives. After falling upon the thorns of life, he may either ask the west wind to take him up, or cry for his tribal morn in the Golden Age: This *is* the first alternative—disillusionment with life after defeat of the will. He will seize this escape provided that he lacks the hardihood of a

Rimbaud, who saw that, given the satisfaction of will as a necessity of the age, the poet must either destroy his will or repudiate poetry for a career of action. But Rimbaud is the exceptional, because he is the perfect, romantic poet.

The other ordinary alternative of the modern allegorist lies in the main Spenserian tradition of ingenuous tale-telling; it is the pure Golden Age of the future, which the poet can envisage with complacency because his will has not gone off into the frustration of romantic irony. He enjoys something like the efficient optimism of science; he asks us to believe that a rearrangement of the external relations of man will not alone make him a little more comfortable, but will remove the whole problem of evil, and usher in perfection. It is this type of crude, physical imagination that we find in Tennyson:

Till the war-drums sound no longer, and the battleflags are furled
In the Parliament of Man, the Federation of the World.

The cult of the will is a specially European or Western cult; it rose after the Middle Ages, and it informs our criticism of society and the arts. For, given the assumption that poetry is only another kind of volition, less efficient than science, it is easy to believe in the superiority of the scientific method. I myself believe in it. For the physical imagination of science is, step by step, perfect, and knows no limit. The physical imagination of poetry, granting it an unlimited range, is necessarily compacted of futile and incredible fictions, which we summarily reject as inferior instruments of the will. And rightly reject, if we assume two things—and our age is convinced that it is impossible to assume anything else: (1) that the only kind of imagination is that of the will, which best realizes its purposes in external constructions or in the control of the external relations of persons and things; (2) that this sole type of imagination will be disillusioned or optimistic, according as it is either imperfectly informed, as in mere poetry, or adequately equipped by science with the "fourfold forms of reason and consequent." That is the view held by a leading school of critics in this country, the most influential of whom has been Mr. Edmund Wilson in *Axel's Castle*, a book written on the assumption that *all* poetry is only an inferior kind of social will.

The critical movement so ably represented by Mr. Wilson is the heresy that I am opposing throughout this essay. That the kind of imaginative literature demanded by this school is the third, and I think necessarily the final, stage in the history of allegory in Western culture, may not be immediately clear.

The school preoccupied with what is called the economic determinism of literature is in the direct line of descent from the crudely moralistic allegory of the Renaissance. The notion that all art is primarily an apology for institutions and classes, though it is now the weapon of the Marxists against "capitalist" literature, has been explicit in our intellectual outlook since the time of Buckle in England, and Taine and Michelet in France. It is an article of faith in the "capitalist" and utilitarian dogma that literature, like everything else, must be primarily, and thus solely, an expression of the will. From such allegory as:

> With him went Danger, clothed in ragged weeds,
>   Made of bear's skin, that him more dreadful made,
> Yet his own face was dreadful, he did need
>   Strange horror, to deform his grisly shade;
>   A net in th' one hand, and a rusty blade
> In th' other was, this Mischief, that Mishap . . .

—from this it is only a step to the sophisticated entities and abstractions of the agitation for social reform, whose vocabulary is an imitation, and an application to conduct, of the terms of physical science. Or rather, I should say, two steps; for the immediate stage of allegory is the romantic irony of the age of Byron and Shelley. The contemporary allegorists have regained something of the easy confidence of their early forerunners; they believe as fully in the positive efficacy of the Marxian dialectic, as Spencer in the negative example of the Seven Deadly Sins.

Yet, the Seven Deadly Sins being now a little threadbare, our new allegorists are quite clear in the recognition that the arts, more especially poetry, have no special function in society. The arts offer to society a pusillanimous instrument for the realization of its will. The better the art, one must add, the more pusillanimous. For art aims at nothing outside itself, and, in the words of Schopenhauer, "is everywhere at its goal." There is no goal for the literature of the will, whose new objective must be constantly redefined in terms of the technology, verbal or mechanical, available at the moment.

The significance of this movement in modern society is perfectly plain: By seizing exclusively those aspects of the total experience that are capable of being put to predictable and successful use, the modern spirit has committed itself to the most dangerous program in Western history. It has committed itself exclusively to this program. We should do well to consider a specimen, by Phelps Putnam, of contemporary romantic irony; the "He" in the passage is the Devil:

> He leaned his elbows on two mountain tops
> And moved his head slowly from side to side,
> Sweeping the plain with his unhurried eyes.
> He was the phoenix of familiar men,
> Of husbands I have known, the horns and all,
> But more, much more—O God, I was afraid.
> I would have hid before the eyes had come.
> Then they were there, and then
> My guts grew warm again in my despair
> And I cried "Pour la Reine" and drew my sword.
> But, Christ, I had no sword.

He had no science; the fictitious sword of the allegorical will that the hero "drew" was incompetent to deal with his desperately practical situation. Our new scientific allegorists rest their case against poetry there. What they neglect to provide for is the hero's failure in case he has a genuine sword of science. For the recognition of that other half of experience, the realm of immitigable evil—or perhaps I had better say in modern abstraction, the margin of error in social calculation—has been steadily lost. The fusion of human success and human error in a vision of the whole of life, *the vision itself being its own goal*, has almost disappeared from the modern world.

IV

I have set forth two propositions about poetry. I will now ask the reader to examine a little more narrowly the second, in the attempt to discriminate between a poetry of the will and a poetry of genuine imagination. We have seen that the poetry of the will takes two forms. There is the romantic, disillusioned irony of Shelley, or for that matter of a poet like Mr. Robinson Jeffers; there is the crude optimism of Tennyson, a moral outlook that has almost vanished from poetry, surviving today as direct political and social propaganda supported by the "social" sciences. My second proposition was a brief commentary on the lines by Shelley:

> Life like a dome of many-colored glass
> Stains the white radiance of eternity

The will asserts a general proposition about the whole of life, but there is no specific, imagined context to support the assertion. As a product of the imagination the passage is incomprehensible; as a practical, that is to say, as a scientific generalization, it is open to the just contempt of the scientific mind. What, then, is the exact purpose and function of such poetry?

In purpose it competes with science; as to function it supports the illusion of moral insight in persons who are incapable of either scientific discipline or poetic apprehension. It is an affirmation of the will in terms that are not a legitimate vehicle of the will. The proper mode of the will—proper, that is, in efficiency, but not necessarily in morals, for the question whether the will should be so expressed at all is a distinct problem—the right mode of the will is some kind of practical effort adequately informed by exact science.

Most modern schools of criticism assume that all poetry is qualitatively the same as the lines by Shelley; they assume this negatively, for the positive assumption is that poetry must of necessity be like science, a quantitative instrument for mastery of the world. This is the interesting theory of Mr. I. A. Richards: because poetry is compacted of "pseudo-statements" it cannot compete with "certified scientific statements," and must be discredited as science moves on to fresh triumphs. This point of view is doubtless inevitable in a scientific age; but it is not an inevitable point of view.

Mr. Richards's theory of the relation between poetry and our beliefs about the world appears novel to some critics. It is the latest version of the allegorical, puritan and utilitarian theory of the arts—a theory that is rendered, by Mr. Richards, the more plausible because it seems to give to the arts a very serious attention. The British utilitarians, a century ago, frankly condemned them. So, with less candor, does Mr. Richards: His desperate efforts to make poetry, after all, useful, consist in justly reducing its "explanations" to nonsense, and salvaging from the wreck a mysterious agency for "ordering our minds." Poetry is a storehouse of ordered emotional energy that properly released might reeducate the public in the principles of the good life. For brevity, I paraphrase Mr. Richards; it should be observed that the idea is set forth in terms of the will.[3]

Yet there is, even according to Mr. Richards, little hope for this kind of education. The "certified scientific statements" about the world make the metaphors, the images, the symbols, all the varieties of "pseudo-statements"—similes like the "dome of many-colored glass"—look extremely foolish, because in the more exact light of science, they are patently untrue. I do not intend here to discuss this theory as a whole, nor to do justice to Mr. Richards's poetic taste, which is superior. One part of the theory, I believe, may be dismissed at once. How can poetry, a tissue of lies, equip the public with "relevant responses" to an environment? Our responses must work; they must be, in at least a provisional sense, scientifically true. What is this mysterious emotional function of poetry that orders our minds with falsehood?

Mr. Richards is, I believe, talking about the unstable fringe of emotion that I have called romantic irony: we have seen that this is what is left to the poet—a lugubrious residue—after he realizes that science is truth and that his own fictions are lies. This residue, alas, organizes and orders nothing whatever. Mr. Richards's underlying assumption about poetry is, like Mr. Edmund Wilson's, embedded in the humanitarian mentality of the age, where it lies too deep for examination.

If the pseudo-statement is motivated by the will (the only intention for it that Mr. Richards can conceive), it is false, and Mr. Richards is right: The poet of this sort expects potatoes to grow better when planted in the dark of the moon.

---

3. The discussion here is based upon Mr. Richards's two principal books: *The Principles of Literary Criticism* (London, 1924) and *Practical Criticism* (London, 1929).

If, on the other hand, a genuine poet uses the pseudo-statement, it is neither true nor false, but is a quality of the total created object: the poem. The power to perceive this total quality has almost disappeared from modern criticism. For all the arts are assumed to be necessarily assertions of the will.

Mr. Richards, like the romantic poet of the age of Byron and Shelley, sees that science has contrived a superior instrument of the will; again like them, he tries to rescue poetry by attributing to it functions of practical volition, functions that he cannot define, but which, in the true "liberal" tradition, he asserts in some realm of private hope against the "truths" of science.

Now it seems to me that the foundations of poetry, and possibly of the other creative arts, are somewhat different. We cannot understand them until we shall have eliminated from our thinking the demands of the category of will with its instrument, the practical intellect.

Let us look at Mr. Richards's famous terms: "certified scientific statement" (science) and "pseudo-statement" (poetry). I will try to show briefly that, for poetry, the certified scientific statement is the half-statement. The pseudo-statement may be, as I have just said, neither true nor false, but a feature of the total quality of the poem. The lines

> Out, out brief candle!
> Life's but a walking shadow; a poor player
> That struts and frets his hour upon the stage,
> And then is heard no more . . .

are certainly not "true": we know that life is not a shadow, it is a vast realm of biological phenomena; nor is it a player. Neither are the lines false: they represent a stage in the dynamic unfolding of Macbeth's character, the whole created image of which is the whole play *Macbeth*, which in its turn is neither true nor false, but *exists as a created object*. None of the pseudo-statements in the play, representing the conflict of will that forms the plot, is either approved or disapproved by the poet. He neither offers us a practical formula for action nor rejects any of the volitional purposes of the characters. He creates the total object of which the pseudo-statements of the will are a single feature, and are therefore neither true nor false. What Mr. Richards's theory (and others like it) comes down to is the uneasy consciousness that such a passage as I have just quoted does not tell us how to keep out of the sort of mess that Macbeth got himself into. The ideal connection of this theory with the traditions of moralistic allegory is quite evident.

Before we may see the certified scientific statement as the half-statement, a further point of Mr. Richards's theory must be noticed. Poets, being ignorant of science and their general ideas false, ought to write poems in which appear no beliefs whatever, but in which, presumably, there is that mysterious ordering of our minds. *The Waste Land* is such a poem—supposedly. But is it? According to the poet himself and to my own simple powers of inspection, it is full of beliefs. Mr. Richards, with admirable aplomb, has seized upon a poem in which large generalizations do not appear, as an instance of his theory: that poets, to keep our respect, must order our minds without lies; that, in, order to avoid saying wrong things, they must say nothing. And this "nothing" is only another species of half-statement. It leads straight to a defense of the recent school of "pure poets" in France,[4] a school that had its meeker followers in England and this country.

This half-statement may be in the pure poets an immersion in the supposedly pure sensations of experience. But in the older romantics of the nineteenth century, it is due to a sentimental escape from the abstractions of science. And indeed both fallacies are due to a misunderstanding of the exact nature of the "certified scientific statement." We saw, in the second section of this essay, how the romantics revolted from science, or one kind of half-statement, giving us romantic irony. This irony has dwindled, in our day, to the other half-statement (to the other activity of the same will) of "pure poetry." It is significant that at the present time we get, from both scientist and pure poet, a renunciation of poetry because it cannot compete with the current version of our objective world, a version that is pre-empted by the demands of the will with its certified scientific statements.

It must be remembered that this kind of statement is invariably the half-statement. It is the statement about a thing, a person, an experience, which relates it to something else, not for the purpose of giving us intensive knowledge of the thing, person, or experience, in itself

---

4. [Tate] See Henri Bremond, *La Poésie Pure* (Paris, 1926).

and as a whole; but to give us, in varying degrees depending upon the exactness of the science under which it is viewed, the half-knowledge that limits us to the control of its extensive relations. If I feed a horse corn every day at noon, I may expect him to do more work in the afternoon than he would do without it. I am controlling the relation between grain and horse under the general proposition: regular feeding of grain increases an animal's capacity for work. The statement must be either true or false.

But the statements in a genuine work of art are neither "certified" nor "pseudo"; the creative intention removes them from the domain of practicality. "In aesthetics," wrote Mr. Leo Stein a few years ago in an excellent book, "we have to do with complex wholes which are never in a rigid state of adjustment."[5] This integral character of the work of art forever resists practical formulation. The aesthetic whole invites indefinitely prolonged attention; whereas the half-statement of science arrests our attention at those features of the whole that may be put to the service of the will. In the following verses the horse cannot be *used*, but as an object arousing prolonged contemplation in its particular setting it may be *known*:

> I set her on my pacing steed,
> And nothing else saw all day long,
> For sidelong she would bend, and sing
> A faëry's song.

The stanza is neither true nor false; it is an object that exists.

I think it ought to be clear by this time that theories like Mr. Richards's, theories covertly or avowedly developed in the interest of social schemes, are not guides to the study of the immense qualitative whole of works of art; they are scientific (more or less) charts, relating the art-object to other objects at the command of the practical will. So it may be said that such theories belong to that perpetually modern impulse to *allegorize* poetry, to abstract for use those features that are available for immediate action, and to repudiate the rest.

It ought to be clear that this is the regular course of science in the whole universe of objects; that with the arts science proceeds consis-

---

5. [Tate] Leo Stein, *The ABC of Esthetics* (New York, 1927).

tently, on principle; that society has developed an instinctive approach to the arts appropriate to the scientific temper of the age.

A man lives in a beautiful house in a beautiful place. Let him discover oil under his land. The oil has been there all the time as a feature of the total scene. But he violates the integrity of the scene by "developing" the oil. Where the house and land had previously existed as a whole of which utility was only one aspect, he abstracts one feature of it for immediate use by means of Mr. Richards's certified scientific half-statements; and destroys its wholeness. Perhaps he was a dreaming kind of man: suppose he had always meant to get out the oil, and had gone about it with an improper method. Suppose that all he could do was to write a poem, like the *Ode to the West Wind*, in which he said: "O Oil, make me thy conduit, even as the earth is!" It would be a poem of the will, and Mr. Richards would have a perfect right to test the scientific efficiency of the formula urged by the poem.

It is not with this kind of poetry, but with another kind that is not a poetry of the will, that I have been concerned; and I have been offering a few commonplaces about its neglect by our advanced critics. Genuine poetry has been written in most ages—including the present—but it is a sort of poetry that was written most completely by Shakespeare. It is the sort of poetry that our "capitalist" and "communist" allegorists have forgotten how to read.

I have sketched some aspects of the poetry of the will, which in the last century and a half has taken two directions that I will summarize again. First, the optimism of science, either pure or social science, an uncritical and positive Platonism. Secondly, the negative Platonism of the romantic spirit, a pessimistic revolt of the individual against the optimism of the scientific will. The quality of volition is practical in both kinds of Platonism. But for isolated figures like Landor, Hopkins, and Dickinson in the last century, and a few today, the creative spirit has been shunted off into obscurity by the heresy of the will.

The quality of poetic vision that I have already in this essay named, with respect to the two forms of will, the middle ground of vision, and, with respect to itself, the vision of the whole, is not susceptible of logical demonstration. We may prepare our minds for its reception by the logical elimination of error. But the kind of criticism that dominates our intellectual life is that of the French mathematician who, after reading a tragedy by Racine, asked: *"Qu'est ce que cela prouve?"* It proves nothing; it creates the totality of experience in its quality; and it has no useful relation to the ordinary forms of action.

Since I have not set out to prove an argument, but to look into arguments that seem to me to be wrong, I will state a conclusion as briefly as possible: that poetry finds its true usefulness in its perfect inutility, a focus of repose for the will-driven intellect that constantly shakes the equilibrium of persons and societies with its unremitting imposition of partial formulas. When the will and its formulas are put back into an implicit relation with the whole of our experience, we get the true knowledge which is poetry. It is the "kind of knowledge which is really essential to the world, the true content of its phenomena, that which is subject to no change, and therefore is known with equal truth for all time." Let us not argue about it. It is here for those who have eyes to see.

7

POETRY:
A NOTE IN ONTOLOGY

JOHN CROWE RANSOM

Among Ransom's most influential essays, "Poetry: A Note in Ontol-
ogy" separates poetry into three kinds, just as Tate's "Three Types of
Poetry" does. Ransom's divisions are informed by his theory of the
"three moments" that he had articulated years before in a letter to
Tate. "[I]n the historical order of experience," he writes, the first
moment is "the original experience—pure of all intellectual content,
unreflective, concrete, and singular; there are no distinctions, and
the subject is identical with the Whole."¹ This moment is followed by
a second, a recognition implicitly acknowledging the loss of the first
but taking something from it: "The feature of the second moment
is, it is now that the record must be taken of the first moment that
has just transpired. This record proceeds inevitably by way of con-
cepts discovered in cognition. It is the beginning of science. Its ends
are practical; but its means are abstractions; and these, it must be
insisted, are subtractions from the whole."² For Ransom, the excel-
lence of man lies in what he calls "the Third Moment," when we
recognize that "[a]ll our concepts and all our histories put together
cannot add up into the wholeness with which we started out."³ Like
religion and morals, poetry is one of the "works of the third moment"

---

1. Ransom, *Selected Letters*, 155.
2. Ibid.
3. Ibid.

that rejoins images to concepts. "Poetry is always the exhibit of Oppo-sition and at the same time Reconciliation between the Conceptual or Formal and the Individual or Concrete."⁴ Or as he puts it in the present essay, "The aesthetic moment appears as a curious moment of suspension; between the Platonism in us, which is militant, always sciencing and devouring, and a starved inhibited aspiration towards innocence which, if it could only be free, would like to respect and know the object as it might of its own accord reveal itself."

Ransom clearly ties the major kinds of poetry to the temporal order of the three moments. "Physical poetry" attempts to recapture the unreflective concreteness of the first moment, but it can never do so. Ransom's descriptions of the "rich and contingent materiality" of the image yield some of his most memorable prose. "Platonic poetry," the second kind, uses images, but only for their conceptual value; as allegory, such poetry is "a discourse in things, but on the under-standing that they are translatable at every point into ideas." Only "metaphysical poetry" fully represents the third moment. He chooses the term in part because of Eliot's revival of Donne and his age, in part because "meta-physical" names precisely what he understands the best poetry to be: not abstract but more than physical. Another term for it is "miracle," and here Ransom makes a point not quite theological, but worth considerable attention by theologians none-theless: "It is the poet and nobody else who gives to the God a nature, a form, faculties, and a history; to the God, most comprehensive of all terms, which, if there were no poetic impulse to actualize or 'find' Him, would remain the driest and deadest among Platonic ideas, with all intension sacrificed to infinite extension."

A poetry may be distinguished from a poetry by virtue of subject-matter, and subject-matter may be differentiated with respect to its ontology, or the reality of its being. An excellent variety of critical doctrine arises recently out of this differentiation, and thus perhaps

---

4. Ibid., 156.

criticism leans again upon ontological analysis as it was meant to do by Kant. The recent critics remark in effect that some poetry deals with things, while some other poetry deals with ideas. The two poetries will differ from each other as radically as a thing differs from an idea. The distinction in the hands of critics is a fruitful one. There is apt to go along with it a principle of valuation, which is the consequence of a temperament, and therefore basic. The critic likes things and intends that his poet shall offer them or likes ideas and intends that he shall offer them and approves him as he does the one or the other. Criticism cannot well go much deeper than this. The critic has carried to the last terms his analysis of the stuff of which poetry is made, and valued it frankly as his temperament or his need requires him to value it.

So philosophical a critic seems to be highly modern. He is; but this critic as a matter of fact is peculiarly on one side of the question. (The implication is unfavorable to the other side of the question.) He is in revolt against the tyranny of ideas, and against the poetry which celebrates ideas, and which may be identified—so far as his usual generalization may be trusted—with the hateful poetry of the Victorians. His bias is in favor of the things. On the other hand the critic who likes Victorian verse, or the poetry of ideas, has probably not thought of anything of so grand a simplicity as electing between the things and the ideas, being apparently not quite capable of the ontological distinction. Therefore he does not know the real or constitutional ground of his liking, and may somewhat ingenuously claim that his predilection is for those poets who give him inspiration, or comfort, or truth, or honest metres, or something else equally "worth while." But Plato, who was not a modern, was just as clear as we are about the basic distinction between the ideas and the things, and yet stands far apart from the aforesaid conscious modern in passionately preferring the ideas over the things. The weight of Plato's testimony would certainly fall on the side of the Victorians, though they may scarcely have thought of calling him as their witness. But this consideration need not conclude the hearing.

I. PHYSICAL POETRY

The poetry which deals with things was much in favor a few years ago with the resolute body of critics. And the critics affected the poets. If necessary, they became the poets, and triumphantly illustrated the new mode. The Imagists were important figures in the history of our poetry, and they were both theorists and creators. It was their intention to present things in their thinginess, or *Dinge* in their *Dinglichkeit*; and to such an extent had the public lost its sense of *Dinglichkeit* that their redirection was wholesome. What the public was inclined to seek in poetry was ideas, whether large ones or small ones, grand ones or pretty ones, certainly ideas to live by and die by, but what the Imagists identified with the stuff of poetry was, simply, things.

Their application of their own principle was sufficiently heroic, though they scarcely consented to be as extreme in the practice as in the theory. They had artistic talent, every one of the original group, and it was impossible that they should make of poetry so simple an exercise as in doctrine they seemed to think it was. Yet Miss Lowell wrote a poem on *Thompson's Lunch Room, Grand Central Station* it is admirable if its intention is to show the whole reach of her courage. Its detail goes like this:

> Jagged greenwhite bowls of pressed glass
> Rearing snow-peaks of chipped sugar
> Above the lighthouse-shaped castors
> Of gray pepper and gray-white salt.

For most of us as for the public idealist, with his "values," this is inconsequential. Unhappily it seems that the things as things do not necessarily interest us, and that in fact we are not quite constructed with the capacity for a disinterested interest. But it must be noted even here that the things are on their good behavior, looking rather well, and arranged by lines into something approaching a military formation. More technically, there is cross-imagery in the snow-peaks of sugar, and in the lighthouse-shaped castors, and cross-imagery involves association, and will presently involve dissociation and thinking. The metre is but a vestige, but even so it means something, for metre is a powerful intellectual determinant marshalling the words and, inevitably, the things. The *Dinglichkeit* of this Imagist specimen, or the realism, was therefore not pure. But it was nearer pure than the world was used to in poetry, and the exhibit was astonishing.

For the purpose of this note I shall give to such poetry, dwelling as exclusively as it dares upon physical things, the name Physical Poetry. It is to stand opposite to that poetry which dwells as firmly as it dares upon ideas.

But perhaps thing *versus* idea does not seem to name an opposition precisely. Then we might phrase it a little differently: image *versus* idea. The idealistic philosophies are not sure that things exist, but they mean the equivalent when they refer to images. (Or they may consent to perceptions or to impressions, following Hume, and following Croce, who remarks that they are pre-intellectual and independent of concepts. It is all the same, unless we are extremely technical.) It is sufficient if they concede that image is the raw material of idea. Though it may be an unwieldy and useless affair for the idealist as it stands, much needing to be licked into shape, nevertheless its relation to idea is that of a material cause, and it cannot be dispossessed of its priority.

It cannot be dispossessed of a primordial freshness, which idea can never claim. An idea is derivative and tamed. The image is in the natural or wild state, and it has to be discovered there, not put there, obeying its own law and none of ours. We think we can lay hold of image and take it captive, but the docile captive is not the real image but only the idea, which is the image with its character beaten out of it.

But we must be very careful: idealists are nothing if not dialectical. They object that an image in an original state of innocence is a delusion and cannot exist, that no image ever comes to us which does not imply the world of ideas, that there is "no percept without a concept." There is something in it. Every property discovered in the image is a universal property, and nothing discovered in the image is marvelous in kind though it may be pinned down historically or statistically as a single instance. But there is this to be understood too: the image which is not remarkable in any particular property is marvelous in its assemblage of many properties, a manifold of properties, like a mine or a field, something to be explored for the properties yet science can manage the image, which is infinite in properties, only by equating it to the one property with which the science is concerned for science at work is always a science; and committed to a special interest. It is not by refutation but by abstraction that science destroys the image. It means to get its "value" out of the image, and we may be sure that it has no use for the image in its original state of freedom. People who are engrossed with their pet "values" become habitual killers. Their game is the images, or the things, and they acquire the ability to shoot them as far off as they can be seen, and do. It is thus that we lose the power of imagination, or whatever faculty it is by which we are able to contemplate things as they are in their rich and contingent materiality. But our dreams reproach us, for in dreams they come alive again. Likewise our memory which makes light of our science by recalling the images in their panoply of circumstance and with their morning freshness upon them.

It is the dream, the recollection, which compels us to poetry, and to deliberate esthetic experience. It can hardly be argued, I think, that the arts are constituted automatically out of original images, and arise in some early age of innocence. (Though Croce seems to support this view, and to make art a pre-adult stage of experience.) Art is based on second love, not first love. In it we make a return to something which we had willfully alienated. The child is occupied mostly with things, but it is because he is still unfurnished with systematic ideas, not because he is a ripe citizen by nature and comes along already trailing clouds of glory. Images are clouds of glory for the man who has discovered that ideas are a sort of darkness. Imagism, that is, the recent historical movement, may resemble a naïve poetry of mere things, but we can read the theoretical pronouncements of Imagists, and we can learn that Imagism is motivated by a distaste for the systematic abstractedness of thought. It presupposes acquaintance with science that famous activity which is "constructive" with respect to the tools of our economic role in this world, and destructive with respect to nature. Imagists wish to escape from science by immersing themselves in images.

Not far off the simplicity of Imagism was, a little later, the subtler simplicity of Mr. George Moore's project shared with several others, in behalf of "pure poetry." In Moore's house on Ebury Street they talked about poetry, with an after-dinner warmth if not an early-morning discretion, and their tastes agreed almost perfectly and reinforced one another. The fruit of these conversations was the volume Pure Poetry. It must have been the most exclusive anthology of English poetry that had yet appeared, since its room was closed to all the poems that dallied visibly with ideas, so that many poems that had been coveted by all other anthologists do not appear there. Nevertheless the book is delicious, and something more deserves to be said for it.

First, that "pure poetry" is a kind of Physical Poetry. Its visible content is a thing-content. Technically, I suppose, it is effective in this character if it can exhibit its material in such a way that an image or set of images and not an idea must occupy the foreground of the reader's attention. Thus:

Full fathom five thy father lies
Of his bones are coral made.

Here it is difficult for anybody (except the perfect idealist who is always theoretically possible and who would expect to take a return from anything whatever) to receive any experience except that of a very distinct image, or set of images. It has the configuration of image, which consists in being sharp of edges, and the modality of image, which consists in being given and non-negotiable, and the density, which consists in being full, a plenum of qualities. What is to be done with it? It is pure exhibit it is to be contemplated perhaps it is to be enjoyed. The art of poetry depends more frequently on this faculty than on any other in its repertory the faculty of presenting images so whole and clean that they resist the catalysis of thought.

And something else must be said, going in the opposite direction. "Pure poetry," all the same, is not as pure as it is claimed to be, though on the whole it is Physical Poetry. (All true poetry is a phase of Physical Poetry.) It is not as pure as Imagism is, or at least it is not as pure as Imagism would be if it lived up to its principles; and in fact it is significant that the volume does not contain any Imagist poems, which argues a difference in taste somewhere. Imagism may take trifling things for its material, presumably it will take the first things the poet encounters, since "importance" and "interest" are not primary qualities which a thing possesses but secondary or tertiary ones which the idealist attributes to it by virtue of his own requirements. "Pure poetry" as Moore conceives it, and as the lyrics of Poe and Shakespeare offer it, deals with the more dramatic materials, and here dramatic means human, or at least capable of being referred to the critical set of human interests. Employing this sort of material the poet cannot exactly intend to set the human economists in us actually into motion, but perhaps he does intend to comfort us with the fleeting sense that it is potentially our kind of material.

In the same way "pure poetry" is nicely metred, whereas Imagism was free. Technique is written on it. And by the way the anthology contains no rugged anonymous Scottish ballad either, and probably for a like reason because it would not be technically finished. Now both Moore and De La Mare are accomplished conservative artists, and what they do or what they approve may be of limited range but it is sure to be technically admirable, and it is certain that they understand what technique in poetry is though they do not define it. Technique takes the thing-content and meters and orders it. Metre is not an original property of things. It is artificial, and conveys the sense of human control, even if it does not wish to impair the thinginess of the things. Metric is a science, and so far as we attend to it we are within the scientific atmosphere. Order is the logical arrangement of things. It involves the dramatic "form" which selects the things, and brings out their appropriate qualities, and carries them through a systematic course of predication until the total impression is a unit of logic and not merely a solid lump of thing-content. The "pure poems" which Moore admires are studied, though it would be fatal if they looked studious. A sustained effort of ideation effected these compositions. It is covered up, and communicates itself only on a subliminal plane of consciousness. But experienced readers are quite aware of it; they know at once what is the matter when they encounter a realism shamelessly passing for poetry, or a well-planned but blundering poetry.

As critics we should have every good will toward Physical Poetry: it is the basic constituent of any poetry. But the product is always something short of a pure or absolute existence, and it cannot quite be said that it consists of nothing but physical objects. The fact is that when we are more than usually satisfied with a Physical Poetry our analysis will probably disclose that it is more than usually impure.

2. PLATONIC POETRY

The poetry of ideas I shall denominate: Platonic Poetry. This also has grades of purity. A discourse which employed only abstract ideas with no images would be a scientific document and not a poem at all, not even a Platonic poem. Platonic Poetry dips heavily into the physical. If Physical Poetry tends to employ some ideation surreptitiously while still looking innocent of idea, Platonic Poetry more than returns the compliment, for it tries as hard as it can to look like Physical Poetry, as if it proposed to conceal its medicine, which is the idea to be propagated, within the sugar candy of objectivity and *Dinglichkeit*. As an instance, it is almost inevitable that I quote a famous Victorian utterance:

> The year's at the spring
> And day's at the morn;
> Morning's at seven;
> The hill-side's dew-pearled;
> The lark's on the wing;
> The snail's on the thorn:
> God's in his heaven—
> All's right with the world!

which is a piece of transparent homiletics for in it six pretty, coordinate images are marched, like six little lambs to the slaughter, to a colon and a powerful text. Now the exhibits of this poetry in the physical kind are always large, and may take more of the attention of the reader than is desired, but they are meant mostly to be illustrative of the ideas. It is on this ground that idealists like Hegel detect something unworthy, like a pedagogical trick, in poetry after all, and consider that the race will abandon it when it has outgrown its childishness and is enlightened.

The ablest arraignment of Platonic Poetry that I have seen, as an exercise which is really science but masquerades as poetry by affecting a concern for physical objects, is that of Mr. Allen Tate in a series of studies recently in *The New Republic*. I will summarize. Platonic

Poetry is allegory, a discourse in things, but on the understanding that they are translatable at every point into ideas. (The usual ideas are those which constitute the popular causes, patriotic, religious, moral, or social.) Or Platonic Poetry is the elaboration of ideas as such, but in proceeding introduces for ornament some physical properties after the style of Physical Poetry which is rhetoric. It is positive when the poet believes in the efficacy of the ideas. It is negative when he despairs of their efficacy, because they have conspicuously failed to take care of him, and utters his personal wail:

I fall upon the thorns of life! I bleed!

This is "Romantic Irony," which comes at occasional periods to interrupt the march of scientific optimism. But it still falls under the category of Platonism; it generally proposes some other ideas to take the place of those which are in vogue.

But why Platonism? To define Platonism we must remember that it is not the property of the historical person who reports dialogues about it in an Academy, any more than "pure poetry" is the property of the talkers who describe it from a house on Ebury Street. Platonism, in the sense I mean, is the name of an impulse that is native to us all, frequent, tending to take a too complete possession of our minds. Why should the spirit of mortal be proud? The chief explanation is that modern mortal is probably a Platonist. We are led to believe that nature is rational and that by the force of reasoning we shall possess it. I have read upon high authority: "Two great forces are persistent in Plato: the love of truth and zeal for human improvement." The forces are one force. We love to view the world under universal or scientific ideas to which we give the name truth and this is because the ideas seem to make not for righteousness but for mastery. The Platonic view of the world is ultimately the predatory, for it reduces to the scientific, which we know. The Platonic Idea becomes the Logos which science worships, which is the Occidental God, whose minions we are, and whose children, claiming a large share in His powers for patrimony.

Now the fine Platonic world of ideas fails to coincide with the original world of perception, which is the world populated by the stubborn and contingent objects, and to which as artists we fly in shame. The sensibility manifested by artists makes fools of scientists, if the latter are inclined to take their special and quite useful form of truth as the whole and comprehensive article. A dandified pagan worldling like Moore can always defeat Platonism, he does it every hour; he can exhibit the savor of his fish and wines, the fragrance of his coffee and cigars, and the solidity of the images in his favorite verse. These are objects which have to be experienced, and cannot be reported, for what is their simple essence that the Platonist can abstract? Moore may sound mystical but he is within the literal truth when he defends "pure poetry" on the ground that the things are constant, and it is the ideas which change—changing according to the latest mode under which the species indulges its grandiose expectation of subjugating nature. The things are constant in the sense that the ideas are never emancipated from the necessity of referring back to them as their original and the sense that they are not altered nor diminished no matter which ideas may take off from them as a point of departure. The way to obtain the true *Dinglichkeit* of a formal dinner or a landscape or a beloved person is to approach the object as such, and in humility then it unfolds a nature which we are unprepared for if we have put our trust in the simple idea which attempted to represent it.

The special antipathy of Moore is to the ideas as they put on their moral complexion, the ideas that relate everything to that insignificant centre of action, the human "soul" in its most Platonic and Pharisaic aspect. Nothing can darken perception better than a repetitive moral earnestness, based on the reputed superiority and higher destiny of the human species. If morality is the code by which we expect the race to achieve the more perfect possession of nature, it is an incitement to a more heroic science, but not to aesthetic experience, nor religious; if it is the code of humility, by which we intend to know nature as nature is, that is another matter but in an age of science morality is inevitably for the general public the former; and so transcendent a morality as the latter is now unheard of. And therefore:

O love, *they* die in yon rich sky,
  They faint on hill or field or river;
Our echoes roll from soul to soul,
  And grow forever and forever.

The italics are mine. These lines conclude an otherwise innocent poem, a candidate for the anthology, upon which Moore remarks: "The Victorian could never reconcile himself to finishing a poem without speaking about the soul, and the lines are particularly vindictive." Vindictive is just. By what right did the Laureate exult in the death of the physical echoes and call upon his love to witness it, but out of the imperiousness of his savage Platonism? Plato himself would have admired this ending, and considered that it redeemed an otherwise vicious poem.

Why do persons who have ideas to promulgate risk the trial by poetry? If the poets are hired to do it, which is the polite conception of some Hegelians, why do their employers think it worth the money, which they hold in public trust for the cause? Does a science have to become a poetry too? A science is the less effective as a science when it muddies its clear waters with irrelevance, a sermon becomes less cogent when it begins to quote the poets. The moralist, the scientist, and the prophet of idealism think evidently that they must establish their conclusions in poetry, though they reach these conclusions upon quite other evidence. The poetry is likely to destroy the conclusions with a sort of death by drowning, if it is a free poetry.

When that happens the Platonists may be cured of Platonism. There are probably two cures, of which this is the better. One cure is by adversity, by the failure of the ideas to work, on account of treachery or violence, or the contingencies of weather, constitution, love, and economics leaving the Platonist defeated and bewildered, possibly humbled, but on the other hand possibly turned cynical and worthless. Very much preferable is the cure which comes by education in the fine arts, erasing his Platonism more gently, leading him to feel that that is not a becoming habit of mind which dulls the perceptions.

The definition which some writers have given to art is: the reference of the idea to the image. The implication is that the act is not for the purpose of honest comparison so much as for the purpose of proving the idea by the image. But in the event the idea is not disproved so much as it is made to look ineffective and therefore foolish. The ideas will not cover the objects upon which they are imposed, they are too attenuated and threadlike for ideas have extension and objects have intension, but extension is thin while intension is thick.

There must be a great deal of genuine poetry which started in the poet's mind as a thesis to be developed, but in which the characters and the situations have developed faster than the thesis, and of their own. The thesis disappears or it is recaptured here and there and at the end, and lodged sententiously with the reader, where every successive reading of the poem will dislodge it again. Like this must be some plays, even some play out of Shakespeare, whose thesis would probably be disentangled with difficulty out of the crowded pageant or some narrative poem with a moral plot but much pure detail perhaps some "occasional" piece by a Laureate or official person, whose purpose is compromised but whose personal integrity is saved by his wavering between the sentiment which is a public duty and the experience which he has in his own right even some proclaimed allegory, like Spenser's, unlikely as that may seem, which does not remain transparent and everywhere translatable into idea but makes excursions into the territory of objectivity. These are hybrid performances. They cannot possess beauty of design, though there may be a beauty in detailed passages. But it is common enough, and we should be grateful. The mind is a versatile agent, and unexpectedly stubborn in its determination not really to be hardened in Platonism. Even in an age of science like the nineteenth century the poetic talents are not so loyal to its apostolic zeal as they and it suppose, and do not deserve the unqualified scorn which it is fashionable to offer them, now that the tide has turned, for their performance is qualified.

But this may be not stern enough for concluding a note on Platonic Poetry. I refer again to that whose Platonism is steady and malignant. This poetry is an imitation of Physical Poetry, and not really a poetry. Platonists practice their bogus poetry in order to show that an image will prove an idea, but the literature which succeeds in this delicate mission does not contain real images but illustrations.

3. METAPHYSICAL POETRY

"Most men," Mr. Moore observes, "read and write poetry between fifteen and thirty and afterwards very seldom, for in youth we are attracted by ideas, and modern poetry being concerned almost exclusively with ideas we live on duty, liberty, and fraternity as chameleons are said to live on light and air, till at last we turn from ideas to things, thinking that we have lost our taste for poetry, unless, perchance, we are classical scholars."

Much is conveyed in this characteristic sentence, even in proportion to its length. As for the indicated chronology, the cart is put after the horse, which is its proper sequence. And it is pleasant to be confirmed in the belief that many men do recant from their Platonism and turn back to things. But it cannot be exactly a *volte-face*, for there are qualifications. If pure ideas were what these men turn from, they would have had no poetry at all in the first period, and if pure things were what they turn to, they would be having not a classical poetry but a pure imagism, if such a thing is possible, in the second.

The mind does not come unscathed and virginal out of Platonism. Ontological interest would have to develop curiously, or wastefully and discontinuously, if men through their youth must cultivate the ideas so passionately that upon its expiration they are done with ideas forever and ready to become as little (and pre-logical) children. Because of the foolishness of idealists are ideas to be taboo for the adult mind? And, as critics, what are we to do with those poems (like *The Canonization* and *Lycidas)* which could not obtain admission by Moore into the anthology but which very likely are the poems we cherish beyond others?

The reputed "innocence" of the aesthetic moment, the "knowledge without desire" which Schopenhauer praises, must submit to a little scrutiny, like anything else that looks too good to be true. We come into this world as aliens come into a land which they must conquer if they are to live. For native endowment we have an exacting "biological" constitution which knows precisely what it needs and determines for us our inevitable desires. There can be no certainty that any other impulses are there, for why should they be? They scarcely belong in the biological picture. Perhaps we are simply an efficient animal species, running smoothly, working fast, finding the formula of life only too easy, and after a certain apprenticeship piling up power and wealth far beyond the capacity of our appetites to use. What will come next? Perhaps poetry, if the gigantic effort of science begins to seem disproportionate to the reward, according to a sense of diminishing returns. But before this pretty event can come to pass, it is possible that every

act of attention which is allowed us is conditioned by a gross and self-
ish interest.

Where is innocence then? The aesthetic moment appears as a curious moment of suspension between the Platonism in us, which is militant, always sciencing and devouring, and a starved inhibited aspiration
towards innocence which, if it could only be free, would like to respect
and know the object as it might of its own accord reveal itself.

The poetic impulse is not free, yet it holds out stubbornly against
science for the enjoyment of its images. It means to reconstitute the
world of perceptions. Finally there is suggested some such formula as
the following:

> *Science gratifies a rational or practical impulse and exhibits the mini-*
> *mum of perception. Art gratifies a perceptual impulse and exhibits the*
> *minimum of reason.*

Now it would be strange if poets did not develop many technical
devices for the sake of increasing the volume of the percipienda or
sensibilia. I will name some of them.

First Device: metre. Metre is the most obvious device. A formal
metre impresses us as a way of regulating very drastically the material,
and we do not stop to remark (that is, as readers) that it has no particular aim except some nominal sort of regimentation. It symbolizes
the predatory method, like a saw-mill which intends to reduce all the
trees to fixed unit timbers, and as business men we require some sign
of our business. But to the Platonic censor in us it gives a false security,
for so long as the poet appears to be working faithfully at his metrical
engine he is left comparatively free to attend lovingly to the things
that are being metered, and metering them need not really hurt them.
Metre is the gentlest violence he can do them, if he is expected to do
some violence.

Second Device: fiction. The device of the fiction is probably no less
important and universal in poetry. Over every poem which looks like
a poem is a sign which reads: This road does not go through to action,
fictitious. Art always sets out to create an "aesthetic distance" between
the object and the subject, and art takes pains to announce that it
is not history. The situation treated is not quite an actual situation,

for science is likely to have claimed that field, and exiled art; but a fictive or hypothetical one, so that science is less greedy and perception may take hold of it. Kant asserted that the aesthetic judgment is not concerned with the existence or non-existence of the object, and may be interpreted as asserting that it is so far from depending on the object's existence that it really depends on the object's non-existence. Sometimes we have a certain melancholy experience. We enjoy a scene which we receive by report only, or dream, or meet with in art but subsequently find ourselves in the presence of an actual one that seems the very same scene only to discover that we have not now the power to enjoy it, or to receive it aesthetically, because the economic tension is upon us and will not indulge us in the proper mood. And it is generally easier to obtain our aesthetic experience from art than from nature, because nature is actual, and communication is forbidden. But in being called fictive or hypothetical the art-object suffers no disparagement. It cannot be true in the sense of being actual, and therefore it may be despised by science. But it is true in the sense of being fair or representative, in permitting the "illusion of reality"; just as Schopenhauer discovered that music may symbolize all the modes of existence in the world; and in keeping with the customary demand of the readers of fiction proper, that it shall be "true to life." The defenders of art must require for it from its practitioners this sort of truth, and must assert of it before the world this dignity. If jealous science succeeds in keeping the field of history for its own exclusive use, it does not therefore annihilate the arts, for they reappear in a field which may be called real though one degree removed from actuality. There the arts perform their function with much less interference, and at the same time with about as much fidelity to the phenomenal world as history has.

Third Device: tropes. I have named two important devices; I am not prepared to offer the exhaustive list. I mention but one other kind, the device which comprises the figures of speech. A proper scientific discourse has no intention of employing figurative language for its definitive sort of utterance. Figures of speech twist accidence away from the straight course, as if to intimate astonishing lapses of rationality beneath the smooth surface of discourse, inviting perceptual attention, and weakening the tyranny of science over the senses. But I skip the several easier and earlier figures, which are timid, and stop on the climactic figure, which is the metaphor; with special reference to its consequence, a poetry which once in our history it produced in a beautiful and abundant exhibit, called Metaphysical Poetry.

And what is Metaphysical Poetry? The term was added to the official vocabulary of criticism by Johnson, who probably took it from Pope, who probably took it from Dryden, who used it to describe the poetry of a certain school of poets, thus: "He [John Donne] affects the metaphysics, not only in his satires, but in his amorous verses, where nature only should reign. . . . In this Mr. Cowley has copied him to a fault." But the meaning of metaphysical which was common in Dryden's time, having come down from the Middle Ages through Shakespeare, was simply: supernatural; *miraculous*. The context of the Dryden passage indicates it.

Dryden, then, noted a miraculism in poetry and repudiated it; except where it was employed for satire, where it was not seriously intended and had the effect of wit. Dryden himself employs miraculism wittily, but seems rather to avoid it if he will be really committed by it; he may employ it in his translations of Ovid, where the responsibility is Ovid's and not Dryden's, and in an occasional classical piece where he is making polite use of myths well known to be pagan errors. In his "amorous" pieces he finds the reign of nature sufficient, and it is often the worse for his amorous pieces. He is not many removes from a naturalist. (A naturalist is a person who studies nature not because he loves it but because he wants to use it, approaches it from the standpoint of common sense, and sees it thin and not thick.) Dryden might have remarked that Donne himself had a change of heart and confined his miraculism at last to the privileged field of a more or less scriptural revelation. Perhaps Dryden found his way to accepting Milton because Milton's miraculism was mostly not a contemporary sort but classical and scriptural, pitched in a time when the age of miracles had not given way to the age of science. He knew too that Cowley had shamefully recanted from his petty miraculism, which formed the conceits, and turned to the scriptural or large order of miraculism to write his heroic (but empty) verses about David; and had written a Pindaric ode in extravagant praise of "Mr. Hobs," whose naturalistic account of nature seemed to render any other account fantastic if not contrary to the social welfare.

Incidentally, we know how much Mr. Hobbes affected Dryden too, and the whole of Restoration literature. What Bacon with his disparagement of poetry had begun, in the cause of science and protestantism, Hobbes completed. The name of Hobbes is critical in any history that would account for the chill which settled upon the poets at the very moment that English poetry was attaining magnificently to the fullness of its powers. The name stood for common sense and naturalism, and the monopoly of the scientific spirit over the mind. Hobbes was the adversary, the Satan, when the latter first intimidated the English poets. After Hobbes his name is legion.

"Metaphysics," or miraculism, informs a poetry which is the most original and exciting, and intellectually perhaps the most seasoned, that we know in our literature, and very probably it has few equivalents in other literatures. But it is evident that the metaphysical effects may be large-scale or they may be small-scale. (I believe that generically, or ontologically, no distinction is to be made between them.) If Donne and Cowley illustrate the small-scale effects, Milton will illustrate the large-scale ones, probably as a consequence of the fact that he wrote major poems. Milton, in the *Paradise Lost*, told a story which was heroic and miraculous in the first place. In telling it he dramatized it, and allowed the scenes and characters to develop of their own native energy. The virtue of a long poem on a "metaphysical" subject will consist in the dramatization or substantiation of all the parts, the poet not being required to devise fresh miracles on every page so much as to establish the perfect "naturalism" of the material upon which the grand miracle is imposed. The *Paradise Lost* possesses this virtue nearly everywhere:

Thus *Adam* to himself lamented loud
Through the still Night, not now, as ere man fell,
Wholsom and cool, and mild, but with black Air
Accompanied, with damps and dreadful gloom,
Which to his evil Conscience represented
All things with double terror: On the ground

Outstretcht he lay, on the cold ground, and oft
Curs'd his Creation, Death as oft accus'd
Of tardie execution, since denounc't
The day of his offence. Why comes not Death,
Said hee, with one thrice acceptable stroke
To end me?

This is exactly the sort of detail for a large-scale metaphysical work, but it would hardly serve the purpose with a slighter and more naturalistic subject with "amorous" verses. For the critical mind Metaphysical Poetry refers perhaps almost entirely to the so-called "conceits" that constitute its staple. To define the conceit is to define small-scale Metaphysical Poetry.

It is easily defined, upon a little citation. Donne exhibits two conceits, or two branches of one conceit in the familiar lines:

Our hands were firmly cemented
By a fast balm which thence did spring;
Our eye-beams twisted, and did thread
Our eyes upon one double string.

The poem which follows sticks to the topic it represents the lovers in precisely that mode of union and no other. Cowley is more conventional yet still bold in the lines:

Oh take my Heart, and by that means you'll prove
    Within, too stor'd enough of love:
Give me but yours, I'll by that change so thrive
    That Love in all my parts shall live.
So powerful is this my change, it render can,
My outside Woman, and your inside Man.

A conceit originates in a metaphor and in fact the conceit is but a metaphor if the metaphor is meant that is, if it is developed so literally that it must be meant, or predicated so baldly that nothing else can be meant. Perhaps this will do for a definition.

Clearly the seventeenth century had the courage of its metaphors, and imposed them imperially on the nearest things, and just as clearly the nineteenth century lacked this courage, and was half-heartedly metaphorical, or content with similes. The difference between the literary qualities of the two periods is the difference between the metaphor and the simile. (It must be admitted that this like other generalizations will not hold without its exceptions.) One period was pithy and original in its poetic utterance, the other was prolix and predictable. It would not quite commit itself to the metaphor even if it came upon one. Shelley is about as vigorous as usual when he says in *Adonaïs*:

> Thou young Dawn,
> Turn all thy dew to splendour. . . .

But splendor is not the correlative of dew, it has the flat tone of a Platonic idea, while physically it scarcely means more than dew with sunshine upon it. The seventeenth century would have said: "Turn thy dew, which is water, into fire, and accomplish the transmutation of the elements." Tennyson in his boldest lyric sings:

> Come into the garden, Maud,
> For the black bat, night, has flown,

and leaves us unpersuaded of the bat. The predication would be complete without the bat, "The black night has flown," and a flying night is not very remarkable. Tennyson is only affecting a metaphor. But later in the same poem he writes:

> The red rose cries, "She is near, she is near";
>   And the white rose weeps, "She is late";
> The larkspur listens, "I hear, I hear";
>   And the lily whispers, "I wait."

And this is a technical conceit. But it is too complicated for this author, having a plurality of images which do not sustain themselves individually. The flowers stand for the lover's thoughts, and have been prepared for carefully in an earlier stanza, but their distinctness is too arbitrary, and these are like a schoolgirl's made-up metaphors. The passage will not compare with one on a very similar situation in *Green Candles*, by Mr. Humbert Wolfe:

> "I know her little foot," gray carpet said:
> "Who but I should know her light tread?"

"She shall come in," answered the open door,
"And not," said the room, "go out any more."

Wolfe's conceit works and Tennyson's does not, and though Wolfe's performance seems not very daring or important, and only pleasant, he employs the technique of the conceit correctly: he knows that the miracle must have a basis of verisimilitude.

Such is Metaphysical Poetry the extension of a rhetorical device; as one of the most brilliant successes in our poetry, entitled to long and thorough examination and even here demanding somewhat by way of a more ontological criticism. I conclude with it.

We may consult the dictionary, and discover that there is a miraculism or supernaturalism in a metaphorical assertion if we are ready to mean what we say, or believe what we hear. Or we may read Mr. Hobbes, the naturalist, who was very clear upon it: "II. The second cause of absurd assertions I ascribe to the giving of names of 'bodies' to 'accidents,' or of 'accidents' to 'bodies,' as they do that say 'faith is infused' or 'inspired,' when nothing can be 'poured' or 'breathed' into anything but body . . . and that 'phantasms' are 'spirits,' etc." Translated into our present terms, Hobbes is condemning the confusion of single qualities with whole things or the substitution of concrete images for simple ideas.

Specifically, the miraculism arises when the poet discovers by analogy an identity between objects which is partial, though it should be considerable, and proceeds to an identification which is complete. It is to be contrasted with the simile, which says "as if" or "like," and is scrupulous to keep the identification partial. In Cowley's passage above, the lover is saying, not for the first time in this literature: "She and I have exchanged our hearts." What has actually been exchanged is affections, and affections are only in a limited sense the same as hearts. Hearts are unlike affections in being engines that pump blood and form body; and it is a miracle if the poet represents the lady's affection as rendering her inside into man. But he succeeds, with this mixture, in depositing with us the image of a very powerful affection.

From the strict point of view of literary criticism it must be insisted that the miraculism which produces the humblest conceit is the same miraculism which supplies to religions their substantive content. (This is said to assert the dignity not of the conceits but of the religions.) It is the poet and nobody else who gives to the God a nature, a form, faculties, and a history; to the God, most comprehensive of all terms, which, if there were no poetic impulse to actualize or "find" Him, would remain the driest and deadest among Platonic ideas, with all intension sacrificed to infinite extension. The myths are conceits, born of metaphors. Religions are periodically produced by poets and destroyed by naturalists. Religion depends for its ontological validity upon a literary understanding, and that is why it is frequently misunderstood. The metaphysical poets, perhaps like their spiritual fathers the medieval Schoolmen, were under no illusions about this. They recognized myth, as they recognized the conceits, as a device of expression; its sanctity as the consequence of its public or social importance.

But whether the topics be Gods or amorous experiences, why do poets resort to miraculism? Hardly for the purpose of controverting natural fact or scientific theory. Religion pronounces about God only where science is silent and philosophy is negative; for a positive is wanted, that is, a God who has His being in the physical world as well as in the world of principles and abstractions. Likewise with the little secular enterprises of poetry too. Not now are the poets so brave, not for a very long time have they been so brave, as to dispute the scientists on what they call their "truth"; though it is a pity that the statement cannot be turned round. Poets will concede that every act of science is legitimate, and has its efficacy. The metaphysical poets of the seventeenth century particularly admired the methodology of science, and in fact they copied it, and their phrasing is often technical, spare, and polysyllabic, though they are not repeating actual science but making those metaphorical substitutions that are so arresting.

The intention of Metaphysical Poetry is to complement science, and improve discourse. Naturalistic discourse is incomplete, for either of two reasons. It has the minimum of physical content and starves the sensibility, or it has the maximum, as if to avoid the appearance of evil, but is laborious and pointless. Platonic Poetry is too idealistic, but Physical Poetry is too realistic, and realism is tedious and does not maintain interest. The poets therefore introduce the psychological device of the miracle. The predication which it permits is clean and quick but it is not a scientific predication. For scientific predication concludes an act of attention but miraculism initiates one. It leaves us looking, marvelling, and revelling in the thick *dinglich* substance that has just received its strange representation.

Let me suggest as a last word, in deference to a common Puritan scruple, that the predication of Metaphysical Poetry is true enough. It is not true like history, but no poetry is true in that sense, and only a part of science. It is true in the pragmatic sense in which some of the generalizations of science are true: it accomplishes precisely the sort of representation that it means to. It suggests to us that the object is perceptually or physically remarkable, and we had better attend to it.

8

LETTER TO THE TEACHER
and
IMAGERY

CLEANTH BROOKS AND ROBERT PENN WARREN

Cleanth Brooks and Robert Penn Warren open their "Letter to the Teacher" in Understanding Poetry *with a forthright challenge: "This book has been conceived on the assumption that if poetry is worth teaching at all it is worth teaching as poetry." Well aware of the possible evasions, they call the teacher to the actual task at hand, and they provide him or her with a highly practical, tightly organized approach, with heavy emphasis on analysis rather than vague appreciation. By implication, learning to read poetry well and to distinguish good from bad helps form taste, which includes thinking and feeling. In the course of the textbook, analyses of individual poems—such as Housman's* To an Athlete Dying Young *and Kilmer's* Trees—*show this formation in action.*

Unlike other essays by Brooks and Warren, the analyses of these poems have a straightforward, even dry quality; they make no attempt to reproduce in prose the affective quality of the poetry. The editors know they are addressing students more interested in science or in business careers than in reading literature. Instead of standing on the desk, as it were, they adopt a hardheaded, no-nonsense prosaic tone, a little gruff, as though they were comparing the way two farmers rotated their crops, or assessing the organization of a factory. They demonstrate that one can talk about and examine the poem itself as

161

a made thing instead of a natural outpouring—a made thing with reasonable laws governing its composition, capable of being judged in terms of its quality. The rough treatment of Trees, undertaken with deadpan earnestness, must have shaken many a pious bosom.

LETTER TO THE TEACHER

This book has been conceived on the assumption that if poetry is worth teaching at all it is worth teaching as poetry. The temptation to make a substitute for the poem as the object of study is usually overpowering. The substitutes are various, but the most common ones are:

Paraphrase of logical and narrative content.

Study of biographical and historical materials.

Inspirational and didactic interpretation.

Of course, paraphrase may be necessary as a preliminary step in the reading of a poem, and a study of the biographical and historical background may do much to clarify interpretation; but these things should be considered as means and not as ends. And though one may consider a poem as an instance of historical or ethical documentation, the poem in itself, if literature is to be studied as literature, remains finally the object for study. Moreover, even if the interest is in the poem as a historical or ethical document, there is a prior consideration: one must grasp the poem as a literary construct before it can offer any real illumination as a document.

When, as a matter of fact, an attempt is made to treat the poem as an object in itself, the result very often is, on the one hand, the vaguest sort of impressionistic comment, or on the other, the study of certain technical aspects of the poem, metrics for instance, *in isolation from other aspects and from the total intention.*

In illustration of these confused approaches to the study of poetry the editors submit the following quotations drawn almost at random from a group of current textbooks.

The sole critical comment on *Ode to a Nightingale* in one popular textbook is:

> The song of the nightingale brings sadness and exhilaration to the poet and makes him long to be lifted up and away from the limitations of life. The seventh stanza is particularly beautiful.

In the same textbook a typical exercise reads:

> What evidences of a love of beauty do you find in Keats's poems?

But one is constrained to voice the following questions:

Is not the real point of importance the relation of the paradox of "exhilaration" and "sadness" to the theme of the poem? As a matter of fact, the question of the theme of the poem is never raised in this textbook.

The seventh stanza is referred to as "beautiful," but on what grounds is the student to take any piece of poetry as "beautiful"?

Even if the exercise quoted is relevant and important, there is a real danger that the suggestion to the student to look for beautiful objects in the poem will tend to make him confuse the mention of beautiful or agreeable objects in poetry with poetic excellence.

Some of the same confusions reappear in another book: "These lyrics [*Ode to the West Wind* and *To a Skylark*] are characterized by a freshness and spontaneity, beautiful figures of speech in abundance, melody, and an unusually skillful adaptation of the form and movement of the verse to the word and the idea. Their melodiousness is sometimes compared with that of Schubert's music."

But in what, for example, does a beautiful comparison consist? The implication is that the beautiful comparison is one which makes use of beautiful objects. Again, when a student has been given no concrete exposition of the "adaptation of form and movement . . . to the word and the idea" of a poem, and has received no inkling of what the "idea" of a particular poem is, what is such a statement expected to mean to him?

Or again: "To the simplicity and exquisite melodiousness of these earlier songs, Blake added mysticism and the subtlest kind of symbolism." One is moved to comment: In the first place, the student can only be made to grasp the function of symbolism in poetry by the most careful investigation of particular instances; certainly, "the subtlest kind of symbolism" should not be flung at him with no further introduction than is provided by this sentence. In the second place, what can the sentence mean on any level? Is it proper to say that any poet "adds" mysticism to anything? And what sort of simplicity is it to which subtle symbolism can be added? Does the *melange* remain simple? And what possible connection is implied here between the "exquisite melodiousness" and the mysticism and symbolism? In any case, the approach to poetry indicated in this sentence raises more problems than it solves.

To glean from another recent textbook: "Emily [Dickinson] the seer teases us into believing that she has dived into the depths where great truths lie and has brought up new and astounding specimens. Many of her bulletins from Immortality seem oracular. Shorn of her matchless imagery they turn out to be puritan platitudes or transcendental echoes. Her definitions of weighty abstractions are unphilosophical. They are quick fancies, created out of a fleeting mood, and are therefore frequently contradictory. But when Emily failed with logic, she succeeded with imagination." It is impossible, apparently, to determine from what principles of poetic criticism these remarks can be derived. The objection that Emily Dickinson's poetry when "shorn of its matchless imagery" would turn out to be platitudes could be raised with equal justification about the most celebrated passages of Shakespeare. The passage rests on a misconception of the relation of "truth" to poetry, and on a confused notion of what constitutes poetic originality. Certainly, to clarify the issue of "truth" and poetic excellence, or of originality and poetic excellence, would be a very ambitious undertaking; but that fact scarcely justifies a complete fogging of the issue.

Occasionally the writer of a textbook will attempt to deal with poetry as a thing in itself worthy of study; and apparently hoping to avoid the sort of vagueness found in the preceding quotation, will isolate certain aspects of poetry for special investigation. In its crudest manifestation this impulse leads to statistical surveys of one kind or another. The student, for instance, is exhorted to count or to classify the figures of speech in a poem; or to define metrical forms.

There is a more sophisticated manifestation of the same impulse, as for example, in the following classification of metrical effects:

> Some of the varied effects *produced by meter* are illustrated in the following stanzas:

Sweet softness—

> Swiftly walk o'er the western wave,
>   Spirit of Night!
> Out of thy misty eastern cave,
> Where all the long and lone daylight,
> Thou wovest dreams of joy and fear,
> Which makes thee terrible, and dear—
> Swift be thy flight!
>
>   —Shelley, *To Night*

Stark simplicity—

> Out of the night that covers me,
>   Black as the pit from pole to pole,
> I thank whatever gods may be
> For my unconquerable soul.
>
>   —Henley, *Invictus*

The author has said flatly concerning these quotations that the effects described are "produced by meter." The statement is completely misleading and rests upon an imperfect understanding of the relation of meter to the other factors in a poem. A clever student would immediately confute the author by pointing out that the line, "Out of thy misty eastern cave," the meter of which is supposed to communicate "soft sweetness," and the line, "Out of the night that covers me," the meter of which is supposed to communicate "stark simplicity," have *exactly* the same meter. In fact, he might point out that many metrical effects are common to selections which communicate very different emotional effects.

This is not to deny that meter is an important factor in poetry, but it is to deny that a specific emotional effect can be tied absolutely to a particular metrical instance. The selections cited do produce different emotional effects, but the basis for the effect can only be given accurately by a study of the relations existing among all the factors, of which meter is only one.

Another instance of the isolation of one technical feature without regard for the whole context and for the particular poet's method is the following observation in a recent textbook:

> Hamlet's "take arms against a sea of troubles" is a classic instance of the poet's failure to visualize what he is saying. Longfellow's mariner, in *A Psalm of Life* "sailing o'er life's solemn main" and at the same time apparently examining "footprints on the sands of time," is another example of confused phrasing.

This passage might be taken as a classic example of the misapplication of an undigested critical principle. We frequently see in textbooks on poetry and in rhetorics the warning against the use of "mixed metaphor." But, of course, in applying this principle one must, in every case, examine the context of the instance, the psychological basis, and the poet's intention. These factors are entirely ignored in the present quotation. For instance, the dramatic situation in the passage from *Hamlet* and the relation of the style to it are dismissed by the high-handed and abstract application of this principle. Incidentally this method would eliminate the following well known passages, among many, from the work of Shakespeare:

> Tomorrow and tomorrow and tomorrow
> Creeps in this petty pace from day to day
> To the last syllable. . . . *Macbeth*

>   If the assassination
> Could trammel up the consequence and catch
> With his surcease, success . . . *Macbeth*

>   Was the hope drunk
> Wherein you dressed yourself? hath it slept since?
> And wakes it now, to look so green and pale . . . *Macbeth*

The critic in question would apparently be embarrassed by the imaginative agility required for reading much of Shakespeare's poetry, especially the poetry of his so-called "great period," simply because he places his reliance on the mechanical and legalistic application of a single principle without reference to context.

As a matter of ironical fact, the image involved in the speech quoted from *Hamlet* can be visualized. One has only to remember the stories of Xerxes, and Cuchulain, one who punished and one who fought the sea, to grasp the point. Furthermore, in justice to *A Psalm of Life*, which is on enough counts a very bad poem, one can indicate that a little more attentive reading will reveal the fact that the mariner who sees the footprints is not actually on the high seas at the moment, but is, as the poem specifically says, a "shipwrecked brother."

The editors of the present book hold that a satisfactory method of teaching poetry should embody the following principles.

1. Emphasis should be kept on the poem as a poem.

2. The treatment should be concrete and inductive.

3. A poem should always be treated as an organic system of relationships, and the poetic quality should never be understood as inhering in one or more factors taken in isolation.

With the hope of giving these principles some vitality the editors have undertaken this book.

This book must stand or fall by the analyses of individual poems which it contains. These analyses are intended to be discussions of the poet's adaptation of his means to his ends: that is, discussions of the relations of the various aspects of a poem to each other and to the total communication intended. Obviously, the analyses presented in the early sections of this book are simple and very incomplete accounts of the problems involved. But the analyses become more difficult as the student is provided with more critical apparatus and becomes more accustomed to the method. The analyses, therefore, form parts of an ascending scale and should not be studied haphazardly.

The general organization of the book is, likewise, determined by this scale of ascending difficulty. The book has seven divisions. Section I deals with poems in which the narrative element is relatively important. Poems of this general nature appear here because the narrative interest seems to afford the broadest and most unspecialized appeal to the ordinary student. The basic question behind the analyses in this section is: *what distinguishes the poetic treatment of a story from the more usual prose treatment?* Section II deals with poems in which the narrative is merely implied or is suppressed in favor of some such interest as that in psychology or character. Section III takes up another approach, that of the poet as observer rather than as narrator. The material in this section ranges from poems which ostensibly are simple, objective descriptions to the last poems, in which description emerges with a definite symbolic force. Section IV takes up one of the more specialized technical problems, that of the nature of rhythm and meter as means of communication. The analyses in this section naturally emphasize the technical considerations of verse, but the attempt is constantly made to indicate the relation of these considerations to the others which the student has already studied. In Section V are considered some of the ways in which tone and attitude are communicated to the reader. The poems of Section VI present some special problems in the use of imagery as a device of communication, and those of Section VII raise questions concerning the function of idea and statement.

Although the poems are arranged in these groups, it is not to be understood that the topics which determine the arrangement are treated in isolation. As a matter of fact, the analyses and questions which are appended to each poem aim at making the student aware of the organic relationship existing among these factors in poetic communication. Obviously, any poem whatsoever would, finally, raise the questions associated with all of these topics. Questions involving imagery, for example, occur even in Section I and are treated in the analyses. Pedagogical convenience, however, demands that special attention be focused on special problems; but, as has been said, it does not demand that those problems be treated in isolation. A poem, then, is placed in any given section because it may be used to emphasize a certain aspect of poetic method and offers, it is hoped, an especially teachable example. But these classifications must be understood as classifications of convenience. Indeed, it might be a fruitful exercise for the students to return to poems in early sections after they have acquired more critical apparatus.

The poems, as has been pointed out, are arranged in a scale of increasing difficulty. Usually, poems of the simplest method and of the broadest general appeal appear in the early sections. But such a scale, of course, cannot be absolute. For example, a poem like *The Ancient Mariner*, which appears in Section I, is on absolute grounds more difficult than many poems appearing in later sections. But it does offer a strong narrative interest. Furthermore, the poems in each section offer a scale of ascending difficulty in regard to the particular problem under discussion. Since this is the case, if poems toward the end of each of the later sections prove too difficult in certain classes, they may be omitted without impairing the general method.

Although the arrangement of poems adopted in this book is one of convenience, it is based on two considerations: first, on aspects of poetic communication, and second, on pedagogical expediency. Therefore, it is hoped that the present arrangement stands on a ground different from the arbitrary and irrational classifications frequently found in textbooks that depart from simple chronological order—classifications such as "lyrics of meditation" and "religious lyrics" and "poems of patriotism," or "the sonnet," the "Ode," the "song," etc.

If one accepts the principle that one must teach by a constant and analytical use of concrete examples, then the nature of the *Introduction* will be readily understood. The *Introduction* does not attempt to arrive at a "definition" of poetry or to explain, for instance, the workings of imagery or meter. It attempts, instead, to dispose of a few of the basic misconceptions with which the teacher is usually confronted in the classroom, and therefore to prepare the student to enter upon an unprejudiced study of the actual poems. Likewise, the *Glossary* of critical terms is based on the idea that the teaching of the book will be by concrete example. The *Glossary* does not provide a set of definitions to be memorized all at once by the student. Rather, it provides definitions and an index of cross references to concrete applications of definitions, which the student can consult as the occasion demands. Even the schematic presentation of metrical terms has been relegated to the *Glossary*, although there it is so organized that it may be studied, if desired, as a consecutive discussion. But even in the case of metrical study, the editors suggest that the general principle of the book be applied.

There are two objections to the method of the present book which may occur to a teacher at this point. It may be objected that this text by its number of analyses attempts to usurp the function of the teacher and to do by the written word what can better be done by the spoken word. Or, second, it may be objected that the judgments of literary value which are involved (and necessarily involved) in the analyses are dogmatic and perhaps often in error.

In answer to the first objection it may be urged that: first, the analyses, if they are at all effective, relieve the teacher of a certain amount of preliminary drudgery and free him for a critical and perhaps more advanced treatment of the un-analyzed poems in each section of the book; second, since, no analyses here could pretend to final completeness, a certain amount of explanation and extension will be required even in treating poems which are analyzed; and third, the fact that a liberal number of analyses are in printed form gives the student an opportunity for a careful private study of the poems in question. With regard to the second objection—the objection that the judgments in the analyses are dogmatic—the editors can only say that no dogmatism is intended. Naturally, they hope that most of their judgments are reasonable, but even if a teacher disagrees with an individual analysis, an explanation of that disagreement should dramatize for the student the basic issues involved. And in fact, the editors feel that disagreement is to be encouraged rather than discouraged in so far as pure impressionism can be eliminated from the debate.

Just as the editors feel that disagreement and debate may be healthful in sharpening the critical instinct of the student, so they feel that the study and analysis of bad and uneven poems will contribute to the same end. A reasonable number of such poems have been included, and a few have been analyzed. The great majority of the poems included in the book, however, represent positive achievement. The modern poems included have not been chosen at random, nor merely on the ground of current fashion. They are intended to represent some of the various lines taken in the development of poetic method in this century. In general, it is hoped that the juxtaposition of good and bad poems, and of new and old poems, will serve to place emphasis on the primary matter of critical reading and evaluation.

Although this book is based on a principle, and is not a casual anthology, and although it is organized in the light of that principle, the final effect, it is hoped, will be to liberate rather than restrict the initiative of the teacher. By positing a principle and a definite objective, the book allows the teacher a great deal of liberty in devising correlative approaches to the general end. Although the book does suggest a variety of exercises for the student, such as analyses modeled on those in the book, comparisons of the prose and poetic versions of the same material, comparisons of poems treating the same theme, etc., the possibility for development along this line is almost infinite and can be adapted to individual needs.

A last word: the editors of this book do not delude themselves that they have here provided, or could elsewhere provide, solutions for any of the fundamental problems of poetic criticism. Nor, least of all, have they provided in this book neat criteria which can be applied in rule-of-thumb fashion. Rather, they hope to present to the student, in proper context and after proper preparation, some of the basic critical problems—with the aim, not of making technical critics, but merely of making competent readers of poetry. At the least, they hope that this book will find some merit in the eyes of those who agree with Louis Cazamian: "that all students of literature should be regarded as historians is an exaggerated and a pernicious assumption. More important still, and much more fruitful than the problems of origins and development, are those of content and significance. What is the human matter, what the artistic value of the work?" So much for the general aim of this book. As for the general method, to quote again from this critic: "it is rightly felt that if the . . . student of literature is to be capable of an intelligent appreciation, he must go beyond the passive enjoyment of what he reads; he must be instructed, partly at least, in the mysteries of the art."

IMAGERY

In many instances we have already commented on various functions of imagery in poetry, and we have seen how important these are. The poems in this section raise no new principles concerning the fundamental nature of poetic imagery, but they have been chosen because they offer the student an opportunity for further analysis. Some poems rely more than others on imagery for conveying their meanings. The following analysis of two lines from Shakespeare's *Venus and Adonis* is made by Samuel Taylor Coleridge, the poet and critic, and has been further expanded by I. A. Richards, a psychologist and critic. This analysis indicates some of the ways in which imagery does its work.

> Look! how a bright star shooteth from the sky
> So glides he in the night from Venus' eye.

How many images and feelings are here brought together without effort and without discord—the beauty of Adonis—the rapidity of his flight—the yearning yet helplessness of the enamoured gazer—and a shadowy ideal character thrown over the whole.[1]

Here, in contrast to the other case, the more the image is followed up, the more links of relevance between the units are discovered. As Adonis to Venus, so these lines to the reader seem to linger in the eye like the after-images that make the trail of the meteor. Here Shakespeare is realizing, and making the reader realize—not by any intensity of effort, but by the fullness and self-completing growth of the response—Adonis's flight as it was to Venus, and the sense of loss, of increased darkness, that invades her. The separable meanings of each word, *Look!* (our surprise at the meteor, hers at his flight), *star* (a light-giver, an influence, a remote and uncontrollable thing) *shooteth* (the sudden, irremediable, portentous fall or death of what had been a guide, a destiny), *the sky* (the source of light and now of ruin), *glides* (not rapidity only, but fatal ease too), *in the night* (the darkness of the scene and of Venus's world now)—all these separable meanings are here brought into one. And as they come together, as the reader's

---

1, Samuel Taylor Coleridge, *Shakespearean Criticism*. Thomas Raysor, ed. Two volumes (London: 1930), I, 213.

mind finds cross-connection after cross-connection between them, he seems, in becoming more aware of them, to be discovering not only Shakespeare's meaning, but something which he, the reader, is himself making. His understanding of Shakespeare is sanctioned by his own activity in it. As Coleridge says: "You feel him to be a poet, inasmuch as for a time he has made you one—an active creative being."[2]

The reader should be on the alert for the implications the imagery in any poem may have and for the relation of imagery to the full intention.

To an Athlete Dying Young
A. E. Housman (1859–1936)

The time you won your town the race
We chaired you through the market-place;
Man and boy stood cheering by,
And home we brought you shoulder-high.

Today, the road all runners come,
Shoulder-high we bring you home,
And set you at your threshold down,
Townsman of a stiller town.

Smart lad, to slip betimes away
From fields where glory does not stay,
And early though the laurel grows
It withers quicker than the rose.

Eyes the shady night has shut
Cannot see the record cut,
And silence sounds no worse than cheers
After earth has stopped the ears:

Now you will not swell the rout
Of lads that wore their honors out,
Runners whom renown outran
And the name died before the man.

---

2. [Brooks and Warren] I. A. Richards, *Coleridge on the Imagination*. (New York: Harcourt-Brace) 1935, 82–84.

So set, before its echoes fade,
The fleet foot on the sill of shade,
And hold to the low lintel up
The still-defended challenge-cup.

And round that early-laureled head
Will flock to gaze the strengthless dead,
And find unwithered on its curls
The garland briefer than a girl's.

In this poem the poet states a paradox: namely, that the early death of the young athlete is a matter for congratulation rather than for sorrow. This is the real theme of the poem. But we should hardly be impressed with the bare statement that it is better to die young rather than old, and even the startling quality of the statement would awaken interest for only a moment. The poet has known better than to state the matter baldly, therefore. He has arranged a little dramatic framework for the statement. In a familiar, almost conversational tone—"Smart lad"—he addresses his congratulations to the young man who is dead; and more than that, he uses the images which are associated with the young man's athletic achievements to describe his death. Indeed, the statement implied by the imagery of the poem is that the young runner has, in dying, won his race again—he has beaten his competitors to the final goal of all of them, death.

Notice, for example, that the funeral is treated exactly as if it were a triumph for the young runner celebrated by his friends. On the day on which he won the race for his town, his friends made a chair for him of their hands and carried him home shoulder-high in triumph. Now on the day of his funeral, they carry him "shoulder-high" again, and they bring him "home." "Smart lad," the poet then calls him, as if he had just finished running a heady race.

The reasons for saying this follow: it is better to die at the prime than to witness one's records broken by someone else. But the poet does not relax his hold on concrete details in making this statement. The laurel, symbol of fame, withers even quicker than does the rose, emblem of beauty. Eyes closed in death cannot see the record broken; to ears stopped with earth, the silence rings as loud as the air filled with cheering. And now the poet returns to the dominant figure of the race. Fame has a habit of outrunning the fastest runner and leaving him behind; the young athlete has not been outrun by his renown.

The figure is developed further in the sixth stanza. The brink of the grave is "the sill of shade" on which the young man has just placed his fleet foot, and the edge of the grave is the "low lintel" up to which the boy holds the "still defended challenge cup." The paradoxes here are especially rich. We think of death as being opposed in every regard to fleetness, and its inertia as incapable of defending anything. Yet by the reasoning which has preceded this stanza, the foot of the dead youth is fleet in death—only in death can he hold his challenge-cup still defended. Others will not be able to wrest it from him. The passage is a fine example of the poet's ability to put things which we ordinarily think of as quite unrelated, or even opposed to each other, into a pattern which gives a meaningful relation where one had not been seen before.

The last stanza exhibits also a fine effect which the poet has prepared for. The stanza catches up the contrast between the laurel and the rose already made in the third stanza. The connection is hinted at in the phrase "early-laureled head." Fame perishes even more quickly than beauty—the garland of laurel withers even faster than the garland of roses which a girl might be supposed to wear. We think of a young girl dead in the first flush of her beauty as an object of pathos, and at the same time think of her as having achieved a sort of triumph at having brought all her beauty untarnished with her into the grave. The poet wishes to get, and does get, something of the same effect for the athlete, and he gets it by suggesting the comparison.

Does he overplay his hand? Does he appear to be trying to extract the last degree of pathos from the situation? The mature reader will feel that the effect of pathos has been secured legitimately, and that the poet is not guilty of sentimentality; that is, that the emotion evoked in the poem is really inherent in the situation and has been developed by the poet for the reader by no unfair means. The pathos is a clean pathos therefore, revealed by a sudden insight but not lingered over for its own sake. One may observe how the firmness of the rhythm of the poem, and the familiar tone of the opening stanzas help to avoid a sentimental effect.

The use of paradox in this poem is also important in this regard, for a paradox tends to provoke a certain mental alertness, a certain awareness which in this case prevents the tone of the poem from becoming too soft. In the same way, and important for the same effect, is the use of symbol (laurel and rose), the use of the particular detail and image, and the use of suggestion rather than flat statement. All of these means are indirect as opposed to the direct prose statement; and this means that the reader must to some extent discover the meaning and the pathos for himself. The reader responds to the situation with force, but legitimately, because he feels that he has been merely helped by the poet to see the real character of the experience.

Trees
Joyce Kilmer (1886–1918)

I think that I shall never see
A poem lovely as a tree.

A tree whose hungry mouth is pressed
Against the sweet earth's flowing breast;

A tree that looks at God all day,
And lifts her leafy arms to pray;

A tree that may in summer wear
A nest of robins in her hair;

Upon whose bosom snow has lain;
Who intimately lives with rain.

Poems are made by fools like me,
But only God can make a tree.

This poem has been very greatly admired by a large number of people. The fact that it has been popular does not necessarily condemn it as a bad poem. But it is a bad poem. First, let us look at it merely on the technical side, especially in regard to the use Kilmer makes of his imagery. Now the poet, in a poem of twelve lines, only makes one fundamental comparison on which the other comparisons are based; this is the same method used by Housman in *To an Athlete Dying Young*.

In *Trees* this fundamental comparison is not definitely stated but is constantly implied. The comparison is that of the tree to a human being. If the tree is compared to a human being, the reader has a right to expect a consistent use to be made of the aspects of the human being which appear in the poem. But look at stanza two:

> A tree whose hungry mouth is pressed
> Against the sweet earth's flowing breast;

Here the tree is *metaphorically (Glossary)* treated as a sucking babe and the earth, therefore, as the mother—a perfectly good comparison that has been made for centuries—the earth as the "great mother," the "giver of life," etc.

But the third stanza introduces a confusion:

> A tree that looks at God all day,
> And lifts her leafy arms to pray;

Here the tree is no longer a sucking babe, but, without warning, is old enough to indulge in religious devotions. But that is not the worst part of the confusion. Remember that the tree is a human being and that in the first stanza the *mouth* of that human being was the *root* of the tree. But now, if the branches are "leafy arms" the tree is a strangely deformed human being. The fourth and fifth stanzas maintain the same anatomical arrangement for the tree as does the third, but they make other unexpected changes: the tree that wears a "nest of robins in her hair" must be a grown-up person, a girl with jewels in her hair; the tree with snow on its bosom is a chaste and pure girl, for so the *associations* of snow with purity and chastity tell the reader; and the tree that "lives with rain" is a chaste and pure young woman who, although vain enough to wear jewels, is yet withdrawn from the complications of human relationships and lives alone with a "nature," i.e., rain, or might be said to be nun-like, an implication made by the religious tone of the poem.

Now it would be quite legitimate for the poet to use any one of the thoughts he wishes to convey about the tree (1. the tree as a babe nursed by mother earth, 2. the tree as a devout person praying all day, 3. the tree as a girl with jewels in her hair, or 4. the tree as a chaste woman alone with nature and God) and to create a metaphor for it, but the trouble is that he tries to convey all of these features by a single basic comparison to a person, and therefore presents a picture thoroughly confused. The poet confuses his reader if the reader tries actually to *see* the images the poet uses or tries to think about their *implications;* and that is exactly what a good poet wants his readers to do, to *visualize* or *feel* or *hear* his images (for there are images of sight, touch, sound, etc.) and then to understand what those images imply, for that is one of the chief ways a poet *communicates* his meaning, a way more important in the long run to most poets than that of the actual flat prose statement of idea.

All of this does not mean of course that a poet *must* take a single comparison and develop it *fully* and *consistently,* or that there must be a strict *transition* from one comparison or image to the next. For instance:

> O my love is like a red, red rose,
> That's newly sprung in June;
> O my love is like the melody
> That's sweetly played in tune.

Although this stanza seems to have in it the same abrupt change in the comparison, there is really a very important difference. Burns does not say that his love is like a rose in the same way that Kilmer says that the tree is like a person; Burns merely implies that his love is beautiful, fragrant, etc. like a rose, or affects him like a rose, but he does not insist on a consistent development of the comparison; he merely wanted to point out the effective part of the comparison, not even thinking, for instance, of the thorns which are not pretty and are painful and which would have caused trouble if he had started a consistent development of the image, as Kilmer does. But without warning Burns then jumps to a melody. Now Kilmer jumps from a sucking babe to a grown person without warning and thereby creates a confusion in the reader's mind. Burns creates no confusion. Why? Because Burns makes an absolute leap from rose to melody with reference to "his love" as the only connecting link, while Kilmer is maintaining a false consistency by a continued reference to a human being. Poets are constantly jumping from one comparison to another quite successfully because they treat each comparison in terms of its own special contribution to the poet's intention.

But in *Trees* there are other difficulties on the technical side. The rhythm is not well chosen. It is monotonous. Each stanza has the same rhythm, with a full pause at the end of a couplet and no pauses within the lines. The effect is sharp and pert, with no impression of thoughtfulness or of competent control on the part of the poet. This is especially inappropriate for a poem which pretends to treat a serious subject. Compare the rhythm, the variety of pauses, etc. of "Trees" with this passage from another poem in the same meter and rime scheme:

> Accept, thou shrine of my dead Saint,
> Instead of dirges this complaint;
> And for sweet flowers to crown thy hearse,
> Receive a strew of weeping verse
> From thy grieved friend, whom thou might'st see
> Quite melted into tears for thee.
>   (From *The Exequy*, by Henry King)

But how seriously does Kilmer treat his "serious subject"? The rhythm does not contribute to a serious approach; nor does the confusion of the treatment of imagery. But let us try to consider his *meaning* or *thought* as such.

The poet is expressing a highly romantic mood in which he pretends that the works of man's mind are not comparable in "loveliness" to the works of Nature. What he wants to say is that he is tired of the works of man and takes refuge in the works of nature, which is quite different from comparing the two things on the basis of "loveliness. . . ." But the two kinds of loveliness, that of art and that of nature, are not comparable; and in the second place "loveliness" is not the word to apply to *Hamlet* by Shakespeare, *Lycidas*, by Milton, *The Canterbury Tales*, by Chaucer, etc. And the tree, as opposed to the poem, is lacking in *meaning* and *expressiveness*; it has those things only in so far as a man can give them to it. Kilmer writes:

> Poems are made by fools like me
> But only God can make a tree.

That is perfectly true, but by the same line of reasoning God makes the poems too, through his agency in man. Or reversing the argument: Bad poems are made by bad poets like Kilmer and good poems are made by good poets like Yeats, Shakespeare, Landor, Milton, etc. Furthermore the paradox created by Kilmer breaks down, because it isn't justified in terms given in the poem; it will not stand inspection. Housman uses a paradox successfully in *To an Athlete Dying Young*, because in the poem he limits the application and illustrates the precise ways in which it contains a truth.

But why has the poem been popular, if so bad? It appeals . . . to a stock response which has nothing to do, as such, with poetry. It praises God and appeals to a religious sentiment. Therefore people who do not stop to look at the poem itself or to study the images in the poem and think about what the poem really says, are inclined to accept the poem because of the pious sentiment, the prettified little pictures (which in themselves appeal to stock responses), and the mechanical rhythm.

9

CRITICISM AS PURE SPECULATION

JOHN CROWE RANSOM

In this essay, originally part of a symposium on "The Intent of the Critic," Ransom shifts his emphasis from the kinds of poetry to the kinds of critical emphasis. He rejects the "psychologistic" and "moralistic" (whether neo-humanist or Marxist) approaches in favor of what he calls "ontological insight." The part of his essay that proved vexing to many was his definition of a poem as "a logical structure having a local texture." Looking back on the 1930s and 1940s from the perspective of 1974, shortly after John Crowe Ransom's death, Allen Tate marveled at the impulse that led three critics of that earlier day (Ransom, Yvor Winters, and Tate himself) to try to "encapsulate poetry"—to derive a "formula" for it. "I am still amazed," he wrote, "that John Ransom, of all people, should come up with 'structure' and 'texture' as critical metaphors."[1] It would be tempting to say that Ransom proposes the radical dualism of "structure" and "texture" ironically, but he does not. In fact, he would defend his formula for the next decade, especially against such later claims of poetic unity as Cleanth Brooks's "The Heresy of Paraphrase" (which follows this essay on page 203). Ransom describes the poem as a "democratic state"—one that gets its business done but does not "despoil its members, the citizens, of the free exercise of their own private and independent character." Prose discourse, on the other

1. Tate, *Memoirs*, 40.

hand, "is a totalitarian state," all of whose parts merely function by "their allotted contributions toward its ends." Ransom refuses to accept Hegel's "concrete universal." In his insistence on noncontradiction—which seems odd after the "miraculism" he espouses in "Poetry: A Note in Ontology"—one might suspect that a stubborn theological doubt informs his denial. Ransom draws back in logical distaste from metaphors of sacramental unity implied by such terms as "the heresy of paraphrase." As Murray Krieger writes, "What is at issue here is whether or not the paraphrase as such exists as a prior element which is then violated."[2]

. . . When we inquire into the "intent of the critic," we mean: the intent of the generalized critic, or critic as such. We will concede that any professional critic is familiar with the technical practices of poets so long as these are conventional, and is expert in judging when they perform them brilliantly, and when only fairly, or badly. We expect a critical discourse to cover that much, but we know that more is required. The most famous poets of our own time, for example, make wide departures from conventional practices: how are they to be judged? Innovations in poetry, or even conventions when pressed to their logical limits, cause the ordinary critic to despair. They cause the good critic to review his aesthetic principles; perhaps to reformulate his aesthetic principles. He tries the poem against his best philosophical conception of the peculiar character that a poem should have.

Mr. T. S. Eliot is an extraordinarily sensitive critic. But when he discusses the so-called metaphysical poetry, he surprises us by refusing to study the so-called conceit which is its reputed basis; he observes instead that the metaphysical poets of the seventeenth century are more like their immediate predecessors than the latter are like the eighteenth- and nineteenth-century poets, and then he goes into a very broad philosophical comparison between two whole "periods" or types of poetry. I think it has come to be understood that his comparison

2. Murray Krieger, *The New Apologists for Poetry* (Minneapolis, MN: University of Minnesota Press, 1956), 84.

is unsound; it has not proved workable enough to assist critics who have otherwise borrowed liberally from his critical principles. (It contains the famous dictum about the "sensibility" of the earlier poets, it imputes to them a remarkable ability to "feel their thought," and to have a kind of "experience" in which the feeling cannot be differentiated from the thinking.) Now there is scarcely another critic equal to Eliot at distinguishing the practices of two poets who are closely related. He is supreme as a comparative critic when the relation in question is delicate and subtle; that is, when it is a matter of close perception and not a radical difference in kind. But this line of criticism never goes far enough. In Eliot's own range of criticism the line does not always answer. He is forced by discontinuities in the poetic tradition into sweeping theories that have to do with aesthetics, the philosophy of poetry; and his own philosophy probably seems to us insufficient, the philosophy of the literary man.

The intent of the critic may well be, then, first to read his poem sensitively, and make comparative judgments about its technical practice, or, as we might say, to emulate Eliot. Beyond that, it is to read and remark the poem knowingly; that is, with an aesthetician's understanding of what a poem genetically "is."

Before I venture, with inadequate argument, to describe what I take to be the correct understanding of poetry, I would like to describe two other understandings which, though widely professed, seem to me misunderstandings. First, there is a smart and belletristic theory of poetry which may be called *psychologistic*. Then there is an altogether staid and commonplace theory which is *moralistic*. Of these in their order.

II

It could easily be argued about either of these untenable conceptions of poetry that it is an act of despair to which critics resort who cannot find for the discourse of poetry any precise differentia to remove it from the category of science. Psychologistic critics hold that poetry is addressed primarily to the feelings and motor impulses; they remind us frequently of its contrast with the coldness, the unemotionality, of science, which is supposed to address itself to the pure cognitive mind. Mr. Richards came out spectacularly for the doctrine, and furnished it with detail of the greatest ingenuity. He very nearly severed the dependence of poetic effect upon any standard of objective knowledge or belief. But the feelings and impulses which he represented as gratified by the poem were too tiny and numerous to be named. He never identified them; they seemed not so much psychological as infra-psychological. His was an esoteric poetic: it could not be disproved. But neither could it be proved, and I think it is safe at this distance to say that eventually his readers, and Richards himself, lost interest in it as being an improvisation, much too unrelated to the public sense of a poetic experience. With other critics psychologism of some sort is an old story, and one that will probably never cease to be told. For, now that all of us know about psychology, there must always be persons on hand precisely conditioned to declare that poetry is an emotional discourse indulged in resentment and compensation for science, the bleak cognitive discourse in its purity. It becomes less a form of knowledge than a form of "expression." The critics are willing to surrender the honor of objectivity to science if they may have the luxury of subjectivity for poetry. Science will scarcely object. But one or two things have to be said about that. In every experience, even in science, there is feeling. No discourse can sustain itself without interest, which is feeling. The interest, of the feeling, is like an automatic index to the human value of the proceeding—which would not otherwise proceed. Mr. Eliseo Vivas is an aesthetician who might be thought to reside in the camp of the enemy, for his affiliations are positivist; yet in a recent essay he writes about the "passion" which sustains the heroic labors of the scientist as one bigger and more intense than is given to most men.

I do not mean to differ with that judgment at all in remarking that we might very well let the passions and the feelings take care of themselves; it is precisely what we do in our pursuit of science. The thing to attend to is the object to which they attach. As between two similar musical phrases, or between two similar lines of poetry, we may often defy the most proficient psychologist to distinguish the one feeling-response from the other; unless we permit him to say at long last that one is the kind of response that would be made to the first line, and the other is the kind of response that would be made to the second line. But that is to do, after much wasted motion, what I have just suggested: to attend to the poetic object and let the feelings take care of themselves. It is their business to "respond." There may be a feeling correlative with the minutest alteration in an object, and adequate to it, but we shall hardly know. What we do know is that the feelings are grossly inarticulate if we try to abstract them and take their testimony in their own language. Since it is not the intent of the critic to be inarticulate, his discriminations must be among the objects. We understand this so well intuitively that the critic seems to us in possession of some esoteric knowledge, some magical insight, if he appears to be intelligent elsewhere and yet refers confidently to the "tone" or "quality" or "value" of the feeling he discovers in a given line. Probably he is bluffing. The distinctness resides in the cognitive or "semantical" objects denoted by the words. When Richards bewilders us by reporting affective and motor disturbances that are too tiny for definition, and other critics by reporting disturbances that are too massive and gross, we cannot fail to grow suspicious of this whole way of insight as incompetent.

Eliot has a special version of psychologistic theory: which looks extremely fertile, though it is broad and nebulous as his psychologistic terms require it to be. He likes to regard the poem as a structure of emotion and feeling. But the emotion is singular, there being only one emotion per poem, or at least per passage: it is the central emotion or big emotion which attaches to the main theme or situation. The feeling is plural. The emotion combines with many feelings; these are our little responses to the single words and phrases, and he does not think of them as being parts of the central emotion or even related to it. The terminology is greatly at fault, or we should recognize at once, I think, a principle that might prove very valuable. I would not answer for the conduct of a technical philosopher in assessing this theory; he might throw it away, out of patience with its jargon. But a lay philosopher who respects his Eliot and reads with all his sympathy might salvage a good thing from it, though I have not heard of anyone doing so. He would *try* to escape from the affective terms, and translate Eliot into more intelligible language. Eliot would be saying in effect that a poem has a central logic or situation or "paraphrasable core" to which an appropriate interest doubtless attaches, and that in this respect the poem is like a discourse of science behind which lies the sufficient passion. But he would be saying at the same time, and this is the important thing, that the poem has also a context of lively local details to which other and independent interests attach; and that in this respect it is unlike the discourse of science. For the detail of scientific discourse intends never to be independent of the thesis (either objectively or affectively) but always functional, and subordinate to the realization of the thesis. To say that is to approach to a structural understanding of poetry, and to the kind of understanding that I wish presently to urge.

III

As for the moralistic understanding of poetry, it is sometimes the specific moralists, men with moral axes to grind, and incidentally men of unassailable public position who cherish that; they have a "use" for poetry. But not exclusively, for we may find it held also by critics who are more spontaneous and innocent: apparently they fall back upon it because it attributes some special character to poetry, which otherwise refuses to yield up to them a character. The moral interest is so much more frequent in poetry than in science that they decide to offer its moralism as a differentia.

This conception of poetry is of the greatest antiquity—it antedates the evolution of close aesthetic philosophy, and persists beside it too. Plato sometimes spoke of poetry in this light—perhaps because it was recommended to him in this light—but nearly always scornfully. In the *Gorgias*, and other dialogues, he represents the poets as moralizing, and that is only what he, in the person of Socrates, is doing at the very moment, and given to doing; but he considers the moralizing of poets as mere "rhetoric," or popular philosophy, and unworthy of the accomplished moralist who is the real or technical philosopher. Plato understood very well that the poet does not conduct a technical or an original discourse like that of the scientist—and the term includes here the moral philosopher—and that close and effective moralizing is scarcely to be had from him. It is not within the poet's power to offer that if his intention is to offer poetry; for the poetry and the morality are so far from being identical that they interfere a little with each other.

Few famous aestheticians in the history of philosophy have cared to bother with the moralistic conception; many critics have, in all periods. Just now we have at least two schools of moralistic critics contending for the official possession of poetry. One is the neohumanist, and Mr. Foerster has identified himself with that. The other is the Marxist, and I believe it is represented in some degree and shade by Mr. Wilson, possibly by Mr. Auden. I have myself taken profit from the discussions by both schools, but recently I have taken more—I suppose this is because I was bought up in a scholastic discipline rather like the neohumanist—from the writings of the Marxist critics. One of the differences is that the neohumanists believe in the "respectable" virtues, but the Marxists believe that respectability is the greatest of vices, and equate respectable with "genteel." That is a very striking difference, and I think it is also profound.

But I do not wish to be impertinent; I can respect both these moralities, and appropriate moral values from both. The thing I wish to argue is not the comparative merits of the different moralities by which poetry is judged, but their equal inadequacy to the reading of the poet's intention. The moralistic critics wish to isolate and discuss the "ideology" or theme or paraphrase of the poem and not the poem itself. But even to the practitioners themselves, if they are sophisticated, comes sometimes the apprehension that this is moral rather than literary criticism. I have not seen the papers of my colleagues in this discussion, for that was against the rules, but it is reported to me that both Mr. Wilson and Mr. Foerster concede in explicit words that criticism has both the moral and the aesthetic branches; Mr. Wilson may call them the "social" and aesthetic branches. And they would hold the critical profession responsible for both branches. Under these circumstances the critics cease to be mere moralists and become dualists; that is better. My feeling about such a position would be that the moral criticism we shall have with us always, and have had always, and that it is easy—comparatively speaking—and that what is hard, and ceded, and indeed more and more urgent after all the failures of poetic understanding, is a better aesthetic criticism. This is the branch which is all but invariably neglected by the wise but morally zealous critics; they tend to forget their dual responsibility. I think I should go so far as to think that, in strictness, the business of the literary critic is exclusively with an aesthetic criticism. The business of the moralist will naturally, and properly, be with something else.

If we have the patience to read for a little while in the anthology, paying some respect to the varieties of substance actually in the poems, we cannot logically attribute ethical character by definition to poetry; for that character is not universal in the poems. And if we have any faith in a community of character among the several arts, we are stopped quickly from risking such a definition for art at large. To claim a moral content for most of sculpture, painting, music or architecture, is to plan something dialectically very roundabout and subtle, or else to be so arbitrary as to invite instant exposure. I should think the former alternative is impractical, and the latter, if it is not stupid, is masochistic.

The moralistic critics are likely to retort upon their accusers by accusing them in turn of the vapid doctrine known as art for art's sake. And with frequent justice; but again we are likely to receive the impression that it is just because art for art's sake, the historic doctrine, proved empty, and availed them so little aesthetically, like all the other doctrines that came into default, that they have fled to their moralism. Moralism does at least impute to poetry a positive substance, as art for art's sake does not. It asserts an autonomy for art, which is excellent; but autonomy to do what? Only to be itself, and to reduce its interpreters to a tautology? With its English adherents in the nineties the doctrine seemed to make only a negative requirement of art, that is, that it should be anti-Victorian as we should say today, a little bit naughty and immoral perhaps, otherwise at least nonmoral, or carefully squeezed dry of moral substance. An excellent example of how two doctrines, inadequate equally but in opposite senses, may keep themselves alive by abhorring each other's errors.

It is highly probable that the poem considers an ethical situation, and there is no reason why it should repel this from its consideration. But, if I may say so without being accused of verbal trifling, the poetic consideration of the ethical situation is not the same as the ethical consideration of it. The straight ethical consideration would be prose; it would be an act of interested science, or an act of practical will. The poetic consideration, according to Schopenhauer, is the objectification of this act of will; that is, it is our contemplation and not our exercise of will, and therefore qualitatively a very different experience; knowledge without desire. That doctrine also seems too negative and indeterminate. I will put the point as I see it in another way. It should be a comfort to the moralist that there is ordinarily a moral composure in the poem, as if the poet had long known good and evil, and made his moral choice between them once and for all. Art is postethical rather than unethical. In the poem there is an increment of meaning which is neither the ethical content nor opposed to the ethical content. The poetic experience would have to stop for the poet who is developing it, or for the reader who is following it, if the situation which is being poetically treated should turn back into a situation to be morally determined; if, for example, the situation were not a familiar one, and one to which we had habituated our moral wills; for it would rouse the moral will again to action, and make the poetic treatment impossible under its heat. Art is more cool than hot, and a moral fervor is as disastrous to it as a burst of passion itself. We have seen Marxists recently so revolted by Shakespeare's addiction to royal or noble *personae* that they cannot obtain aesthetic experience from the plays; all they get is a moral agitation. In another art, we know, and doubtless we approve, the scruple of the college authorities in not permitting the "department of fine arts" to direct the collegians in painting in the nude. Doctor Harms Sachs, successor to Freud, in a recent number of his *American Imago*, gives a story from a French author as follows:

> He tells that one evening strolling along the streets of Paris he noticed a row of slot machines which for a small coin showed pictures of women in full or partial undress. He observed the leering interest with which men of all kind and description, well dressed and shabby, boys and old men, enjoyed the peep show. He remarked that they all avoided one of these machines, and wondering what uninteresting pictures it might show, he put his penny in the slot. To his great astonishment the generally shunned picture turned out to be the Venus of Medici. Now he begins to ponder: Why does nobody get excited about her? She is decidedly feminine and not less naked than the others which hold such strong fascination for everybody. Finally he finds a satisfactory answer: they fight shy of her because she is beautiful.

And Doctor Sachs, though in his own variety of jargon, makes a number of wise observations about the psychic conditions precedent to the difficult apprehension of beauty. The experience called beauty is beyond the powerful ethical will precisely as it is beyond the animal passion, and indeed these last two are competitive, and coordinate. Under the urgency of either we are incapable of appreciating the statue or understanding the poem.

IV

The ostensible substance of the poem may be anything at all which words may signify: an ethical situation, a passion, a train of thought, a flower or landscape, a thing. This substance receives its poetic increment. It might be safer to say it receives some subtle and mysterious alteration under poetic treatment, but I will risk the cruder formula: the ostensible substance is increased by an x, which is an increment. The poem actually continues to contain its ostensible substance, which is not fatally diminished from its prose state: that is its logical core, or paraphrase. The rest of the poem is x, which we are to find.

We feel the working of this simple formula when we approach a poetry with our strictest logic, provided we can find deliverance from certain inhibiting philosophical prepossessions into which we have been conditioned by the critics we have had to read. Here is Lady Macbeth planning a murder with her husband:

> When Duncan is asleep—
> Whereto the rather shall his hard day's journey
> Soundly invite him—his two chamberlains
> Will I with wine and wassail so convince,
> That memory, the warder of the brain,
> Shall be a fume, and the receipt of reason
> A limbec only; when in swinish sleep
> Their drenched natures lie as in a death,
> What cannot you and I perform upon
> The unguarded Duncan? what not put upon
> His spongy officers, who shall bear the guilt
> Of our great quell?[3]

---

3. [Ransom] I. vii. 61–72.

It is easy to produce the prose argument or paraphrase of this speech; it has one upon which we shall all agree. But the passage is more than its argument. Any detail, with this speaker, seems capable of being expanded in some direction which is not that of the argument. For example, Lady Macbeth says she will make the chamberlains drunk so that they will not remember their charge, nor keep their wits about them. But it is indifferent to this argument whether memory according to the old psychology is located at the gateway to the brain, whether it is to be disintegrated into fume as of alcohol, and whether the whole receptacle of the mind is to be turned into a still. These are additions to the argument both energetic and irrelevant—though they do not quite stop or obscure the argument. From the point of view of the philosopher they are excursions into particularity. They give, in spite of the argument, which would seem to be perfectly self-sufficient, a sense of the real density and contingency of the world in which arguments and plans have to be pursued. They bring out the private character which the items of an argument can really assume if we look at them. This character spreads out in planes at right angles to the course of the argument, and in effect gives to the discourse another dimension, not present in a perfectly logical prose. We are expected to have sufficient judgment not to let this local character take us too far or keep us too long from the argument.

All this would seem commonplace remark, I am convinced, but for those philosophically timid critics who are afraid to think that the poetic increment is local and irrelevant, and that poetry cannot achieve its own virtue and keep undiminished the virtues of prose at the same time. But I will go a little further in the hope of removing the sense of strangeness in the analysis. I will offer a figurative definition of a poem.

A poem is, so to speak, a democratic state, whereas a prose discourse—mathematical, scientific, ethical, or practical and vernacular—is a totalitarian state. The intention of a democratic state is to perform the work of state as effectively as it can perform it, subject to one reservation of conscience: that it will not despoil its members, the citizens, of the free exercise of their own private and independent characters. But the totalitarian state is interested solely in being effective, and regards the citizens as no citizens at all; that is, regards them as functional members whose existence is totally defined by their allotted contributions to its ends; it has no use for their private characters, and therefore no provision for them. I indicate of course the extreme or polar opposition between two polities, without denying that a polity may come to us rather mixed up.

In this trope the operation of the state as a whole represents of course the logical paraphrase or argument of the poem. The private character of the citizens represents the particularity asserted by the parts in the poem. And this last is our x.

For many years I had seen—as what serious observer has not—that a poem as a discourse differentiated itself from prose by its particularity, yet not to the point of sacrificing its logical cogency or universality. But I could get no further. I could not see how real particularity could get into a universal. The object of aesthetic studies became for me a kind of discourse, or a kind of natural configuration, which like any other discourse or configuration claimed universality, but which consisted actually, and notoriously, of particularity. The poem was concrete, yet universal, and in spite of Hegel I could not see how the two properties could be identified as forming in a single unit the "concrete universal." It is usual, I believe, for persons at this stage to assert that somehow the apparent diffuseness or particularity in the poem gets itself taken up or "assimilated" into the logic, to produce a marvelous kind of unity called a "higher unity," to which ordinary discourse is not eligible. The belief is that the "idea" or theme proves itself in poetry to be even more dominating than in prose by overcoming much more energetic resistance than usual on the part of the materials, and the resistance, as attested in the local development of detail, is therefore set not to the debit but to the credit of the unifying power of the poetic spirit. A unity of that kind is one which philosophers less audacious and more factual than Hegel would be loath to claim. Critics incline to call it, rather esoterically, an "imaginative" rather than a logical unity, but one supposes they mean a mystical, an ineffable, unity. I for one could neither grasp it nor deny it. I believe that is not an uncommon situation for poetic analysts to find themselves in.

It occurred to me at last that the solution might be very easy if looked for without what the positivists call "metaphysical prepossessions." Suppose the logical substance remained there all the time, and was in no way specially remarkable, while the particularity came in by accretion, so that the poem turned out partly universal, and partly particular, but with respect to different parts. I began to remark the dimensions of a poem, or other work of art. The poem was not a mere moment in time, nor a mere point in space. It was sizable, like a house. Apparently it had a "plan," or a central frame of logic, but it had also a huge wealth of local detail, which sometimes fitted the plan functionally or served it, and sometimes only subsisted comfortably under it; in either case the house stood up. But it was the political way of thinking which gave me the first analogy which seemed valid. The poem was like a democratic state, in action, and observed both macroscopically and microscopically.

The house occurred also, and provided what seems to be a more negotiable trope under which to construe the poem. A poem is a *logical structure* having a *local texture*. These terms have been actually though not systematically employed in literary criticism. To my imagination they are architectural. The walls of my room are obviously structural; the beams and boards have a function; so does the plaster, which is the visible aspect of the final wall. The plaster might have remained naked, aspiring to no character, and purely functional. But actually it has been painted, receiving color; or it has been papered, receiving color and design, though these have no structural value; and perhaps it has been hung with tapestry, or with paintings, for "decoration." The paint, the paper, the tapestry are texture. It is logically unrelated to structure. But I indicate only a few of the textural possibilities in architecture. There are not fewer of them in poetry.

The intent of the good critic becomes therefore to examine and define the poem with respect to its structure and its texture. If he has nothing to say about its texture he has nothing to say about it specifically as a poem, but is treating it only insofar as it is prose.

I do not mean to say that the good critic will necessarily employ my terms.

V

Many critics today are writing analytically and with close intelligence, in whatever terms, about the logical substance or structure of the poem, and its increment of irrelevant local substance or texture. I believe that the understanding of the ideal critic has to go even further than that. The final desideratum is an ontological insight, nothing less. I am committed by my title to a representation of criticism as, in the last resort, a speculative exercise. But my secret committal was to speculative in the complete sense of—ontological.

There is nothing especially speculative or ontological in reciting, or even appraising, the logical substance of the poem. This is its prose core—its science perhaps, or its ethics if it seems to have an ideology. Speculative interest asserts itself principally when we ask why we want the logical substance to be compounded with the local substance, the good lean structure with a great volume of texture that does not function. It is the same thing as asking why we want the poem to be what it is.

It has been a rule, having the fewest exceptions, for aestheticians and great philosophers to direct their speculations by the way of overstating and overvaluing the logical substance. They are impressed by the apparent obedience of material nature, whether in fact or in art, to definable form or "law" imposed upon it. They like to suppose that in poetry, as in chemistry, everything that figures in the discourse means to be functional, and that the poem is imperfect in the degree that it contains items, whether by accident or intention, which manifest a private independence. It is a bias with which we are entirely familiar, and reflects the extent to which our philosophy hitherto has been impressed by the successes of science in formulating laws which would "govern" their objects. Probably I am here reading the state of mind of yesterday rather than of today. Nevertheless we know it. The worldview which ultimately forms itself in the mind so biased is that of a world which is rational and intelligible. The view is sanguine, and naïve. Hegel's worldview, I think it is agreed, was a subtle version of this, and if so, it was what determined his view of art. He seemed to make the handsomest concession to realism by offering to knowledge a kind of universal which was not restricted to the usual abstracted aspects of the material, but included all aspects, and was a concrete universal. The concreteness in Hegel's handling was not honestly, or at any rate not fairly, defended. It was always represented as being in process of pointing up and helping out the universality. He could look at a work of art and report all its substance as almost assimilated to a ruling "idea." But at least Hegel seemed to distinguish what looked like two ultimate sorts of substance there, and stated the central aesthetic problem as the problem of relating them. And his writings about art are speculative in the sense that he regarded the work of art not as of great intrinsic value necessarily, but as an object lesson or discipline in the understanding of the world process, and as its symbol.[4]

I think of two ways of constructing poetry with respect to its ultimate purpose; of which the one is not very handsome nor speculatively interesting, and the other will appear somewhat severe.

The first construction would picture the poet as a sort of epicure, and the poem as something on the order of a Christmas pudding, stuffed with what dainties it will hold. The pastry alone, or it may be the cake, will not serve; the stuffing is wanted too. The values of the poem would be intrinsic, or immediate, and they would include not only the value of the structure but also the incidental values to be found in the texture. If we exchange the pudding for a house, they would include not only the value of the house itself but also the value of the furnishings. In saying intrinsic or immediate, I mean that the poet is fond of the precise objects denoted by the words, and writes the poem for the reason that he likes to dwell upon them. In talking about the main value and the incidental values I mean to recognize the fact that the latter engage the affections just as truly as the former. Poetic discourse therefore would be more agreeable than prose to the epicure or the literally acquisitive man; for prose has but a single value, being about one thing only; its parts have no values of their own, but only instrumental values, which might be reckoned as fractions of the single value proportionate to their contributions to it. The prose is one-valued and the poem is many-valued. Indeed, there will certainly be poems whose texture contains many precious objects, and aggregates a greater value than the structure.

---

4. [Ransom] See Hegel, *The Philosophy of Fine Art*, above,. 518–31.

So there would be a comfortable and apparently eligible view that poetry improves on prose because it is a richer diet. It causes five or six pleasures to appear, five or six good things, where one had been before; an alluring consideration for robustious, full-blooded, bourgeois souls. The view will account for much of the poem, if necessary. But it does not account for all of it, and sometimes it accounts for less than at other times.

The most impressive reason for the bolder view of art, the speculative one, is the existence of the "pure," or "abstractionist," or non-representational works of art; though these will probably occur to us in other arts than poetry. There is at least one art, music, whose works are all of this sort. Tones are not words, they have no direct semantical function, and by themselves they mean nothing. But they combine to make brilliant phrases, harmonies, and compositions. In these compositions it is probable that the distinction between structure or functional content, on the one hand, and texture or local variation and departure, on the other, is even more determinate than in an impure art like poetry. The world of tones seems perfectly inhuman and impracticable; there is no specific field of experience "about which" music is telling us. Yet we know that music is powerfully affective. I take my own musical feelings, and those attested by other audients, as the sufficient index to some overwhelming human importance which the musical object has for us. At the same time it would be useless to ask the feelings precisely what they felt; we must ask the critic. The safest policy is to take the simplest construction, and try to improvise as little fiction as possible. Music is not music, I think, until we grasp its effects both in structure and in texture. As we grow in musical understanding the structures become always more elaborate and sustained, and the texture which interrupts them and sometimes imperils them becomes more bold and unpredictable. We can agree in saying about the works of music that these are musical structures, and they are richly textured; we can identify these elements, and perhaps precisely. To what then do our feelings respond? To music as structural composition itself; to music as manifesting the structural principles of the world; to modes of structure which we feel to be ontologically possible, or even probable. Schopenhauer construed music very much in that sense. Probably it will occur to us that musical compositions bear close analogy therefore to operations in pure mathematics. The mathematicians confess that their constructions are "nonexistential"; meaning as I take it, that the constructions testify with assurance only to the structural principles, in the light of which they are possible but may not be actual, or if they are actual may not be useful. This would define the mathematical operations as speculative: as motivated by an interest so generalized and so elemental that no word short of ontological will describe it.

But if music and mathematics have this much in common, they differ sharply in their respective worldviews or ontological biases. That of music, with its prodigious display of texture, seems the better informed about the nature of the world, the more realistic, the less naïve. Perhaps the difference is between two ontological educations. But I should be inclined to imagine it as rising back of that point: in two ontological temperaments.

There are also, operating a little less successfully so far as the indexical evidences would indicate, the abstractionist paintings, of many schools, and perhaps also works of sculpture; and there is architecture. These arts have tried to abandon direct representational intention almost as heroically as music. They exist in their own materials and indicate no other specific materials; structures of color, light, space, stone—the cheapest of materials. They too can symbolize nothing of value unless it is structure or composition itself. But that is precisely the act which denotes will and intelligence; which becomes the act of fuller intelligence if it carefully accompanies its structures with their material textures; for then it understands better the ontological nature of materials.

Returning to the poetry. It is not all poems, and not even all "powerful" poems, having high index ratings, whose semantical meanings contain situations important in themselves or objects precious in themselves. There may be little correlation between the single value of the poem and the aggregate value of its contents—just as there is no such correlation whatever in music. The "effect" of the poem may be astonishingly disproportionate to our interest in its materials. It is true, of course, that there is no art employing materials of equal richness with poetry, and that it is beyond the capacity of poetry to employ indifferent materials. The words used in poetry are the words the race has already formed, and naturally they call attention to things and events that have been thought to be worth attending to. But I suggest that any poetry which is "technically" notable is in part a work of abstractionist art, concentrating upon the structure and the texture, and the structure-texture relation, out of a pure speculative interest.

At the end of *Love's Labour's Lost* occurs a little diversion which seems proportionately far more effective than that laborious play as a whole. The play is over, but Armado stops the principals before they disperse to offer them a show:

> ARMADO But, most esteemed greatness, will you hear the dialogue that the two learned men have compiled in praise of the owl and the cuckoo? It should have followed in the end of our show.
> KING Call them forth quickly; we will do so.
> ARMADO Holla! approach. *(Reenter, Holofemes, etc.)* This side is Hiems, Winter, this Ver, the Spring; the one maintained by the owl, the other by the cuckoo. Ver, begin.

THE SONG

SPRING When daisies pied and violets blue
And lady-smocks all silver-white
And cuckoo-buds of yellow hue
Do paint the meadows with delight,
The cuckoo then, on every tree,
Mocks married men; for thus sings he,
Cuckoo;
Cuckoo, cuckoo: O word of fear,
Unpleasing to a married ear!

When shepherds pipe on oaten straws,
And merry larks are ploughmen's clocks,
When turtles tread, and rooks, and daws,
And maidens bleach their summer smocks,
The cuckoo then, on every tree,
Mocks married men; for thus sings he,
Cuckoo;

Cuckoo, cuckoo: O word of fear,
Unpleasing to a married ear!

WINTER When icicles hang by the wall,
And Dick the shepherd blows his nail,
And Tom bears logs into the hall,
And milk comes frozen home in pail,
When blood is nipped and ways be foul,
Then nightly sings the staring owl,
Tu-who;
Tu-whit, tu-who, a merry note,
While greasy Joan doth keel the pot.

When all aloud the wind doth blow,
And coughing drowns the parson's saw,
And birds sit brooding in the snow,
And Marian's nose looks red and raw,
When roasted crabs hiss in the bowl,
Then nightly sings the staring owl,
Tu-who;
Tu-whit, tu-who, a merry note,
While greasy Joan doth keel the pot.

ARMADO The words of Mercury are harsh after the songs of Apollo.
You that way—we this way. *(Exeunt.)*[5]

The feeling index registers such strong approval of this episode that
a critic with ambition is obliged to account for it. He can scarcely
account for it in terms of the weight of its contents severally.

At first glance Shakespeare has provided only a pleasant little caricature of the old-fashioned (to us, medieval) debate between personi-
fied characters. It is easygoing, like nonsense; no labor is lost here.
Each party speaks two stanzas and concludes both stanzas with the
refrain about his bird, the cuckoo or the owl. There is next to no generalized argument, or dialectic proper. Each argues by citing his characteristic exhibits. In the first stanza Spring cites some flowers; in the
second stanza, some business by country persons, with interpolation of

5. [Ransom] V. ii. 893–941.

some birds that make love. Winter in both his stanzas cites the country business of the season. In the refrain the cuckoo, Spring's symbol, is used to refer the lovemaking to more than the birds; and this repeats itself, though it is naughty. The owl is only a nominal symbol for Winter, an "emblem" that is not very emblematic, but the refrain manages another reference to the kitchen, and repeats itself, as if Winter's pleasures focused in the kitchen.

In this poem texture is not very brilliant, but it eclipses structure. The argument, we would say in academic language, is concerned with "the relative advantages of Spring and Winter." The only logical determinateness this structure has is the good coordination of the items cited by Spring as being really items peculiar to Spring, and of the Winter items as peculiar to Winter. The symbolic refrains look like summary or master items, but they seem to be a little more than summary and in fact to mean a little more than they say. The argument is trifling on the whole, and the texture from the point of view of felt human importance lacks decided energy; both which observations are to be made, and most precisely, of how many famous lyrics, especially those before the earnest and self-conscious nineteenth century! The value of the poem is greater than the value of its parts: that is what the critic is up against.

Unquestionably it is possible to assemble very fine structures out of ordinary materials. The good critic will study the poet's technique, in confidence that here the structural principles will be discovered at home. In this study he will find as much range for his activities as he desires.

Especially must he study the metrics, and their implications for structural composition. In this poem I think the critic ought to make good capital of the contrast between the amateurishness of the pleasant discourse as meaning and the hard determinate form of it phonetically. The meter on the whole is out of relation to the meaning of the poem, or to anything else specifically; it is a musical material of low grade, but plastic and only slightly resistant material, and its presence in every poem is that of an abstractionist element that belongs to the art.

And here I will suggest another analogy, this one between Shakespeare's poem and some ordinary specimen of painting. It does not matter how old-fashioned or representational the painting is, we shall

all, if we are instructed in the tradition of this art, require it to exhibit along with its represented object an abstract design in terms of pure physical balance or symmetry. We sense rather than measure the success of this design, but it is as if we had drawn a horizontal axis and a vertical axis through the center of the picture, and required the painted masses to balance with respect to each of these two axes. This is an over-simple statement of a structural requirement by which the same details function in two worlds that are different, and that do not correlate with each other. If the painting is of the Holy Family, we might say that this object has a drama, or an economy, of its own; but that the physical masses which compose it must enter also into another economy, that of abstract design; and that the value of any unit mass for the one economy bears no relation to its value for the other. The painting is of great ontological interest because it embodies this special dimension of abstract form. And turning to the poem, we should find that its represented "meaning" is analogous to the represented object in the painting, while its meter is analogous to the pure design.

A number of fascinating speculative considerations must follow upon this discovery. They will have to do with the most fundamental laws of this world's structure. They will be profoundly ontological, though I do not mean that they must be ontological in some recondite sense; ontological in such a homely and compelling sense that perhaps a child might intuit the principles which the critic will arrive at analytically, and with much labor.

I must stop at this point, since I am desired not so much to anticipate the critic as to present him. In conclusion I will remark that the critic will doubtless work empirically, and set up his philosophy only as the drift of his findings will compel him. But ultimately he will be compelled. He will have to subscribe to an ontology. If he is a sound critic his ontology will be that of his poets; and what is that? I suggest that the poetic world view is Aristotelian and "realistic" rather than Platonic and "idealistic." He cannot follow the poets and still conceive himself as inhabiting the rational or "tidy" universe that is supposed by the scientist.

10

The Heresy of Paraphrase

Cleanth Brooks

In the summer 1947 issue of the Kenyon Review, *John Crowe Ransom responded to the publication of Cleanth Brooks's* The Well-Wrought Urn, *where "The Heresy of Paraphrase" first appeared, by pointing out the central paradox of the New Criticism that he himself had named earlier in the decade. On the one hand, critics had released from the poem "a kind of centrifugal energy, whereby its meaning expands with a little encouragement." On the other hand, here was Brooks, who had done as much as anyone besides William Empson to establish the New Criticism, "seriously attempting now to see poems as wholes, and to conceive the difficult object, the unitary poem," as Ransom put it. "But how will he reassemble and integrate the meanings when he has made it his first duty to dissipate them?" Ransom did not think it was possible, despite Brooks's fascination with one formulation in particular. "He has always liked to stand and marvel at paradoxes," Ransom remarked, making Brooks look like a country visitor beset by the vision of a duck-billed platypus at the zoo. "We do not rest in a paradox," said Brooks's old teacher. "We resolve it."[1]*

Yet in advocating the poem's unity in "The Heresy of Paraphrase,"

---

1. John Crowe Ransom, "Poetry: I, The Formal Analysis." From *Selected Essays of John Crowe Ransom*, Thomas Daniel Young and John Hindle, eds. (Baton Rouge: Louisiana State University Press, 1984), 193.

Brooks clearly means to challenge Ransom's troubling distinction between a "logical structure" and a "local texture" in "Criticism as Pure Speculation." For Brooks, most critical "distempers" come from confusing what one can say about a poem "for the essential core of the poem itself." The critic should rather attempt to comprehend the whole: "The unity is achieved by a dramatic process, not a logical; it represents an equilibrium of forces, not a formula." In making his point, Brooks takes aim directly at the word "irrelevance," which Ransom uses to distinguish the texture of the poetry from what can be paraphrased: "The truth is that the apparent irrelevancies which metrical pattern and metaphor introduce do become relevant when we realize that they function in a good poem to modify, qualify, and develop the total attitude which we are to take in coming to terms with the total situation."

The ten poems that have been discussed[2] were not selected because they happened to express a common theme or to display some particular style or to share a special set of symbols. It has proved, as a matter of fact, somewhat surprising to see how many items they do have in common: the light symbolism as used in *L'Allegro—Il Penseroso* and in the *Intimations* ode, for example; or, death as a sexual metaphor in *The Canonization* and in *The Rape of the Lock*; or the similarity of problem and theme in the *Intimations* ode and *Among School Children*.

On reflection, however, it would probably warrant more surprise if these ten poems did not have much in common. For they are all poems which most of us will feel are close to the central stream of the tradition. Indeed, if there is any doubt on this point, it will have to do with only the first and last members of the series [Donne's *The Canonization* and Yeats's *Among School Children*]—poems whose relation

2. Donne, *The Canonization*; Shakespeare, *Macbeth*; Milton, *L'Allegro* and *Il Penseroso*; Herrick, *Corinna's Going a-Maying*; Pope, *The Rape of the Lock*; Gray, *Elegy Written in a Country Churchyard*; Wordsworth, *Ode: Imitations of Immortality from Recollections of Early Childhood*; Keats, *Ode on a Grecian Urn*; Tennyson, *Tears, Idle Tears*; and Yeats, *Among School Children*.

to the tradition I shall, for reasons to be given a little later, be glad to waive. The others, it will be granted, are surely in the mainstream of the tradition.

As a matter of fact, a number of the poems discussed in this book were not chosen by me but were chosen for me. But having written on these, I found that by adding a few poems I could construct a chronological series which (though it makes no pretension to being exhaustive of periods or types) would not leave seriously unrepresented any important period since Shakespeare. In filling the gaps I tried to select poems which had been held in favor in their own day and which most critics still admire. There were, for example, to be no "metaphysical" poems beyond the first exhibit and no "modern" ones other than the last. But the intervening poems were to be read as one has learned to read Donne and the moderns. One was to attempt to see, in terms of this approach, what the masterpieces had in common rather than to see how the poems of different historical periods differed—and in particular to see whether they had anything in common with the "metaphysicals" and with the moderns.

The reader will by this time have made up his mind as to whether the readings are adequate. (I use the word advisedly, for the readings do not pretend to be exhaustive, and certainly it is highly unlikely that they are not in error in one detail or another.) If the reader feels that they are seriously inadequate, then the case has been judged; for the generalizations that follow will be thoroughly vitiated by the inept handling of the particular cases on which they depend.

If, however, the reader does feel them to be adequate, it ought to be readily apparent that the common goodness which the poems share will have to be stated, not in terms of *content* or *subject matter* in the usual sense in which we use these terms, but rather in terms of structure. The "content" of the poems is various, and if we attempt to find one *quality* of content which is shared by all the poems—a "poetic" subject matter or diction or imagery—we shall find that we have merely confused the issues. For what is it to be poetic? Is the schoolroom of Yeats's poem poetic or unpoetic? Is Shakespeare's "new-borne babe / Striding the blast" poetic whereas the idiot of his "Life is a tale tolde by an idiot" is unpoetic? If Herrick's "budding boy or girl" is poetic, then why is not that monstrosity of the newspaper's society page, the "society bud," poetic too?

To say this is not, of course, to say that all materials have precisely the same potentialities (as if the various pigments on the palette had the same potentialities, any one of them suiting the given picture as well as another). But what has been said, on the other hand, requires to be said: for, if we are to proceed at all, we must draw a sharp distinction between the attractiveness or beauty of any particular item taken, as such and the "beauty" of the poem considered as a whole. The latter is the effect of a total pattern, and of a kind of pattern which can incorporate within itself items intrinsically beautiful or ugly, attractive or repulsive. Unless one asserts the primacy of the pattern, a poem becomes merely a bouquet of intrinsically beautiful items.

But though it is in terms of structure that we must describe poetry, the term *structure* is certainly not altogether satisfactory as a term. One means by it something far more internal than the metrical pattern, say, or than the sequence of images. The structure meant is certainly *not form* in the conventional sense in which we think of form as a kind of envelope which "contains" the "content." The structure obviously is everywhere conditioned by the nature of the material which goes into the poem. The nature of the material sets the problem to be solved, and the solution is the ordering of the material.

Pope's *Rape of the Lock* will illustrate: the structure is not the heroic couplet as such, or the canto arrangement; for, important as is Pope's use of the couplet as one means by which he secures the total effect, the heroic couplet can be used—has been used many times—as an instrument in securing very different effects. The structure of the poem, furthermore, is not that of the mock-epic convention, though here, since the term *mock-epic* has implications of attitude, we approach a little nearer to the kind of structure of which we speak.

The structure meant is a structure of meanings, evaluations, and interpretations; and the principle of unity which informs it seems to be one of balancing and harmonizing connotations, attitudes, and meanings. But even here one needs to make important qualifications: the principle is not one which involves the arrangement of the various elements into homogeneous groupings, pairing like with like. It unites the like with the unlike. It does not unite them, however, by the simple process of allowing one connotation to cancel out another nor does it reduce the contradictory attitudes to harmony by a process of subtraction. The unity is not a unity of the sort to be achieved by the reduction and simplification appropriate to an algebraic formula. It is a positive unity, not a negative; it represents not a residue but an achieved harmony.

The attempt to deal with a structure such as this may account for the frequent occurrence in the preceding chapters of such terms as *ambiguity, paradox, complex of attitudes,* and—most frequent of all, and perhaps most annoying to the reader—*irony.* I hasten to add that I hold no brief for these terms as such. Perhaps they are inadequate. Perhaps they are misleading. It is to be hoped in that case that we can eventually improve upon them. But adequate terms—whatever those terms may turn out to be—will certainly have to be terms which do justice to the special kind of structure which seems to emerge as the common structure of poems so diverse as *The Rape of the Lock* and *Tears, Idle Tears.*

The conventional terms are much worse than inadequate: they're positively misleading in their implication that the poem constitutes a "statement" of some sort, this statement being true or false, and expressed more or less clearly or eloquently or beautifully; for it is from this formula that most of the common heresies about poetry derive. The formula begins by introducing a dualism which thenceforward is rarely overcome, and which at best can be overcome only by the most elaborate and clumsy qualifications. Where it is not overcome, it leaves the critics lodged upon one or the other of the horns of a dilemma: the critic is forced to judge the poem by its political or scientific or philosophical truth; or, he is forced to judge the poem by its form has conceived externally and detached from human experience. Mr. Alfred Kazin, for example, to take an instance from a recent and popular book, accuses the "new formalist"—his choice of that epithet is revealing—of excepting the latter horn of the dilemma because he notices that they have refused the former. In other words, since they refuse to write poems by their messages, he assumes that they are compelled to write them by their formal embellishments.

The omnipresence of this dilemma, a false dilemma, I believe, will also account for the fact that so much has been made in the preceding chapters of the resistance which any good poem sets up against all attempts to paraphrase it. The point is surely not that we cannot describe adequately enough for many purposes with the poem in general is "about" and what the general effect of the poem is: *The Rape of the Lock* is *about* the foibles of an eighteenth-century belle. The effective *Corinna's Going a-Maying* is one of gaiety tempered by the poignance of the fleetingness of youth. We can very properly use paraphrases as pointers and as shorthand references provided that we know what we are doing. But it is highly important that we know what we are doing and that we see plainly that paraphrase is not the real core of meaning which constitutes the essence of the poem.

For the imagery and the rhythm are not merely the instruments by which this fancied core-of-meaning-which-can-be-expressed-in-a-paraphrase is directly rendered. Even in the simplest poem their mediation is not positive incorrect. Indeed, whatever statement we may seize upon his incorporating the "meaning" of the poem, immediately the imagery and the rhythm seem to set up tensions with it, warping and twisting it, qualifying and revising it. This is true of Wordsworth's *Ode* no less than of Donne's *Canonization*. To illustrate: if we say that the *Ode* celebrates the spontaneous "naturalness" of the child, there is the poem itself to indicate that nature has a more sinister aspect—that the process by which the poetic lamb becomes the dirty old sheep or the child racing over the meadows becomes the balding philosopher is a process that is thoroughly "natural." Or, if we say that the thesis of the *Ode* is that the child brings into the natural world a supernatural glory which acquaintance with the world eventually and inevitably quenches in the light of common day, there is the last stanza and the drastic qualifications which it asserts: it is significant that the thoughts that he too deep for tears are mentioned in this sunset stanza of the *Ode* and that they are thoughts, not of the child, but of the man.

We have precisely the same problem if we make our example *The Rape of the Lock*. Does the poet assert that Belinda is a goddess? Or does he say that she is a brainless chit? Whichever alternative we take, there are elaborate qualifications to be made. Moreover, if the simple propositions offered seem in their forthright simplicity to make too easy the victory of the poem over any possible statement of its meaning, then let the reader try to formulate a proposition that will say what the poem "says." As his proposition approaches adequacy, he will find, not only that it has increased greatly in length, but that it has begun to fill itself up with reservations and qualifications—and most significant of all—the formulator will find that he has himself begun to fall back upon metaphors of his own in his attempt to indicate what the poem "says." In sum, his proposition, as it approaches adequacy, ceases to be a proposition.

Consider one more case, *Corinna's Going a-Maying*. Is the doctrine preached to Corinna throughout the first four stanzas true? Or is it damnably false? Or is it a "harmless folly"? Here perhaps we shall be tempted to take the last option as the saving mean—what the poem really *says*—and my account of the poem at the end of the third chapter is perhaps susceptible of this interpretation—or misinterpretation. If so, it is high time to clear the matter up. For we mistake matters grossly if we take the poem to be playing with opposed extremes, only to point the golden mean in a doctrine which, at the end, will correct the falsehood of extremes. The reconcilement of opposites which the poet characteristically makes is not that of a prudent splitting of the difference between antithetical over-emphases.

It is not so in Wordsworth's poem nor in Keats's nor in Pope's. It is not so even in this poem of Herrick's. For though the poem reflects, if we read it carefully, the primacy of the Christian mores, the pressure exerted throughout the poem is upon the pagan appeal; and the poem ends, significantly, with a reiteration of the appeal to Corinna to go a-Maying, an appeal which, if qualified by the Christian view, still, in a sense, has been deepened and made more urgent by that very qualification. The imagery of loss and decay, it must be remembered, comes in this last stanza after the admission that the May-Day rites are not a real religion but a "harmless folly."

If we are to get all these qualifications into our formulation of what the poem says—and they are relevant—then, our formulation of the "statement" made by Herrick's poem will turn out to be quite as difficult as that of Pope's mock-epic. The truth of the matter is that all such formulations lead away from the center of the poem—not toward it; that the "prose-sense" of the poem is not a rack on which the stuff of the poem is hung; that it does not represent the "inner" structure or the "essential" structure or the "real" structure of the poem. We may use—and in many connections must use—such formulations as more or less convenient ways of referring to parts of the poem. But such formulations are scaffoldings which we may properly for certain purposes, throw about the building. We must not mistake them for the internal and essential structure of the building itself.

Indeed, one may sum up by saying that most of the distempers of criticism come about from yielding to the temptation to take certain remarks which we make *about* the poem—statements about what it says or about what truth it gives or about what formulations it illustrates—for the essential core of the poem itself. As W. M. Urban puts it in his *Language and Reality*:

> The general principle of the inseparability of intuition and expression holds with special force for the aesthetic intuition. Here it means that form and content, or content and medium, are inseparable. The artist does not first intuit his object and then find the appropriate medium. It is rather in and through his medium that he intuits the object.

So much for the process of composition. As for the critical process: "To pass from the intuitible to the nonintuitible is to negate the function and meaning of the symbol." For it "is precisely because the more universal and ideal relations cannot be adequately expressed directly that they are indirectly expressed by means of the more intuitible." The most obvious examples of such error (and for that reason those which are really least dangerous) are those theories which frankly treat the poem as propaganda. The most subtle (and the most stubbornly rooted in the ambiguities of language) are those which, beginning with the "paraphrasable" elements of the poem, refer the other elements of the poem finally to some role subordinate to the paraphrasable elements. (The relation between all the elements must surely be an organic one—there can be no question about that. There is, however, a very serious question as to whether the paraphrasable elements have primacy.)

Mr. Winters's position will furnish perhaps the most respectable example of the paraphrastic heresy. He assigns primacy to the "rational meaning" of the poem. "The relationship, in the poem, between rational statement and feeling," he remarks in his latest book, "is thus seen to be that of motive to emotion." He goes on to illustrate his point by a brief and excellent analysis of the following lines from Browning: "So wore night; the East was gray, / White the broad-faced hemlock flowers. . . ."

"The verb *wore*" he continues,

> means literally that the night passed, but it carries with it connotations of exhaustion and attrition which belong to the condition of the protagonist; and grayness is a color which we associate with such a condition. If we change the phrase to read: "Thus night passed," we shall have the same rational meaning, and a meter quite as respectable, but no trace of the power of the line: the connotation *of wore* will be lost, and the connotation of *gray* will remain in a state of ineffective potentiality.

But the word *wore* does not mean *literally* "that the night passed," it means literally "that the night *wore*"—whatever *wore* may mean, and as Winters's own admirable analysis indicates, *wore* "means," whether *rationally* or *irrationally*, a great deal. Furthermore, "So wore night" and "Thus night passed" can be said to have "the same rational meaning" only if we equate *rational meaning* with the meaning of a loose paraphrase. And can a loose paraphrase be said to be the "motive to emotion"? Can it be said to "generate" the feelings in question? (Or, would Mr. Winters not have us equate *rational statement* and *rational meanings*.)

Much more is at stake here than any quibble. In view of the store which Winters sets by rationality and of his penchant for poems which make their evaluations overtly, and in view of his frequent blindness to those poems which do not—in view of these considerations, it is important to see that what "So wore night" and "Thus night passed" have in common as their "rational meaning" is not the "rational meaning" of each but the lowest common denominator of both. To refer the structure of the poem to what is finally a paraphrase of the poem is to refer it to something outside the poem.

To repeat, most of our difficulties in criticism are rooted in the heresy of paraphrase. If we allow ourselves to be misled by it, we distort the relation of the poem to its "truth," we raise the problem of belief in a vicious and crippling form, we split the poem between its "form" and its "content"—we bring the statement to be conveyed into an unreal competition with science or philosophy or theology. In short, we put our questions about the poem in a form calculated to produce the battles of the last twenty-five years over the "use of poetry."[3]

If we allow ourselves to be misled by the heresy of paraphrase, we run the risk of doing even more violence to the internal order of the poem itself. By taking the paraphrase as our point of stance, we misconceive the function of metaphor and meter. We demand logical coherences where they are sometimes irrelevant, and we fail frequently to see imaginative coherences on levels where they are highly relevant.

But what would be a positive theory? We tend to embrace the doctrine of a logical structure the more readily because, to many of us, the failure to do so seems to leave the meaning of the poem hopelessly up in the air. The alternative position will appear to us to lack even the relative stability of an Ivory Tower: it is rather commitment to a free balloon. For, to deny the possibility of pinning down what the poem "says" to some "statement" will seem to assert that the poem really says nothing. And to point out what has been suggested in earlier chapters and brought to a head in this one, namely, that one can never measure a poem against the scientific or philosophical yardstick for the reason that the poem, when laid along the yardstick, is never the "full poem" but an abstraction from the poem—such an argument will seem to such readers a piece of barren logic-chopping—a transparent dodge.

Considerations of strategy then, if nothing more, dictate some positive account of what a poem is and does. And some positive account can be given, though I cannot promise to do more than suggest what a poem is, nor will my terms turn out to be anything more than metaphors.[4]

_____

3. [Brooks] I do not, of course, intend to minimize the fact that some of these battles have been highly profitable, or to imply that the foregoing paragraphs could have been written except for the illumination shed by the discussions of the last twenty-five years.

4. [Brooks] For those who cannot be content with metaphors (or with the particular metaphors which I can give) I recommend René Wellek's excellent "The Mode of Existence of a Literary Work of Art," *The Southern Review* (Spring 1942). I shall not try to reproduce here as

The essential structure of a poem (as distinguished from the rational or logical structure of the "statement" which we abstract from it) resembles that of architecture or painting: it is a pattern of resolved stresses. Or, to move closer still to poetry by considering the temporal arts, the structure of a poem resembles that of a ballet or musical composition. It is a pattern of resolutions and balances and harmonizations developed through a temporal scheme.[5]

Or, to move still closer to poetry, the structure of a poem resembles that of a play. This last example, of course, risks introducing once more the distracting element, since drama, like poetry, makes use of words. Yet, on the whole, most of us are less inclined to force the concept of "statement" on drama than on a lyric poem: for the very nature of drama is that of something "acted out"—something which arrives at its conclusion through conflict—something which builds conflict into its very being. The dynamic nature of drama, in short, allows us to regard it as an action rather than as a formula for action or as a statement about action. For this reason, therefore, perhaps the most helpful analogy by which to suggest the structure of poetry is that of the drama, and for many readers at least, the least confusing way in which to approach a poem is to think of it as a drama.

a handy, thumbnail definition his account of a poem as "a stratified system of norms," for the definition would be relatively meaningless without the further definitions which he assigns to the individual terms in this chapter, but I believe that the generalizations about poetry outlined here can be thoroughly accommodated to the position which his essay sets forth.

5. [Brooks] In recent numbers of *Accent*, two critics for whose work I have high regard have emphasized the dynamic character of poetry. Kenneth Burke argues that if we are to consider a poem as a poem, we must consider it as a "mode of action." R. P. Blackmur asks us to think of it as gesture, "the outward and dramatic play of inward and imagined meaning." I do not mean to commit either of these critics to my own interpretation of dramatic or symbolic action; and I have, on my own part, several rather important reservations with respect to Mr. Burke's position. But there are certainly large areas of agreement among our positions. The reader might also compare the account of poetic structure given in this chapter with the following passage from Susanne Langer's *Philosophy in a New Key*:

> . . . though the material of poetry is verbal, its import is not the literal assertion made in the words, but *the way the assertion is made*, and this involves the sound, the tempo, the aura of associations of the words, the long or short sequences of ideas, the wealth or poverty of transient imagery that contains them, the sudden arrest of fantasy by pure fact, or of familiar fact by sudden fantasy, the suspense of literal meaning by a sustained ambiguity resolved in a long-awaited key word, and the unifying, all-embracing artifice of rhythm.

214 of Cleanth Brooks

The general point, of course, is not that either poetry or drama
makes no use of ideas, or that either is "merely emotional"—whatever
that is—or that there is not the closest and most important relationship
between the intellectual materials which they absorb into their structure and other elements in the structure. The relationship between the
intellectual and the nonintellectual elements in a poem is actually far
more intimate than the conventional accounts would represent it to
be: the relationship is not that of an idea "wrapped in emotion" or a
"prose-sense decorated by sensuous imagery."

The dimension in which the poem moves is not one which excludes
ideas, but one which does include attitudes. The dimension includes
ideas, to be sure; we can always abstract an "idea" from a poem—even
from the simplest poem—even from a lyric so simple and unintel-
lectual as

> Western wind, when wilt thou blow
> That the small rain down can rain?
> Christ, that my love were in my arms
> And I in my bed again!

But the idea which we abstract—assuming that we can all agree on
what that idea is—will always be *abstracted*: it will always be the projection of a plane along a line or the projection of a cone upon a plane.

If this analogy proves to be more confusing than illuminating let us
return to the analogy with drama. We have argued that any proposition asserted in a poem is not to be taken in abstraction but is justified,
in terms of the poem, if it is justified at all, not by virtue of its scientific
or historical or philosophical truth, but is justified in terms of a principle analogous to that of dramatic propriety. Thus, the proposition
that "Beauty is truth, truth beauty" is given its precise meaning and
significance by its relation to the total context of the poem.

This principle is easy enough to see when the proposition is asserted
overtly in the poem—that is, when it constitutes a specific detail of the
poem. But the reader may well ask: is it not possible to frame a proposition, a statement, which will adequately represent the total meaning of the poem; that is, is it not possible to elaborate a summarizing
proposition which will "say," briefly and in the form of a proposition,

what the poem "says" as a poem, a proposition which will say it fully and will say it exactly, no more and no less? Could not the poet, if he had chosen, have framed such a proposition? Cannot we as readers and critics frame such a proposition?

The answer must be that the poet himself obviously did not—else he would not have had to write his poem. We as readers can attempt to frame such a proposition in our effort to understand the poem; it may well help toward an understanding. Certainly, the efforts to arrive at such propositions can do no harm *if we do not mistake them for the inner core of the poem*—if we do not mistake them for "what the poem *really* says." For, if we take one of them to represent the essential poem, we have to disregard the qualifications exerted by the total context as of no account, or else we have assumed that we can reproduce the effect of the total context in a condensed prose statement.[6]

But to deny that the coherence of a poem is reflected in a logical paraphrase of its "real meaning" is not, of course, to deny coherence to poetry; it is rather to assert that its coherence is to be sought elsewhere. The characteristic unity of a poem (even of those poems which may accidentally possess a logical unity as well as this poetic unity) lies in the unification of attitudes into a hierarchy subordinated to a total and governing attitude. In the unified poem, the poet has "come to terms" with his experience. The poem does not merely eventuate in a logical conclusion. The conclusion of the poem is the working out of the various tensions—set up by whatever means—by propositions,

---

6. [Brooks] We may, it is true, be able to adumbrate what the poem says if we allow ourselves enough words, and if we make enough reservations and qualifications, thus attempting to come nearer to the meaning of the poem by successive approximations and refinements, gradually encompassing the meaning and pointing to the area in which it lies rather than realizing it. The earlier chapters of this book, if they are successful, are obviously illustrations of this process. But such adumbrations will lack, not only the tension—the dramatic force—of the poem; they will be at best crude approximations of the poem. Moreover—and this is the crucial point—they will be compelled to resort to the methods of the poem—analogy, metaphor, symbol, etc.—in order to secure even this near an approximation.

Urban's comment upon this problem is interesting: he says that if we expand the symbol,

> we lose the "sense" or value of the symbol as *symbol*. The solution . . . seems to me to lie in an adequate theory of interpretation of the symbol. It does not consist in substituting *literal* for symbol sentences, in other words substituting "blunt" truth for symbolic truth, but rather in deepening and enriching the meaning of the symbol.

metaphors, symbols. The unity is achieved by a dramatic process, not a logical; it represents an equilibrium of forces, not a formula. It is "proved" as a dramatic conclusion is proved: by its ability to resolve the conflicts which have been accepted as the *données* of the drama.

Thus, it is easy to see why the relation of each item to the whole context is crucial, and why the effective and essential structure of the poem has to do with the complex of attitudes achieved. A scientific proposition can stand alone. If it is true, it is true. But the expression of an attitude, apart from the occasion which generates it and the situation which it encompasses, is meaningless. For example, the last two lines of the *Intimations* ode, "To me the meanest flower that blows can give / Thoughts that do often lie too deep for tears," when taken in isolation—I do not mean quoted in isolation by one who is even vaguely acquainted with the context—makes a statement which is sentimental if taken in reference to the speaker, and one which is patent nonsense if taken with a general reference. The man in the street (of whom the average college freshman is a good enough replica) knows that the meanest flower that grows does not give him thoughts that he too deep for tears; if he thinks about the matter at all, he is inclined to feel that the person who can make such an assertion is a very fuzzy sentimentalist.

We have already seen the ease with which the statement "Beauty is truth, truth beauty" becomes detached from its context, even in the hands of able critics; and we have seen the misconceptions that ensue when this detachment occurs. To take one more instance: the last stanza of Herrick's *Corinna*, taken in isolation, would probably not impress the average reader as sentimental nonsense. Yet it would suffer quite as much by isolation from its context as would the lines from Keats's *Ode*. For, as mere statement, it would become something flat and obvious—of course our lives are short! And the conclusion from the fact would turn into an obvious truism for the convinced pagan, and, for the convinced Christian, equally obvious, though damnable, nonsense.

Perhaps this is why the poet, to people interested in hard-and-fast generalizations, must always seem to be continually engaged in blurring out distinctions only after provoking and unnecessary delays. But this last position is merely another variant of the paraphrastic heresy:

to assume it is to misconceive the end of poetry—to take its meanderings as negative, or to excuse them (with the comfortable assurance
that the curved line is the line of beauty) because we can conceive the
purpose of a poem to be only the production, in the end, of a proposition—of a statement.

But the meanderings of a good poem (they are meanderings only
from the standpoint of the prose paraphrase of the poem) are not negative, and they do not have to be excused; and most of all, we need to see
what their positive function is; for unless we can assign them a positive
function, we shall find it difficult to explain why one divergence from
"the prose line of the argument" is not as good as another. The truth
is that the apparent irrelevancies which metrical pattern and metaphor
introduce do become relevant when we realize that they function in a
good poem to modify, qualify, and develop the total attitude which we
are to take in coming to terms with the total situation.

If the last sentence seems to take a dangerous turn toward some
special "use of poetry"—some therapeutic value for the sake of which
poetry is to be cultivated—I can only say that I have in mind no special ills which poetry is to cure. Uses for poetry are always to be found,
and doubtless will continue to be found. But my discussion of the
structure of poetry is not being conditioned at this point by some new
and special role which I expect poetry to assume in the future or some
new function to which I would assign it. The structure described—
a structure of "gestures" or attitudes—seems to me to describe the
essential structure of both the *Odyssey* and *The Waste Land*. It seems to
be the kind of structure which the ten poems considered in this book
possess in common.

If the structure of poetry is a structure of the order described, that
fact may explain (if not justify) the frequency with which I have had to
have recourse, in the foregoing chapters, to terms like *irony* and *paradox*. By using the term *irony*, one risks, of course, making the poem
seem arch and self-conscious, since *irony*, for most readers of poetry, is
associated with satire, *vers de société*, and other "intellectual" poetries.
Yet, the necessity for some such term ought to be apparent; and *irony* is
the most general term that we have for the kind of qualification which
the various elements in a context receive from the context. This kind

of qualification, as we have seen, is of tremendous importance in any poem. Moreover, *irony* is our most general term for indicating that recognition of incongruities—which, again, pervades all poetry to a degree far beyond what our conventional criticism has been heretofore willing to allow.

Irony in this general sense, then, is to be found in Tennyson's *Tears, Idle Tears* as well as in Donne's *Canonization*. We have, of course, been taught to expect to find irony in Pope's *Rape of the Lock*, but there is a profound irony in Keats's *Ode on a Grecian Urn*; and there is irony of a very powerful sort in Wordsworth's *Intimations* ode. For the thrusts and pressures exerted by the various symbols in this poem are not avoided by the poet: they are taken into account and played, one against the other. Indeed, the symbols—from a scientific point of view—are used perversely: it is the child who is the best philosopher; it is from a kind of darkness—from something that is "shadowy"—that the light proceeds; growth into manhood is viewed, not as an extrication from, but as an incarceration within, a prison.

There should be no mystery as to why this must be so. The terms of science are abstract symbols which do not change under the pressure of the context. They are pure (or aspire to be pure) denotations; they are defined in advance. They are not to be warped into new meanings. But where is the dictionary which contains the terms of a poem? It is a truism that the poet is continually forced to remake language. As Eliot has put it, his task is to "dislocate language into meaning."

And, from the standpoint of a scientific vocabulary, this is precisely what he performs: for, rationally considered, the ideal language would contain one term for each meaning, and the relation between term and meaning would be constant. But the word, as the poet uses it, has to be conceived of, not as a discrete particle of meaning, but as a potential of meaning, a nexus or cluster of meanings.

What is true of the poet's language in detail is true of the larger wholes of poetry. And therefore, if we persist in approaching the poem as primarily a rational statement, we ought not to be surprised if the statement seems to be presented to us always in the ironic mode. When we consider the statement immersed in the poem, it presents itself to us, like the stick immersed in the pool of water, warped and bent.

Indeed, whatever the statement, it will always show itself as deflected away from a positive, straightforward formulation.

It may seem perverse, however, to maintain, in the face of our revived interest in Donne, that the essential structure of poetry is not logical. For Donne has been appealed to of late as the great master of metaphor who imposes a clean logic on his images beside which the ordering of the images in Shakespeare's sonnets is fumbling and loose. It is perfectly true that Donne makes a great show of logic; but two matters need to be observed. In the first place, the elaborated and "logical" figure is not Donne's only figure or even his staple one. "Telescoped" figures like "Made one another's hermitage" are to be found much more frequently than the celebrated comparison of the souls of the lovers to the legs of a pair of compasses. In the second place, where Donne uses "logic," he regularly uses it to justify illogical positions. He employs it to overthrow a conventional position or to "prove" an essentially illogical one.

Logic, as Donne uses it, is nearly always an ironic logic to state the claims, of an idea or attitude which we have agreed, with our everyday logic, is false. This is not to say, certainly, that Donne is not justified in using his logic so, or that the best of his poems are not "proved" in the only senses in which poems can be proved.

But the proof is not a logical proof. *The Canonization* will scarcely prove to the hard-boiled naturalist that the lovers, by giving up the world, actually attain a better world. Nor will the argument advanced in the poem convince the dogmatic Christian that Donne's lovers are really saints.

In using logic, Donne as a poet is fighting the devil with fire. To adopt Robert Penn Warren's metaphor (which, though I lift it somewhat scandalously out of another context, will apply to this one):

> The poet, somewhat less spectacularly [than the saint], proves his vision by submitting it to the fires of irony—to the drama of the structure in the hope that the fires will refine it. In other words, the poet wishes to indicate that his vision has been earned, that it can survive reference to the complexities and contradictions of experience.

The same principle that inspires the presence of irony in so many of our great poems also accounts for the fact that so many of them seem to be built around paradoxes. Here again the conventional associations of the term may prejudice the reader just as the mention of Donne may prejudice him. For Donne, as one type of reader knows all too well, was of that group of poets who wished to impress their audience with their cleverness. All of us are familiar with the censure passed upon Donne and his followers by Dr. Johnson, and a great many of us still retain it as our own, softening only the rigor of it and the thoroughness of its application, but not giving it up as a principle.

Yet there are better reasons than that of rhetorical vainglory that have induced poet after poet to choose ambiguity and paradox rather than plain, discursive simplicity. It is not enough for the poet to analyze his experience as the scientist does, breaking it up into parts, distinguishing part from part, classifying the various parts. His task is finally to unify experience. He must return to us the unity of the experience itself as man knows it in his own experience. The poem, if it be a true poem is a simulacrum of reality—in this sense, at least, it is an "imitation"—by *being* an experience rather than any mere statement about experience or any mere abstraction from experience.

Tennyson cannot be content with *saying* that in memory the poet seems both dead *and* alive; he must dramatize its life-in-death for us, and his dramatization involves, necessarily, ironic shock and wonder. The dramatization demands that the antithetical aspects of memory be coalesced into one entity which—if we take it on the level of statement—is a paradox, the assertion of the union of opposites. Keats's Urn must express a life which is above life and its vicissitudes, but it must also bear witness to the fact that its life is not life at all but is a kind of death. To put it in other terms, the Urn must, in its role as historian, assert that myth is truer than history. Donne's lovers must reject the world in order to possess the world.

Or, to take one further instance: Wordsworth's light must serve as the common symbol for aspects of man's vision which seem mutually incompatible—intuition and analytic reason. Wordsworth's poem, as a matter of fact, typifies beautifully the poet's characteristic problem itself. For even this poem, which testifies so heavily to the way in which the world is split up and parceled out under the growing light of reason, cannot rest in this fact as its own mode of perception, and still be a poem. Even after the worst has been said about man's multiple vision, the poet must somehow prove that the child is father to the man, that the dawn light is still somehow the same light as the evening light.

If the poet, then, must perforce dramatize the oneness of the experience, even though paying tribute to its diversity, then his use of paradox and ambiguity is seen as necessary. He is not simply trying to spice up, with a superficially exciting or mystifying rhetoric, the old stale stockpot (though doubtless this will be what the inferior poet does generally and what the real poet does in his lapses). He is rather giving us an insight which preserves the unity of experience and which, at its higher and more serious levels, triumphs over the apparently contradictory and conflicting elements of experience by unifying them into a new pattern.

Wordsworth's *Intimations* ode, then, is not only a poem, but, among other things, a parable about poetry. Keats's *Ode on a Grecian Urn* is quite obviously such a parable. And, indeed, most of the poems which we have discussed in this study may be taken as such parables.

In one sense, Pope's treatment of Belinda raises all the characteristic problems of poetry. For Pope, in dealing with his "goddess," must face the claims of naturalism and of common sense which would deny divinity to her. Unless he faces them, he is merely a sentimentalist. He must do an even harder thing: he must transcend the conventional and polite attributions of divinity which would be made to her as an acknowledged belle. Otherwise, he is merely trivial and obvious. He must "prove" her divinity against the common-sense denial (the brutal denial) and against the conventional assertion (the polite denial). The poetry must be wrested from the context: Belinda's lock, which is what the rude young man wants and which Belinda rather prudishly defends and which the naturalist asserts is only animal and which displays in its curled care the style of a particular era of history, must be given a place of permanence among the stars.

11

THE THEMES OF ROBERT FROST

ROBERT PENN WARREN

Robert Penn Warren's famous essay "Pure and Impure Poetry" has recently been reprinted by Garrick Davis in Praising It New *as one of the key texts of the New Criticism. Less well-known is Warren's 1947 essay on Robert Frost, which has much to say on the later stages of the debate about what poetry is. The most obvious irony, of course, is that a Southern critic is commenting on the emblematic Yankee, the man who had already become a kind of parody of himself by the 1940s (at least in his public persona) and who would not again receive such serious critical attention for what he actually was until Randall Jarrell's essays in* Poetry and the Age *a decade later. Warren does not mention the quarrels between Cleanth Brooks and John Crowe Ransom over the "paraphrasable core" of a poem, but certainly a "theme" comes closest to being subject to paraphrase. Warren takes up Frost in particular, one might surmise, because his poems are essentially about the "interpenetration" between the logical structure of things and the "irrelevancies" that Ransom finds to be the "local texture" of poetry. As Warren writes of Frost's* Birches, *"The poet has undertaken to define for us both the distinction between and the interpenetration of two worlds, the world of nature and the world of the ideal, the heaven and the earth, the human and the non-human (oppositions which appear in various relationships), by developing images gradually from the literal descriptive level of reference to the symbolic level of reference."*

In other words, precisely by looking at the themes of individual poems taken together, Warren comes upon a way of paraphrasing that is not heretical and a way of talking about unity as interpenetration without reference to religious metaphors. In Frost, Warren uncovers a poet who explicitly calls himself an anti-Platonist—"platonism" being the key term both for Tate and Ransom in defining poetry that has lost the ontology of the image. Warren's description of the movement from the literal level to the symbolic level anticipates, to some degree, the direction that Allen Tate takes several years later in "The Symbolic Imagination."

A large body of criticism has been written on the poetry of Robert Frost, and we know the labels which have been used: nature poet, New England Yankee, symbolist, humanist, skeptic, synecdochist, anti-Platonist, and many others. These labels have their utility, true or half true as they may be. They point to something in our author. But the important thing about a poet is the kind of poetry he writes. We are not interested primarily in his "truth" as such—as label, as samplerwork—but in the degree to which it is an organizing and vitalizing principle in his poem. For only in so far as it operates as such a principle—in so far as the poem becomes truly expressive—does the truth have meaning at all.

In any case, I do not want to begin by quarreling with the particular labels. Instead, I want to begin with some poems and try to see how their particular truths are operative within the poems themselves. I know perfectly well that there are some readers of poetry who object to this process. They say that it is a profanation, that they simply want to enjoy the poem. We all want to enjoy the poem. And we can be comforted by the fact that the poem, if it is true poem, will, like the baby's poor kitty-cat, survive all the pinching and prodding and squeezing which love will lavish upon it. It will have nine lives too. Further, and more importantly, the perfect intuitive and immediate grasp of a poem in the totality of its meaning and structure—the thing we desire—may come late rather than early—on the fiftieth reading rather than on the first. Perhaps we must be able to look forward as well as back as we move through the poem—be able to sense the complex of relationships and implications—before we can truly have that immediate grasp.

But we know that some poets flinch when faced with any critical discussion of their poems. The critic may so readily turn into the dogmatist who wants to extract the message from the poem and throw the poem away—just as the sentimentalist wants to enjoy his own feelings provoked by the poem and throw the poem away. Frost himself has been especially shy of the dogmatists and has not shown too much sympathy with a reader who, to quote him, "stands at the end of a poem ready in waiting to catch you by both hands with enthusiasm and drag you off your balance over the last punctuation mark into more than you meant to say."

Or we have the case of Yeats. An admirer sent Yeats an interpretation of one of his poems, and asked if it was right. Yeats replied, grudgingly, that it was, but added that he did not think poets ought to interpret their own poems, or give the green light to the interpretations of other people, for this would serve to limit the poems. A good poem is a massive, deep, and vital thing, but this does not imply that a poem is a stimulus to which any response, so long as it is intense, is appropriate. It does not mean that the poem is merely a body of material which the reader may fancifully reorder according to his whim. But it does imply that, though the poem is a controlled focus of experience, within the terms of that control many transliterations are possible as variants of the root attitude expressed. (There are many ways to state the theme of a poem.)

To turn to the poems: the poets may make their protests and reservations, but discussions will continue. As a starting point I am taking one of Frost's best-known and most widely anthologized pieces, *Stopping by Woods on a Snowy Evening*. But we shall not be content to dwell exclusively on this poem, attractive as it is, for it will quite naturally lead us into some other poems. It will lead us to the other poems because it represents but one manifestation of an impulse very common in Frost's poetry. Here is the poem:

Whose woods these are I think I know.
His house is in the village though;

He will not see me stopping here
To watch his woods fill up with snow.

My little horse must think it queer
To stop without a farmhouse near
Between the woods and frozen lake
The darkest evening of the year.

He gives his harness bells a shake
To ask if there is some mistake.
The only other sound's the sweep
Of easy wind and downy flake.

The woods are lovely, dark and deep.
But I have promises to keep,
And miles to go before I sleep,
And miles to go before I sleep.

Now, the poem we are dealing with may be said to be simple—that is, the event presented is, in itself, simple and the poet says, quite simply, what the event presumably means. But this does not mean that the implications of the event are not complex; the area of experience touched upon by the poem is "suggestive" or "haunting." And all good poems, even the simplest, work, it seems to me, in exactly that way. They drop a stone into the pool of our being, and the ripples spread.

The poem does, in fact, look simple. A man driving by a dark woods stops to admire the scene, to watch the snow falling into the special darkness. He remembers the name of the man who owns the woods and knows that the man, snug in his house in the village, cannot begrudge him a look. He is not trespassing. The little horse is restive and shakes the harness bells. The man decides to drive on, because, as he says, he has promises to keep—he has to get home to deliver the groceries for supper—and he has miles to go before he can afford to stop, before he can sleep.

At the literal level that is all the poem has to say. But if we read it at that level, we shall say, and quite rightly, that it is the silliest stuff we ever saw. That is what the Amazon queen in Shakespeare's *Midsummer Night's Dream* said to her husband as she watched the play Bottom and his fellows were giving in honor of her marriage. But Theseus, her husband, replied: "The best in this kind are but shadow and the worst are no worse if imagination amend them." We shall try to be a little less literal-minded than the Amazon queen and shall try to see what reality our little poem is a shadow of.

> Whose woods these are I think I know.
> His house is in the village though;
> He will not see me stopping here
> To watch his woods fill up with snow.

With that first stanza we have a simple contrast, the contrast between the man in the village, snug at his hearthside, and the man who stops by the woods. The sane, practical man has shut himself up against the weather; certainly he would not stop in the middle of the weather for no reason at all. But, being a practical man, he does not mind if some fool stops by his woods so long as the fool merely looks and does not do any practical damage, does not steal firewood or break down fences. With this stanza we seem to have a contrast between the sensitive and the insensitive man, the man who uses the world and the man who contemplates the world. And the contrast seems to be in favor of the gazer and not the owner—for the purposes of the poem at least. In fact, we may even have the question: Who is the owner, the man who is miles away or the man who can really see the woods?

With the second stanza another contrast emerges:

> My little horse must think it queer
> To stop without a farmhouse near
> Between the woods and frozen lake
> The darkest evening of the year.

Here we have the horse-man contrast. The horse is practical too. He can see no good reason for stopping, not a farmhouse near, no oats available. The horse becomes an extension, as it were, of the man in the village—both at the practical level, the level of the beast which cannot understand why a man would stop, on the darkest evening of the year, to stare into the darker darkness of the snowy woods. In other words, the act of stopping is the specially human act, the thing that differentiates the man from the beast. The same contrast is continued into the third stanza—the contrast between the impatient shake of the harness bells and the soothing whish of easy wind and downy flake.

To this point we would have a poem all right, but not much of a poem. It would set up the essential contrast between, shall we say, action and contemplation, but it would not be very satisfying because it would fail to indicate much concerning the implications of the contrast. It would be a rather too complacent poem, too much at ease in the Zion of contemplation.

But in the poem the poet actually wrote, the fourth and last stanza brings a very definite turn, a refusal to accept either term of the contrast developed to this point.

> The woods are lovely, dark and deep.
> But I have promises to keep,
> And miles to go before I sleep,
> And miles to go before I sleep.

The first line proclaims the beauty, the attraction of the scene—a line lingering and retarded in its rhythm. But with this statement concerning the attraction—the statement merely gives us what we have already dramatically arrived at by the fact of the stopping—we find the repudiation of the attraction. The beauty, the peace, is a sinister beauty, a sinister peace. It is the beauty and peace of surrender—the repudiation of action and obligation. The darkness of the woods is delicious—but treacherous. The beauty which cuts itself off from action is sterile; the peace which is a peace of escape is a meaningless and, therefore, a suicidal peace. There will be beauty and peace at the end of the journey, in the terms of the fulfillment of the promises, but that will be an earned beauty stemming from action.

In other words, we have a new contrast here. The fact of the capacity to stop by the roadside and contemplate the woods sets man off from the beast, but in so far as such contemplation involves a repudiation of the world of action and obligation it cancels the definition of man which it had seemed to establish. So the poem leaves us with that paradox, and that problem. We can accept neither term of the original contrast, the poem seems to say; we must find a dialectic which will accommodate both terms. We must find a definition of our humanity which will transcend both terms.

This theme is one which appears over and over in Frost's poems—the relation, to state the issue a little differently, between the fact and the dream. In another poem, *Mowing*, he puts it this way, 'The fact is the sweetest dream that labor knows." That is, the action and the reward cannot be defined separately, man must fulfill himself, in action, and the dream must not violate the real. But the solution is not to sink into the brute—to act like the little horse who knows that the farmhouses mean oats—to sink into nature, into appetite. But at the same time, to accept the other term of the original contrast in our poem, to surrender to the pull of the delicious blackness of the woods, is to forfeit the human definition, to sink into nature by another way, a dangerous way which only the human can achieve. So our poem, which is supposed to celebrate nature, may really be a poem about man defining himself by resisting the pull into nature. There are many poems on this subject in Frost's work. In fact, the first poem in his first book is on this subject and uses the same image of the dark wood with its lethal beauty. It is called *Into My Own*.

> One of my wishes is that those dark trees,
> So old and firm they scarcely show the breeze,
> Were not, as 'twere, the merest mask of gloom,
> But stretched away until the edge of doom.
>
> I should not be withheld but that some day
> Into their vastness I should steal away,
> Fearless of ever finding open land,
> Or highway where the slow wheel pours the sand.
>
> I do not see why I should e'er turn back,
> Or those should not set forth upon my track
> To overtake me, who should miss me here
> And long to know if still I held them dear.
>
> They would not find me changed from him they knew—
> Only more sure of all I thought was true.

Here the man enters the dark wood but manages to carry his humanity with him; he remains more sure of all he had thought was true.
And thus the poem becomes a kind of parable of the position of the
artist, the man who is greatly concerned with the flux of things, with
the texture of the world, with, even, the dark "natural" places of man's
soul. He is greatly concerned with those things, but he manages to
carry over, in terms of those things, the specifically human.

From *Into My Own* let us turn to a late poem, which again gives us
the man and the dark wood and the invitation to come into the lethal
beauty. This one is called *Come In*.

> As I came to the edge of the woods,
> Thrush music—hark!
> Now if it was dusk outside,
> Inside it was dark,
>
> Too dark in the woods for a bird
> By sleight of wing
> To better its perch for the night,
> Though it still could sing.
>
> The last of the light of the sun
> That had died in the west
> Still lived for one song more
> In a thrush's breast.
>
> Far in the pillared dark
> Thrush music went—
> Almost like a call to come in
> To the dark and lament.
>
> But no, I was out for stars:
> I would not come in.
> I meant not even if asked,
> And I hadn't been.

In this woods, too, there is beauty, and an invitation for the man to
come in. And, as in *Stopping by Woods on a Snowy Evening*, he declines
the invitation. Let us develop a little more fully the implications of the

contrast between the two poems. The thrush in the woods cannot now do anything to alter its position. Practical achievement is at an end—the sleight of wing (a fine phrase) can do no good. But it still can sing. That is, the darkness can still be conquered in the very lament. In other words, the poet is prepared to grant here that a kind of satisfaction, a kind of conquest, is possible by the fact of expression, for the expression is, in itself, a manifestation of the light which has been withdrawn. Even in terms of the lament, in terms of the surrender to the delicious blackness, a kind of ideal resolution—and one theory of art, for that matter—is possible. (We remember that it was a thing for a man to do and not for a horse to do to stop by the other dark woods.)

But here the man, as before, does not go into the woods. He will not make those terms with his destiny, not, in any case, unless forced to do so. (The thrush cannot do otherwise, but a man can, perhaps, and if he can do otherwise he more fully defines himself as man.) No, the man is out for stars, as he says. Which seems to say that man, by his nature (as distinguished from bird), is not dependent upon the day; he can find in the night other symbols for his aspiration. He will not lament the passing of the day, but will go out for stars.

> I would not come in.
> I meant not even if asked,
> And I hadn't been.

What are we to take as the significance of this last little turn? Is it merely a kind of coyness, a little ironical, wry turn, without content, a mere mannerism? (And in some of Frost's poems we do have the mere mannerism, a kind of self-imitation.) Why had not the man been asked to come in? The thrush's song had seemed to be an invitation. But it had not been an invitation after all. For the bird cannot speak to the man. It has not the language of man. It can speak only in terms of its own world, the world of nature and the dark woods, and not in terms of the man who is waiting for the darkness to define the brilliance of the stars. So here we have again the man-nature contrast (but we must remember that nature is in man, too), the contrast between the two kinds of beauty, and the idea that the reward, the dream, the ideal, stems from action and not from surrender of action.

Let us leave the dark-wood symbol and turn to a poem which, with other materials, treats Frost's basic theme. This is *After Apple-Picking*, the poem which I am inclined to think is Frost's masterpiece, it is so poised, so subtle, so poetically coherent in detail.

> My long two-pointed ladder's sticking through a tree
> Toward heaven still,
> And there's a barrel that I didn't fill
> Beside it, and there may be two or three
> Apples I didn't pick upon some bough.
> But I am done with apple-picking now.
> Essence of winter sleep is on the night,
> The scent of apples: I am drowsing off.
> I cannot rub the strangeness from my sight
> I got from looking through a pane of glass
> I skimmed this morning from the drinking trough
> And held against the world of hoary grass.
> It melted, and I let it fall and break.
> But I was well
> Upon my way to sleep before it fell,
> And I could tell
> What form my dreaming was about to take.
> Magnified apples appear and disappear,
> Stem end and blossom end,
> And every fleck of russet showing clear.
> My instep arch not only keeps the ache,
> It keeps the pressure of a ladder-round.
> I feel the ladder sway as the boughs bend.
> And I keep hearing from the cellar bin
> The rumbling sound
> Of load on load of apples coming in.
> For I have had too much
> Of apple-picking: I am overtired
> Of the great harvest I myself desired.
> There were ten thousand thousand fruit to touch,
> Cherish in hand, lift down, and not let fall.
> For all

That struck the earth,
No matter if not bruised or spiked with stubble,
Went surely to the cider-apple heap
As of no worth.
One can see what will trouble
This sleep of mine, whatever sleep it is.
Were he not gone,
The woodchuck could say whether it's like his
Long sleep, as I describe its coming on,
Or just some human sleep.

The items here—ladder in apple tree, the orchard, drinking trough, pane of ice, woodchuck—all have their perfectly literal meanings—the echo of their meaning in actuality. And the poem, for a while anyway, seems to be commenting on that actual existence those items have. Now, some poems make a pretense of living only in terms of that actuality. For instance, *Stopping by Woods on a Snowy Evening* is perfectly consistent at the level of actuality—a man stops by the woods, looks into the woods, which he finds lovely, dark and deep, and then goes on, for he has promises to keep. It can be left at that level, if we happen to be that literal-minded, and it will make a sort of sense. However, *After Apple-Picking* is scarcely consistent at the level of actuality. It starts off with a kind of consistency, but something happens. The hero of the poem says that he is drowsing off—and in broad daylight, too. He says that he has a strangeness in his sight which he drew from the drinking trough. So the literal world dissolves into a kind of dream world—the literal world and the dream world overlapping, as it were, like the two sets of elements in a superimposed photograph. What is the nature of this dream world? And what is its relation to the literal world, the world of real apples and the aching instep arch and the real woodchuck?

The poem opens with a few lines which seem to apply wholeheartedly to the literal world:

My long two-pointed ladder's sticking through a tree
Toward heaven still,
And there's a barrel that I didn't fill

234 of Robert Penn Warren

Beside it, and there may be two or three
Apples I didn't pick upon some bough.

It is all literal enough. We even observe the very literal down-to-earth word "sticking" and the casualness of the tone of the whole passage. In fact, it would be hard to say this more simply than it is said. Even the rhymes are unobtrusive, and all the more so because all of the lines except one are run-on lines. But let us, in the light of the rest of the poem, look more closely. The ladder, we observe, has been left sticking "toward heaven still." That is, as we have said, casual and commonplace enough, but we suddenly realize it isn't merely that, when we remember the poem is about the kind of heaven the poet wants, the kind of dream-after-labor he wants—and expects.

So, to break the matter down into crude statement and destroy the quality of the suggestive-in-the-commonplace, we have a kind of preliminary appearance of the theme which concerns the relation of labor and reward, earth and heaven. With our knowledge of the total poem, we can look back, too, at the next several lines and reread them: Maybe I missed something in my life, in my labor, the poet says, but not much, for I tried quite conscientiously to handle carefully every item of my harvest of experience, to touch with proper appreciation everything that came to hand. Maybe I did miss a few things, he seems to say, but I did the best I could, and on the whole did pretty well.

But now the harvest is over, he says, and the "essence of winter sleep is on the night, the scent of apples." He is aware of the conclusion, the successful conclusion of his effort, and in that awareness there is a strangeness in his sight. He is now looking not into the world of effort but the world of dream, of the renewal. It is misty and strange, as seen through the pane of ice, but still it has the familiar objects of the old world of effort, but the objects now become strange in their very familiarity. He is poised here on the frontier between the two worlds, puzzling about their relationship. But he can already tell, he says, what will be the content of the dream world, the world of reward for labor now accomplished.

And I could tell
What form my dreaming was about to take.

Magnified apples appear and disappear,
Stem end and blossom end,
And every fleck of russet showing clear.

The dream will relive the world of effort, even to the ache of the instep
arch where the ladder rung was pressed. But is this a cause for regret or
for self-congratulation? Is it a good dream or a bad dream? The answer
is not to be found in statement, for as far as the statement goes he says:

For I have had too much
Of apple-picking: I am overtired
Of the great harvest I myself desired.

No, we must look for the answer in the temper of the description
he gives of the dream—the apples, stem end and blossom end, and
every fleck of russet showing clear. The richness and beauty of the
harvest—magnified now—is what is dwelt upon. In the dream world
every detail is bigger than Me, and richer, and can be contemplated in
its fullness. And the accent here is on the word contemplated. Further,
even as the apple picker recalls the details of labor which made him
overtired, he does so in a way which denies the very statement that the
recapitulation in dream will "trouble" him. For instance, we have the
delicious rhythm of the line,

I feel the ladder sway as the boughs bend.

It is not the rhythm of nightmare, but of the good dream. Or we
find the same temper in the next few lines in which the poet returns
to the fact that he, in the real world, the world of effort, had carefully
handled and cherished each fruit, and *cherished* is not the word to use if
the labor is mere labor, the brutal act. So even though we find the poet
saying that his sleep will be troubled, the word *troubled* comes to us
colored by the whole temper of the passage, ironically qualified by that
temper. For he would not have it otherwise than troubled, in this sense.
To quote again:

One can see what will trouble
This sleep of mine, whatever sleep it is.
Were he not gone,

> The woodchuck could say whether it's like his
> Long sleep, as I describe its coming on,
> Or just some human sleep.

Well, what does the woodchuck have to do with it? How does he enter the poem, and with what credentials? His sleep is contrasted with "just some human sleep." The contrast, we see, is on the basis of the dream. The woodchuck's sleep will be dreamless and untroubled. The woodchuck is simply in the nature from which man is set apart. The animal's sleep is the sleep of oblivion. But man has a dream which distinguishes him from the woodchuck. But how is this dream related to the literal world, the world of the woodchuck and apple harvests and daily experience? It is not a dream which is cut off from that literal world of effort—a heaven of ease and perpetual rewards, in the sense of rewards as coming after and in consequence of effort. No, the dream, the heaven, will simply be a reliving of the effort—magnified apples, stem end and blossom end, and every fleck, every aspect of experience, showing clear.

We have been considering the literal world and the dream world as distinct, for that is the mechanism of the poem, the little myth of the poem. But here it may be well to ask ourselves if the poet is really talking about immortality and heaven—if he is really trying to define the heaven he wants and expects after this mortal life. No, he is only using that as an image for his meaning, a way to define his attitude. And that attitude is an attitude toward the here and now, toward man's conduct of his life in the literal world. So we must make another transliteration.

This attitude has many implications. And this leads us to a rather important point about poetry. When we read a poem merely in terms of a particular application of the attitude involved in it, we almost always read it as a kind of cramped and mechanical allegory. A poem defines an attitude, a basic view, which can have many applications. It defines, if it is a good poem, a sort of strategic point for the spirit from which experience of all sorts may be freshly viewed.

But to return to this poem: What would be some of the implied applications? First, let us take it in reference to the question of any sort of ideal which man sets up for himself, in reference to his dream. By this application the valid ideal would be that which stems from and involves the literal world, which is arrived at in terms of the literal world and not by violation of man's nature as an inhabitant of that literal world. Second, let us take it in reference to man's reward in this literal world. By this application we would arrive at a statement like this: Man must seek his reward in his fulfillment through effort and must not expect reward as something coming at the end of effort, like the oats for the dray horse in the trough at the end of the day's pull. He must cherish each thing in his hand. Third, let us take it in reference to poetry, or the arts. By this application, which is really a variant of the first, we would find that art must stem from the literal world, from the common body of experience, and must be a magnified "dream" of that experience as it has achieved meaning, and not a thing set apart, a mere decoration.

These examples, chosen from among many, are intended merely to point us back into the poem—to the central impulse of the poem itself. But they are all summed up in this line from *Mowing*, another of Frost's poems: "The fact is the sweetest dream that labor knows." However, we can step outside of the poems a moment and find a direct statement from the anti-Platonic Frost. He is comparing himself with E. A. Robinson, but we can see the application to the thematic line which has been emerging in the poems we have been considering.

> I am not the Platonist Robinson was. By Platonist I mean one who believes what we have here is an imperfect copy of what is in heaven. The woman you have is an imperfect copy of some woman in heaven or in someone else's bed. Many of the world's greatest—maybe all of them—have been ranged on that romantic side. I am philosophically opposed to having one Iseult for my vocation and another for my avocation. . . . Let me not sound the least bit smug. I define a difference with proper humility. A truly gallant Platonist will remain a bachelor as Robinson did from unwillingness to reduce any woman to the condition of being used without being idealized.

Smug or not—and perhaps the poet protests his humility a little too much—the passage does give us a pretty clear indication of Frost's position. And the contrast between "vocation" and "avocation" which he uses leads us to another poem in which the theme appears, *Two Tramps in Mud Time*. The last stanza is talking about the relation of "love" and "need" as related to an activity—which may be transliterated into "dream" and "fact" if we wish:

> But yield who will to their separation,
> My object in living is to unite
> My avocation and my vocation
> As my two eyes make one in sight.
> Only where love and need are one,
> And the work is play for mortal stakes,
> Is the deed ever really done
> For Heaven and the future's sakes.

And we may notice that we have, in line with our earlier poems on the theme, the apparently contrasting terms "mortal stakes" and "Heaven."

In conclusion, I may cite *Desert Places*, which is a late and more bleakly stoical version of *Stopping by Woods on a Snowy Evening*, and *Birches*, which is almost a variant of *After Apple-Picking*. Here are the closing lines of *Birches*:

> So was I once myself a swinger of birches.
> And so I dream of going back to be.
> It's when I'm weary of considerations,
> And life is too much like a pathless wood
> Where your face burns and tickles with the cobwebs
> Broken across it, and one eye is weeping
> From a twig's having lashed across it open.
> I'd like to get away from earth awhile
> And then come back to it and begin over.
> May no fate willfully misunderstand me
> And half grant what I wish and snatch me away
> Not to return. Earth's the right place for love:
> I don't know where it's likely to go better.
> I'd like to go by climbing a birch tree,
> And climb black branches up a snow-white trunk
> Toward heaven, till the tree could bear no more,
> But dipped its top and set me down again.

That would be good both going and coming back.
One could do worse than be a swinger of birches.

For the meaning, in so far as it is abstractly paraphrasable as to theme: Man is set off from nature by the fact that he is capable of the dream, but he is also of nature, and his best dream is the dream of the fact, and the fact is his position of labor and fate in nature though not of her. For the method: The poet has undertaken to define for us both the distinction between and the interpenetration of two worlds, the world of nature and the world of the ideal, the heaven and the earth, the human and the non-human (oppositions which appear in various relationships), by developing images gradually from the literal descriptive level of reference to the symbolic level of reference.

It may be said quite truly in one sense that this interpenetration, this fusion, of the two worlds is inherent in the nature of poetry—that whenever we use a metaphor, even in ordinary conversation, we remark on the interpenetration in so far as our metaphor functions beyond the level of mere mechanical illustration. But the difference between the general fact and these poems is that the interpenetration of the two worlds, in varying ranges of significance, is itself the theme of the poems. We can whimsically say that this does not prove much. Even the most vindictive Platonist could not do very differently, for in so far as he was bound to state his Platonic theme in words—words, which belong to our world of fact and contingency—he would be unwittingly celebrating the un-Platonic interpenetration of the two worlds. But there is a practical difference if not an ultimate one. We might get at it this way: The process the poet has employed in all of these poems, but most fully and subtly I think in *After Apple-Picking*, is to order his literal materials so that, in looking back upon them as the poem proceeds, the reader suddenly realizes that they have been transmuted. When Shakespeare begins a sonnet with the question, "Shall I compare thee to a summer's day?" and proceeds to develop the comparison, "Thou art more lovely and more temperate," he is assuming the fact of the transmutation, of the interpenetration of the worlds, from the very start. But in these poems, Frost is trying to indicate, as it were, the very process of the transmutation, of the interpenetration. That, and what that implies as an attitude toward all our activities, is the very center of these poems, and of many others among his work.

12

POETRY AS TRADITION

DONALD DAVIDSON

When Murray Krieger published The New Apologists for Poetry
*in 1956, he sounded the death knell of the New Criticism, according
to Frank Lentricchia.[1] Krieger discusses Tate and Ransom at length
in his book, and he includes a number of references to Robert Penn
Warren, but the other original member of the Fugitive-Agrarians,
Donald Davidson, gets no mention at all. By 1956, Davidson had
been out of the mainstream quarrels for almost two decades, in part
because he retained a loyalty to the South that the others had long
before modified or abandoned. "Poetry as Tradition," first presented
as a lecture in 1956, situates the discussion of poetry in a large context
and brings some ventilation to the increasingly airless quarrels over
"the autonomous and autotelic nature of the single, lonely poem"[2]
that seemed to bedevil Brooks and Ransom through the 1940s.*

    *Davidson criticizes his fellow poets and critics, first of all, for
losing the large audience that poetry had enjoyed a century before.
In particular, he holds up Ransom's reasoning as problematic. Wor-
ried that scientists would accuse poets of mere affectation, Ransom
insisted upon making the style of poetry "impregnable," according to
Davidson. The problem, of course, was that poetry therefore became*

---

1. Frank Lentricchia, *After the New Criticism* (Chicago: University of Chicago Press, 1980),
213 ff.
2. Ibid., 3.

a specialty for a few, not a matter of wide enjoyment for a whole people: "[T]he impregnable or guarded style, whether it precedes or follows defensive criticism, does not increase the general currency of poetry and is not intended to. . . . Mainly it reaches only the literary elite of poets, critics, professors of English, and the students who are electing certain courses and have to submit to it." Davidson reminds his readers that in the great ages of poetry—until the time of Pope— poetry was more a living, spoken art than an artifact on the page. It gives him no consolation to see poetry preserved in textbooks: "This is for poetry a kind of death-in-life, to exist only on the printed page, not on the lips of men, not to be carried by their voices and therefore almost never carried in their memories, rarely in their hearts."

Looking back over a hundred years of poetry, from Poe and Baude- laire to Eliot, Yeats, Frost, Ransom, and Tate, we can easily distin- guish certain features that mark off the poetry we call "modern" from the poetry that preceded it. The sharp dissociation of the poet from society, the low valuation put by society upon poetry as an art, and the rise of experimental modes of poetry, accompanied by a parallel development of an enormous body of criticism—these are the features whose history must be traced, whose causes must be probed, if poetry, as we commonly say, is to be "understood" in modern terms.

These phenomena are of course interrelated. The dissociation of the poet from society, already in definite prospect in the sixteenth century, has become more painfully apparent as society has accepted the dominance of science and consequently has become indisposed to accept poetry as truth. If poetry comes to be regarded as a trifling fic- tion, of no use as compared with the dicta of physical science, the gap between the poet and society widens to a chasm. The experimentalism of the modern poets may represent a conscious or unconscious effort, in one group of tendencies, to bridge the chasm by making the style and subject matter of poetry conform to the fluid, highly unstable social regime created by the rule of science—a regime in which popu- lar fashions must change in step with the changing hypotheses of science and the accompanying economic figurations that are the response of applied science. Or, by countertendency, the chasm is accepted as permanent, and experimentalism becomes the celebrated ivory tower to which the poet retires. In other terms, poetry becomes a specialty, one among the many specialties forced upon society by the modern regime. Then it can be practiced and understood only by specialists, who are only too likely to be college professors and critics.

Meanwhile, poetry has to be defended, and it is chiefly in his role as defender of his art that the poet becomes literary critic. The task is inescapable, and it cannot be left to the scholar and the nonpoet critic if the true role of the poet and the meaning of his art are to be asserted with sufficiently compelling force. From Sidney's defense, on through Wordsworth's *Preface to Lyrical Ballads* and Coleridge's *Biographia Literaria*, and down to Eliot's essays, Yeats's reminiscences, the discourses of Frost at his poetry readings, and the prose works of Ransom, Brooks, Warren, and Tate, the defense of poetry has been steadily and brilliantly waged. It necessarily becomes more broadly expository and philosophical as the common ground of understanding between the poet and his audiences approaches zero as a limit.

And the poets themselves, or the poet-critics, become almost the sole defenders. No help comes from the physical scientist, the social scientist, or the businessman, who has become their too-willing ally. The professional world of education, now committed to antihumanism and firmly indentured to the service of science, is not interested. The clergy, who in the Middle Ages were often the friends and preservers, if also the censors, of poetry, have gone over to the enemy. This is a notable defection and heresy. To the promulgators of secular and socialized religion, poetry has ceased to have much meaning. With dismay we can observe how the modern cleric, explaining to his flock that the Scriptures at certain cardinal points are merely symbolic, is in this way asserting that they are mere poetry, and *therefore* not Truth.

It is not surprising, then, that the criticism of poetry, increasing vastly in our time, sometimes explanatory, more often polemical, is nearly always in principle a defense of poetry, conducted by the poet and his last remaining allies, the critics, against a regime hostile or indifferent to poetry. Nor is it surprising that the defense often takes the form of direct counterattack upon the regime itself. In this phase of operations the poet may well become an outright traditionalist in religion, politics, and economics. He examines the defects of modern civilization. He develops a sense of catastrophe. With an insight far more accurate than the forecasts of professional social philosophers, he begins to plot the lines of stress and strain along which disaster will erupt. He predicts the ruin of modern secularized society and makes offers of salvation. These are unheard or unheeded. Then upon the deaf ears and faceless bodies of modern society he invokes the poet's curse.

In form, this curse may be as deceptively facetious as the famous last sentence of Sidney's apology: "That while you live you live in love, and never get favor for lacking skill of a sonnet; and when you die, your memory die from the earth for want of an epitaph." Or as Eliot's "This is the way the world ends/Not with a bang but with a whimper." Or it may be Allen Tate's more explicit

> All are born Yankees of the race of men
> And this, too, now the country of the damned.

Or, in another vein, the curse may proliferate into broader indictment, containing a positive as well as a negative, such as may be found in the desperately voluminous prose works of Richard Wagner in the nineteenth century or the restrained vehemence of the symposia of the Southern "Agrarians" of the twentieth century.

However framed, the poet's curse cannot be dismissed as a trifling eccentricity. The historical record will show that it has seldom, if ever, failed to work. A civilization that says to the poet, "Go up, thou baldhead!" by that act proves itself ripe for comminatory sentence. Rejection of poetry is the sign that the civilization is preparing its own doom. And after the catastrophe, whether sudden or only a decline and fall, all that survives is the rejected poetry, the religion if any, and whatever else, being immaterial tradition, is not subject to physical destruction. The rest is nothing but ruins to be picked over by archaeologist and historian.

II

But if such, in epitome, is the history of modern poetry, it does not seem encouraging. It would be unrealistic not to reexamine the grounds on which the modern defense of poetry is being offered. If it is a valid defense, why does not poetry gain in currency and influence rather than diminish as it obviously is diminishing?

The Elizabethan defense of poetry was a highly successful defense, for it may be said to have created, or helped to create, not only a new poetry but also a new audience for poetry. Wordsworth and Coleridge, who rode in the whirlwind and directed the storm of English romanticism, repeated the success of the Elizabethans, though not until after they had suffered some initial defeats—as generally happened to romantic experimentalists. Our more modern poets have succeeded in only one phase of the battle. They have created a new poetry—or poetries—and their defense, working in critical reflex, has undoubtedly aided the perfection of their art. But they have not created a new audience. On the contrary, they have lost most of the audience that existed for poetry a hundred years ago. That audience, which as late even as fifty years ago, was attending in large numbers the performance of Tennyson and Browning, or at least of the Fitzgerald who found his way in limp leather to many a parlor table, has abruptly dwindled to a faithful, well-schooled few. The show is financially on the rocks; the poet-author-actors would starve if not supported by Guggenheim fellowships and lectureships in creative writing.

Obscurity of style and meaning is most often mentioned as the chief cause of the exit of the audience. To this the poets retort that they are no more obscure than Donne or Milton or Dante and indeed are much more clear and explicit than, say, the intolerably vague Shelley or the intolerably verbose Browning. And they are right. More serious might be the charge that they are eclectic, as Stark Young defines eclectic. In their poetry there is often a good deal of the "lustre of the artist" without a perfectly equivalent illumination of the subject. In much of their poetry—and this is true of many poems of apparently innocent simplicity, as in the poems of Frost—we cannot get at the subject until we master the style in all its intricate implications. Comprehension of the style is the condition on which we get the subject, which is not to be abstracted as an element separate from the poem in its absolute totality. For such poetry, what Joseph Conrad makes Marlow say about a story may well apply: the meaning of the poem is not a kernel lying at its center, but is in the wrappings that must be unfolded one by one as much as it is in the center.

The style has a distortion peculiar to modern art. The metrical system is shattered into dissonance or avoided altogether. "Prose effects" are deliberately cultivated. In some extreme instances typographical oddities are used to accent the patterns of dissonance, of divergence from the tradition. "Poeticisms" and "cliches" are avoided. Metaphor becomes intricately symbolic; and its closely woven inferential and referential scheme, worked into both the texture and the structure of the poem, puts a severe tax upon the most devoted reader's attention. The poem must be pondered like a problem; it is not made to be read aloud, but must be studied in secluded contemplation.

The total result is what may be called the "guarded style"— guarded, that is, against any suspicion of romanticism or sentimentality, and in this way made objective truth. Much of the New Criticism, particularly that part of it which has been elaborated in the essays of John Crowe Ransom, is concerned with the necessity of purging poetry of any betrayers of the art who weaken the cause by mere repetition of past conventions, or by assuming that prettiness of language, efflorescence of rhetoric, or loud assertion of laudable sentiments is enough to make poetry valid. At the heart of Mr. Ransom's statement of the case is his apprehension that science—or at least the scientific mind—is only too ready to point to poetic rhetoric as affectation and to seize upon it as evidence that poetry, as compared with science, is mere pretense and that therefore poets cannot be trusted to pronounce on the serious business of life. The style of poetry, then, must be made impregnable against such attack.

But the impregnable or guarded style, whether it precedes or follows defensive criticism, does not increase the general currency of poetry and is not intended to. The aesthetic argument does not reach a wide public. Mainly it reaches only the literary elite of poets, critics, professors of English, and the students who are electing certain courses and have to submit to it. The general public does not know that science is hostile to poetry, and furthermore harbors a suspicion, inherited from some old rumors about the behavior of Byron or Poe, that poets are queer. The guarded style does nothing to dispel the suspicion. A Virginian or Mississippian may faintly remember his Shakespeare and somewhat uncertainly essay to quote Shakespeare. He may carry in his head some distant echo of Pinckney's "I fill this cup to one made up / Of loveliness alone"; but, unless specially schooled, he may feel himself becoming a stranger to poetry when his son returns from studying under Ransom at Kenyon or Brooks at Yale and tells him that *The Dry Salvages* and *Sailing to Byzantium* are great poems, and that the following lines, also from a great poem, deal with the predicament of a young man, a modern, who is musing beside a Confederate grave-yard as Gray once mused in an English country churchyard:

Night is the beginning and the end
And in between the ends of distraction
Waits mute speculation, the patient curse
That stones the eyes, or like the jaguar leaps
For his own image in a jungle pool, his victim.

The father at this point is likely to remember only that poets are queer. His ancestors, a hundred years ago, may have indulged Mr. Poe, even though Mr. Poe was queer. But the arrangements of our time will give him little opportunity to indulge Mr. Allen Tate, whom he will probably never meet, and whose *Ode to the Confederate Dead* will not be bound in limp leather to ornament his parlor table. In fact he will have no parlor; his new dwelling is of the ranch-house design. This same father—who must be drafted here to represent the hypothetical audience of the modern poets—may also have an uneasy apprehension, if he attempts to read the books that his son brings back from Kenyon or Yale, that Messrs. Eliot, Yeats, Ransom, Tate, et al. are disagreeably reproachful toward the regime that he, the father, is committed to uphold and that he derives revenue from.

The apprehension, which somehow filters through the barrier of the obscure, guarded style, is certainly justified. Much more definitely than the Elizabethans and the Romantics, the modern poets are Ish-maelitish dissenters toward the society that they must as contemporaries inhabit. A hundred years ago John Stuart Mill took comfort from the poetry of William Wordsworth and openly confessed the fact that Wordsworth had made a new man of him. This result could hardly have been achieved by Wordsworth's verbal eloquence alone. There must have been—and indeed there was—some common metaphysical ground between Wordsworth the poet and Mill the political economist. Between the modern political—economists and the modern poets there is no such common ground. Every serious poem by Messrs. Eliot, Yeats, Frost, Tate, and their most able contemporaries is in fact a reproach, direct or implied, against the modern political economists—that is to say, the social scientists in general. It is difficult to imagine a member of the Academy of Political and Social Science as turning to these poets for restoration of spirits. The social scientists know the poets are not on their side. And even when a poet does appear on their side—as Mr. Archibald MacLeish has done—they would almost rather he wouldn't. What will people think if they have a poet in their ranks volleying verses instead of surveys?

Thus the modern defenders of poetry have lost a resource that their predecessors enjoyed. They cannot do much proselyting for poetry and cannot enlarge the area that they defend. Sometimes, frankly admitting the limitation, they are content to say that the role of poetry is now minor and that they must therefore devote themselves to the perfection of the minor poem. But in any case, they do not cease to compose poetry or to defend it. This display of valor is as necessary as it is admirable. Yet meanwhile the audience, or the age in general, flows around them and goes on about its concerns, very much as the mass armies of World War I flowed around the "strong points" of the famous Western Front, leaving them to be slowly reduced to rubble by artillery and mortar fire from the rear, or else simply to "wither on the vine."

Whether the strong points occupied by the modern poets can be held long enough to be relieved by a general counter-offensive, I would not undertake to say. But, to carry the military figure further,

I would argue that the defense of poetry has been made on too narrow a front and lacks a real defense in depth.

III

The modern defense of poetry is a defense of poetry in its literary character only. It refers to the poetry of the printed page, or even more definitely to the poetry composed *for* the printed page, the poetry received by the solitary, silent reader who ponders it in voiceless seclusion. It is a defense of poetry as a literary tradition, not of poetry as a tradition that includes, with much else, a literary tradition.

Poetry of the strictly literary tradition is a fairly new phenomenon, uncertainly developed amid the shifting hazards of post-Renaissance culture, a rare specialty that has tended to become ever more rare and more special. In the great tradition of poetry, the fact of publication, whether in manuscript books or printed books, is an incidental result, not a determining cause, of the public authority of poetry. But to the modern poets the printed page has become a determinant. This unacknowledged factor has had much to do with the form and style of modern poetry. Failure to reckon with it has caused modern poets, turned critics, to direct their defense to what is really but one small segment of the great tradition which they constantly invoke.

It is splendid for T. S. Eliot to argue that the poetry of Western civilization from Homer to the present is one continuous body of tradition into which the modern poet should strive to incorporate his own art, even if, to do so, he has to use the dubious, revolutionary means of dislocating language, syntax, and grammar. But the implied contention that *The Wasteland* extends the tradition of Homer and Dante is not valid unless the *Iliad, Odyssey,* and *Divine Comedy* are to be taken as published books, just as *The Wasteland* is a published book. But the fact that Homer's and Dante's works have been repeatedly printed does not reduce them to the status of mere books. They are much more. The essential Homer lies outside the tradition that we think of as literary, nor does the existence of manuscripts and vast libraries of annotated editions, made for practical purposes of record and study, convert the poetry of Homer into a literary poetry. Whether it was in any sense a written poetry is something of a moot question. The important thing is that the Homeric epics were composed for oral performance and that the rhapsodes memorized them and for centuries recited, declaimed, or chanted them from memory.

The epic of the great tradition is not a book in the post-Renaissance sense. The epic of Dante, standing as it does in a critical period of the Middle Ages, is more of a book than the Homeric epics are; but a purely literary tradition could not have begotten *The Divine Comedy*. Of the three great masters to whom Eliot professes close allegiance—Dante, Donne, and Baudelaire—only Baudelaire belongs wholly to the purely literary tradition and wrote books of poetry rather than composed poems. John Donne is a learned poet, but both Elizabethan drama, as a spoken medium, and Elizabethan song strongly affect his composition. He was not published as a poet in his lifetime. Shakespeare was the author of stage plays, and published no books except the minor experimental poems, *Venus and Adonis* and *The Rape of Lucrece*. His sonnets were published, but in a pirated edition, not with his consent. Chaucer may be claimed as a literary poet, but his style, so far as it actually is literary, is the style of an age that, as to poetry, was strongly influenced by nonliterary elements. A manuscript book of Chaucer's poems, like the manuscript books of classic Greece and imperial Rome, was a very different affair from a modern printed book. It can hardly be said that the form and style of Chaucer or any other pre-Renaissance poet were determined by the book as a medium of publication. All such poetry in a sense is pre-literary, for it stems from a culture in which the literary art is not yet severable from its associations with oral narrative and practical song.

This poetry is not only the poetry of tradition. It is tradition itself. If the Bible is approached as a mere book, even though it be called the Good Book, it is continually in danger of becoming only "literature." The Bible as "the Word of God" is a different thing entirely—the sacred though tangible and convenient instrument of Divine Revelation handed down as truth, and therefore in the highest sense tradition. The difference between Catholic and Protestant as to the merit of Biblical authority as such occurs, we should note, at the period when book-publication of the Bible is facilitated by the advance of printing, and this is also the period when poets, sometimes hesitantly, sometimes with only disguised reluctance, begin to write books of poetry.

The separation of poetry as literature from poetry as a tradition embodying both literary and nonliterary features begins, that is, in the late sixteenth century, when printer and publisher appear as entrepreneurs between the poet and his audience. That the separation was definitely beginning by 1557 we know from the complaint voiced by Richard Tottel in his preface to the first printed anthology of English lyric poetry: "It resteth now (gentle reder) that thou thinke it not evill doon, to publish, to the honor of the English tong, and for the profit of the studious of Englishe eloquence, those workes which the ungentle horders up of such treasure have heretofore envied thee." Mr. Hyder Rollins takes this as Tottel's complaint against the "anti-publication complex" of the Tudor poets who were courtiers or affected the manners of courtiers. But Tottel could just as well have been apologizing to the public for his impudence in printing in book form the "songs and sonnets" which everyone knew were intended for singing or for private circulation in manuscript.

The great triumphs of Elizabethan lyric poetry were the songs composed for actual performance as songs during the Golden Age of English vocal music. To recover the original texts of most of these songs, we must go either to the numerous songbooks of the period and disentangle the words, as Canon Fellowes has done, from their dispersed positions among the vocal parts; or else, with less difficulty, edit them from the songbooks of the lutanist school or from the fairly late printed editions of stage plays, masks, and interludes. The so-called antipublication complex of the poets was so firmly established that poets generally refrained from any published collection of their lyric and dramatic verses. The temptation to publish was nevertheless there, and we know that Ben Jonson, for one, yielded to it and was joked about it, if the evidence of Sir John Suckling's "A Session of the Poets," published in 1646, is to be credited:

> The first that broke silence was good old Ben,
> Prepared before with Canary wine,

> And he told them plainly he deserved the bays,
> For his were called Works, where others were but Plays.

"Works" is a literary title; "Plays" is nonliterary.

So far as literary poetry is concerned, we can trace the two tendencies, really counter to one another, yet intermingled, in the lists of songbooks and miscellanies published from 1557 to the beginning of the Puritan revolution. The songbooks, beginning in 1588 with William Byrd's *Psalms, Sonnets, and Songs,* and ending, say, with Bateson's *Second Set of Madrigals,* 1618, give us lyric poetry allied with music, in its oral, non-literary character. But the miscellanies, which contain songs without tunes, emphasize the literary character and are definitely books of poems.

It would be reasonable to assume that poetry took no great harm at first from its appearance in that great novelty, the printed book. At first the relationship of book to poem was not very different from the relationship of manuscript to poem during the previous centuries. It was a relationship of pure convenience. The printed book offered greater convenience than the manuscript and naturally had its appeal both to poet and to audience. Easy reproduction of copies by the printer's press meant extension of audience and ultimately made the poetry book an article of commerce, profitable both to author and to printer.

By the time we reach Pope, the relationship between book and poem is beginning to change. Pope was, no doubt, the first real bestseller among the poets, and therefore the first to achieve financial independence through publication. From Pope's time to ours the book becomes more and more a determinate of the poetry, with, other causes of course intermingling to sequester poetry as a purely literary art. From this time on there is hardly any survival of poetry as a non-literary or even half-literary art. Only ballad and folk song survive at the oral level to remind us that genuine poetry can flourish without benefit of publication.

It seems obvious that if the whole tradition of poetry is to be taken into account, the modern defense of poetry is very unenterprising in developing a critical strategy that serves very well to defend Dryden or Coleridge or Eliot, but that ignores the vast resources poetry had at command during the centuries and that cannot adequately defend or even fully explain the poetry which made use of those resources. In the former centuries, not only did music and sweet poetry agree, but poetry was all-penetrative, and prose was a poor second or worse in the grand competition.

In our own bookish, entirely literary age the gains of poetry are relatively small, perhaps, in proportion to its losses. The gains are chiefly in flexibility of style, and they occur mainly in the province of the short or quasi-lyrical poem, of which, from Donne to Dylan Thomas, we have a great number. This poetry now accepts the printed page as its essential medium, and it is not otherwise accessible or approachable. It is seldom quoted except in critical essays. It is all but incapable of oral dissemination. Only on the printed page can it be pondered, grasped, and absorbed. It cannot flourish widely, and in fact has no large-scale circulation now except in school and college textbooks. Therefore, it does not filter down from the highest cultural levels to the lowest, as the preliterary poetry did, nor can it, like that earlier poetry, recruit its strength by drawing upon a deep-rooted folk culture.

The losses of poetry, under the literary regime, are in fact spectacular and disheartening.

We have lost the epic entirely. In the three centuries since the appearance of Milton's *Paradise Lost* Western civilization has not produced a single great epic poem. We have had long poetical works of epical dimensions, like Goethe's *Faust*, Wordsworth's *Prelude*, Hardy's *The Dynasts*, Bridges's *The Testament of Beauty*, but not one of these is a true epic. These long poems, and all others of their character, are books that happen to be written in verse. They are distinctly literary works, quasi-dramas, quasi-essays, which project a poet's highly personal and subjective interpretation of experience. They have no capacity for existing independent of the printed page. They could not survive the tests which Homer, Vergil, and Dante have successfully endured.

Whether Milton can survive may now be doubtful. His epic, it is true, uses a highly developed literary style. Yet it is much more than a purely literary venture. If Milton, like T. S. Eliot, had had only the context of a literary tradition to support him, his epic could never have been composed. It would have been an extended verse-essay like *The Testament of Beauty* or an extended quasi-lyric like *The Wasteland*. Milton, a belated Elizabethan, was farther away from the non-literary tradition of narrative poetry than Dante, but he still felt its influence. *Paradise Lost* carries the implication of spoken performance. It was in fact first conceived as drama, and it still bears the marks of dramatic intention in its declamatory idiom—the famous "Miltonic blank verse"—and in the structure of its "scenes." Milton as music-lover also felt the alliance of poetry with its sister art, and some of his peculiar metrical practices, as Mr. William Hunter has shown, are best understood in the light of Milton's habituation to the seventeenth-century style of rendering psalms and hymns. Furthermore, since Milton the epic poet, like the Homer of fable, was blind, he dictated rather than wrote his epic.

But beyond all these considerations, which link Milton with the poetry of preliterary tradition, his epic is tradition itself in its content and impact. From it, the eighteenth-century poets abstracted some remnants of the Miltonic style—and nothing more. They failed to understand and accept it as tradition. The cause of their failure is implied in Pope's *Rape of the Lock*, the cartoon of an epic which tells us that British society was cultivating formality but losing all sense of form, with the implication now clear to us, if not to that society, that to repudiate tradition is to lose the sense of form. On the other hand, at a wider cultural level Milton's epic had the impact of tradition in giving Protestantism a certain power of visualization that austere Calvinism utterly lacked and could never impart by doctrinal means. The Heaven and Hell of Protestant England and America for some centuries have been at least as much Miltonic as scriptural in their visualized images. That the debt to Milton is unconscious is all the more a tribute to the power of genuine epic. The all-penetrative though somewhat strange compound—classical, Hebraic, Christian, and occult—of Milton's vision substitutes its own eidōla for the images of "Papist" tradition that Puritan fanaticism discarded. And so the enemies of "mythology" accept, without realizing it, an Adam and Eve, a Satan, a Michael, that Milton may almost be said to have invented. No purely literary work of the last three centuries has achieved comparable results.

In losing the epic, we have also lost narrative poetry in general. This loss has occurred gradually, but it is now definite. The short story is now the preferred vehicle for minor narratives, the novel for major narratives. Both of these rejoice in the printed book and periodical, without which they could never have developed or even come into existence.

We have lost poetic drama. Prose rather than verse has long been the accepted medium for the stage play. In its rise it exactly parallels the preference for realism and naturalism on the stage. Poetry dare not show its face in the theater except in opera—which must generally be in an Italian, French, or German libretto—or in revivals of plays composed as Shakespeare's were, when verse was the accepted medium and when drama and poetry were inseparable.

This loss of poetry as a dramatic medium begins in England, significantly, just about at the time when poetry was passing over from its preliterary period into its literary development. The perfection of dramatic verse by Shakespeare and his contemporaries is approximately coincident with the beginning of the decline of dramatic verse or, one can almost say, its abrupt extinction.

But there would seem to be no good reason to blame this attainment of perfection as itself the cause of the decline. Literary historians are not very convincing in their explanations of the shift from dramatic verse to dramatic prose; in fact they do not seem to exhibit sufficient concern over the phenomenon. In particular, they fail to note that the identification of poetry with book publication, which is definite by the time of Cowley, dissociates the art of poetry from spoken performance, and therefore from stage use. From this time on, the capacity to write verse for the stage diminishes as the capacity to write literary or bookish verse increases. Verse dramas no longer succeed on the stage. Even as literary pieces they tend to become tour de forces, and may have thin claims to merit on either literary or dramatic grounds.

In our own time, it is true, there have been some notable attempts to recover the stage for poetry. But Eliot's *Murder in the Cathedral*, for one instance, is far better as a book than as a play. Its merits are literary rather than dramatic. At a performance one is quickly aware that the poet's capacity in literary composition, concededly impressive, is interfering with rather than assisting the dramatic action. It is a patchwork of soliloquies and splendid "imaginary conversations" that offers the semblance but not the dramatic reality of a play.

Finally, we have all but completely lost the alliance of poetry with music. Poetry as practical song no longer is composed at the higher levels of art, except in grand opera. The tradition of poetry as song survives only in our heritage of folk song, secular and sacred, of the centuries past when no cultural gulf separated the true poet from the good musician, and when there was not, as now, one audience for poetry, another for music. Robert Herrick's *Advice to Virgins to Make Much of Time*, said to have been the most popular song of the seventeenth century, is a last convincing example of a good lyric by a sophisticated poet which is also a good song, current as song and not merely "read" as poetry. The period when a lyric by Sidney or Shakespeare or even Donne might, as a matter of course, be set by musicians as fine as Morley, Willbye, or Alfonso Ferrabosco was ending, of course, before Herrick's arrival. The songs of Robert Burns, more than a century later, are a recrudescence of an earlier tradition, lingering in Scotland and Ireland, but rather thoroughly stifled in England by the rise of science, commerce, industrialism, and abstraction.

By the nineteenth century the alliance between music and poetry tapers to a thin sentimental vein, as in the romantic effusions of Thomas Moore. Some of Tennyson's lyrics have had music forced upon them, but they do not "set" well. The death of the alliance is marked as certain by the emergence of the comic operas of Gilbert and Sullivan, in which parody and burlesque dominate. The songs of *Pinafore* or *The Mikado* are a far cry from any of those that Shakespeare wrote for his plays or that appear, for example, in Nash's *Summer's Last Will and Testament*. We can see that the only medium in which the English-speaking public will accept a union of the talents of Gilbert and Sullivan is a bantering, humorous, satirical medium. The old tradition must put on the mask of light comedy if it is to be accepted at all. Beyond this stage of degeneration lies only, as we know, the steady descent into vulgarization, sentimentality, and finally outright laundry and obscenity that mark popular song in our own century.

The vogue of Schubert's *lieder* may be cited as an exception to the general tendency. But a moment's reflection shows that this vogue represents a triumph of music as music rather than of music and poetry as sister arts. Heine's *Die Grenadiere* and Goethe's *Erlkonig* require the technical genius of a Schumann-Heink, accompanied by a virtuoso pianist, for full realization as art songs, and are then essentially music. They are not very accessible to amateurs; they do not survive on the popular tongue. They have had no enduring influence upon our general culture, which has been steadily drifting away from *lieder*. Goethe's lyrics, true enough, could be set as songs by a great musician, but they are actually literary exploitations of a traditional form, not poetry as tradition itself. As poems they lead a book existence quite dissociated from their occasional musical performance.

Today there are hardly any poets of merit who can or will write a literary ballad or would even consider composing a song lyric. It is unimaginable to readers of Eliot or Tate that those poets would be caught composing lyrics that actually could be used in a Rogers and Hammerstein type of Broadway musical. The distance between the literary poet of today and the jukebox might have to be measured in astronomical light-years, but it would be a fair measure of the cultural distance between the finest poetry of the twentieth century and the general audience. That is what we mean when we say our culture is falling apart.

IV

Whether the gains achieved by modern literary poetry, with its extraordinary command over nuances and hidden implications and its quality of absolute self-containment, overbalance the losses that I have enumerated, I do not undertake to say. The defense of this poetry has been well argued by Eliot, Ransom, Tate, Brooks, and other able poets and critics. Within the terms of the argument as it has been conducted for the past three decades or more, it is as conclusive as a defense can be.

There remains the question: What next?

The possibilities of poetry as a literary art seem now to have been as thoroughly explored and exploited as we could expect them to be. In that direction there are no more fields to conquer. There are no literary techniques that the modern poets do not already have at their command. In fact we may have now reached the point of diminishing returns for literary techniques as such. The poetry of the book may have reached its limit and finished its term. The publishers of books seem, to take that for granted; they no longer welcome the poets to their lists. The admission of modern poetry to the textbooks of school and college classes may be, in a sense, as much an entombment as a triumph. This is for poetry a kind of death-in-life, to exist only on the printed page, not on the lips of men, not be carried by their voices and therefore almost never carried in their memories, rarely in their hearts.

In its submission to the printed page poetry is taking the greatest risk it has ever taken—the risk of extinction. Books as instruments of record and convenience have their legitimate use, but it is of a relative nature; they are a means, not an end. As instruments of such relative character, books are highly perishable. What is imperishable in them is what passes over in to human life, unconsciously retained or consciously, even devoutly, treasured in memory and handed on from one memory to another.

The poet is not in the plight of the encyclopedist, who must be provided with his set of alphabetized volumes, periodically brought up to date in new editions, or else fail to exist. Nor is the poet in the plight of the novelist. Divorced from the book, prose fiction cannot flourish or even exist in the literary form wrought by the author; so divorced, it can survive only as a told story, which is a very different thing. What story could be remembered and told out of the printed pages of Dostoevsky, James, Proust, Joyce, or Hemingway? But poetry, like its sister arts of drama and music, can always reduce the book to its true function as an instrument of convenience and exist, even flourish, as an oral art, or as an art combining oral and literary features. The long persistence of meter, rhyme, and other formal elements of verse are the strongest parts of the proof of this great capacity. They ally poetry with memory; they are the marks of poetry that not only derives from tradition but is tradition. It is not surprising that modern poets, habituating themselves to the printed page, have often discarded entirely the formal elements of verse, or else so irregularized them that they are hardly recognizable as formal elements. But thus to bind the great art of poetry to typography is to surrender the major part of the once vast province of poetry in favor of the dubious security of the library.

A poetry that puts itself in a position not to be recited, not to be sung, hardly ever to be read aloud from the page where it stands, and almost never to be memorized, is nearing the danger edge of absurdity. It not only cannot become tradition in the large sense. It is risking the loss of the literary tradition which it now too hopefully magnifies.

In his *Idea of a Theatre* Francis Fergusson says:

> A drama, as distinguished from a lyric, is not primarily a composition in the verbal medium; the words result, as one might put it, from the underlying structure of incident and character. As Aristotle remarks, "the poet, or *maker*, should be the maker of plots rather than of verses, since he is a poet because he imitates and what he imitates are actions."

I would amend this profound observation at one point and make it read "A drama, as distinguished from a *merely literary lyric.* . . ." For the spoken or sung poem actually has many of the properties that Mr. Fergusson, following Aristotle, ascribes to drama.

There is no place for poetry to go next unless it reasserts its old independence of the book and finds a way to restore some of its former oral character. That such independence may be very difficult to regain is conceded. But that is a problem for our civilization no less than for our poetry. A civilization cannot feed in the flourish of nonperishable things. Only in perishable things at its center can give it life. Nothing is more imperishable than poetry. In comparison, the material works of science and industry are but fleeting trifles. No civilization of the past has ever lived without poetry. Our civilization can hardly be an exception.

The Sacramental South

As my final word, I think we should have found a larger word than agrarian, for it was this whole country's Christian inheritance that was threatened, and still is. But let there be no misunderstanding. We still are subjects of Christendom. Only we have reached its Satanic phase. I can't believe that any society is strong which holds physical property as its quest. There is only one comfort, and it is the only thing that has been promised: the gates of Hell will not finally prevail.

—Andrew Lytle, 1980

THE SACRAMENTAL SOUTH
INTRODUCTION

As early as 1930, Allen Tate spoke of the South in religious terms. In his objection to the title *I'll Take My Stand*, he pointed to the broader significance of the kind of culture the Agrarians wanted to preserve, and his essay for the volume spoke of the inadequacy of Southern religion to sustain that way of life after a military defeat. He argued that the Old South was "a feudal society without a feudal religion."[1] Although Southern politicians could quote scripture to justify slavery, the Old South "tried to encompass its destiny within the terms of Protestantism, in origin, a non-agrarian and trading religion; hardly a religion at all, but a result of secular ambition."[2] But if not Protestantism, what? Probably no suggestion (except for immediate integration of the races) could have more offended feeling in the South, but Tate clearly points to Catholicism, especially the medieval Church, as the missing element in the Old South, and he lays out the problem with a lucid analysis:

> They [antebellum Southerners] had a religious life, but it was not
> enough organized with a right mythology. In fact, their rational life
> was not powerfully united to the religious experience, as it was in

1. Allen Tate, "Remarks on the Southern Religion." From Twelve Southerners, *I'll Take My Stand: The South and the Agrarian Tradition* (Baton Rouge: Louisiana State University Press, 1977), 166.
2. Ibid., 168.

medieval society, and they are a fine specimen of the tragic pitfall upon which the Western mind has always hovered. Lacking a rational system for the defense of their religious attitude and its base in a feudal society, they elaborated no rational system whatever, no full-grown philosophy; so that, when the post-bellum temptations of the devil, who is the exploiter of nature, confronted them, they had no defense. Since there is, in the Western mind, a radical division between the religious, the contemplative, the qualitative, on the one hand, and the scientific, the natural, the practical on the other, the scientific mind always plays havoc with the spiritual life when it is not powerfully enlisted in its cause; it cannot be permitted to operate alone.[3]

Both Robert Brinkmeyer and Peter A. Huff have shown the influence of the antimodernist thinkers of the Catholic Revival on Tate at this early stage of his thought.[4] Already, at the time of the Agrarian movement, he saw that what was best in the South pointed beyond itself toward a civilization with a philosophically and theologically grounded doctrine.

Everything in his view of an integrated culture—especially given the example of T. S. Eliot—depended on religion. Ironically, though, he remained incapable of faith. In 1929, when he wrote to Donald Davidson from Paris, "I am more and more heading towards Catholicism," Tate's actual conversion was still two decades in the future. The reasons that he gave Davidson seem almost entirely intellectual: "We have reached a condition of the spirit where no further compromise is possible. That is the lesson taught us by the Victorians who failed to unite naturalism and the religious spirit; we've got to do away with one or the other; and I can never capitulate to naturalism."[5] But Catholicism also attracted him because it was so embedded in an organic way of life already for the most part lost in America, but certainly

3. Tate, "Remarks," 173.
4. Robert H. Brinkmeyer Jr., *Three Catholic Writers of the Modern South* (Oxford, MS: University of Mississippi Press, 2000). Peter A. Huff, *Allen Tate and The Catholic Revival* (Mahwah, NJ: Paulist Press, 1996).
5. Donald Davidson and Allen Tate. *The Literary Correspondence of Donald Davidson and Allen Tate*, John Tyree Fain and Thomas Daniel Young, eds. (Athens, GA: University of Georgia Press, 1974), 223.

enjoyed at times in the American South and still present as well in rural France—for example, in the faith of Félicité, the heroine of Flaubert's "A Simple Heart."

In a letter to Andrew Lytle, Tate describes the picnic at Cassis in southern France that became the basis of his poem *The Mediterranean*. Not only was the location spectacular—"a calanque, or deep gorge where the water was like a lake, and perfectly transparent at a depth of thirty feet and where the cliffs, almost, perpendicular rise for three hundred feet"—but they enjoyed a meal, a "peasant's feast," of seven successive courses prepared by a local cook, "the fourteenth recorded generation of his family, who have always been small landowners."[6] The wine they drank (the best in Provence, not for sale) was made by another old peasant in the neighborhood, and Tate describes at length the courteous leave-taking of this old man: "He was like a shepherd in Theocritus, and indeed I felt afterwards that this same feast had been given in that same place since the time of Homer. There has never been a machine age in Southern France and there never will be. It appears that the reason why the peasants are so fine down here is their complete independence. France as a nation and the political organization of Europe may fall, but these people will never change."[7]

Was it because their Catholicism sustained them? Tate does not make the argument here; he simply notes that, unlike those in the New South of his day, the peasants of southern France retain their way of life, untempted by technology: "And that's why our notion is right—independence on the land. And that is why France is our model for that idea at the present time. I intend to study this subject in order to write about it effectively: their idea here is the same as ours—the land not for profit but for enjoyment of civilized life."[8]

Tate's wife, Caroline Gordon, converted to Catholicism in 1947, three years before Tate did. Her trajectory, which certainly influenced his own, centers on the gradual discovery of an underlying narrative of redemption. In an important essay on Caroline Gordon's fiction published in 1957, Louise Cowan pointed out a defining feature of the

6. Andrew Lytle and Allen Tate, *The Lytle-Tate Letters*, Thomas Daniel Young and Elizabeth Sarcone, eds. (Oxford, MS: University of Mississippi Press, 1987), 40.
7. Ibid.
8. Ibid.

South that perhaps began to be evident only with the work of Gordon and Tate in the late 1940s and early 1950s—about the same time that Flannery O'Connor, Gordon's disciple in the art of fiction, began to make her mark.

> Modern Southern writers in general have regarded their task as the discovery of an already existent pattern in actual experience rather than as the imposition of an ideal pattern upon experience. Their unanimity of attitude is not traceable to a conscious aesthetic (for there has been no traditional Southern theory of art), but to an instinctively coherent way of dealing with the world, a way inherited from their culture and underlying their own personal vision of life. This worldview can best be described, I think, by the word "*sacramental*," since it is a way of looking at the physical universe as existing both in its own right and as a sign. But, to the Southerner, matter is not in any simple fashion an embodiment of spirit. Objects and creatures are real in themselves, and yet they are also mysteries, reflecting God and each other in a network of resemblances which at times illumine and at times veil the relationship between the creator and his creations. The mode of thought resulting from this attitude is analogical, and, though it is of course far older than the American South, it is not encountered consistently elsewhere in literature written in English since the seventeenth century.[9]

Notably, Cowan does not restrict this description of the world's significant givenness to Southern *Catholic* writers. It is always implicit. Ransom's view of the image in its ontology of "rich and contingent materiality," for example, becomes more fully comprehensible in this context, both as Southern and as more than Southern. Opposition to industrial technology, also known as "the devil, who is the exploiter of nature," as Tate puts it, comes into perspective as well. One does not exploit a world one understands as sacramental.

Over half a century after Tate described the peasants at Cassis, Andrew Lytle wrote the foreword to *The Southern Mandarins*, the

9. Louise Cowan, "Nature and Grace in Caroline Gordon." From *Studies in Medieval, Renaissance, American Literature: A Festschrift*, Betsy Colquitt, ed. (Fort Worth: Texas Christian University Press, 1971), 173.

collection of letters that Caroline Gordon wrote to her friend Sally Wood in the 1920s and 1930s. In it, Lytle recollects that the twelve contributors to *I'll Take My Stand* "by common agreement saw what was needed: to restore what was lost, if possible, and restrain further subversion of not only southern but the general well-being. They reaffirmed the history of their inherited European culture. It had a name, but the name had fallen into disuse. It was, of course, Christendom."[10] It took several decades, but as he came to recognize the sacramental vision implicit in the South, Tate's understanding of the Old South as half of a whole that would have been completed by Catholic doctrine emerges in a different light, now "thingly," full of *dinglichkeit*: things point beyond themselves when they most intensely dwell in their own natures. They cannot otherwise be what they are. In their being present, they bear the traces of presence itself, as Thomas Aquinas taught. The world's body is always a sign, capable of bearing within it a Dantean richness of meaning, a manifold of levels. Tate's own movement fully into this recognition comes in his essay "The Symbolic Imagination," especially in his startling comparison of St. Catherine of Siena's sacramental faith to the poetic practice of Dante. But crucial to his understanding as well is the contrast with Poe, the displaced Southerner who perfectly embodies—or disembodies—the "angelism" whose nature Tate learned from Jacques Maritain. Caroline Gordon's "Some Readings and Misreadings" not only insists upon the artist's "patient, passionate portrayal of natural objects," but also implicitly points to a way of understanding the South "in hope." Flannery O'Connor's "The Catholic Novelist in the Protestant South," compiled from two lectures, adds to the central vision of the South as a potent, densely symbolic given.

10. Sally Wood, *The Southern Mandarins: Letters of Caroline Gordon to Sally Wood, 1937–1944* (Baton Rouge: Louisiana State University Press, 1984), 4.

13

OUR COUSIN, MR. POE[1]

ALLEN TATE

During a long period of illness in his childhood, Allen Tate immersed himself in the strange, suffocating world of Edgar Allan Poe, the greatest Southern writer of the nineteenth century. Not only did he read the famous poems and the short stories with their premature burials, their imploding psychic worlds, their various horrors of vampirism, but he plunged with relish into Poe's theoretical works, such as The Colloquy of Monos and Una *and* Eureka. *Not until he approached fifty did Tate actually manage to address the whole force of Poe within his imagination, and he was able to do so then in his two major essays on Poe only because his friend Jacques Maritain had supplied him with the concept he needed: "angelism."[2] Tate sees in Poe an heir of Cartesian thought who made an exemplary attempt to treat even mortality itself as a weak concession to convention, one to be overcome by an amplified assertion of the will. Lovers in Poe, rather like the Catharist heretics in Denis de Rougemont's* Love in the Western World, *try to circumvent the specific limitations of the*

1. [Tate] Address delivered before the Poe Society of Baltimore on the centenary of Poe's death (October 7, 1949), and repeated as a Bergen lecture at Yale University (November 14, 1949).
2. "Science as Descartes conceives it is a human science which would be at the same time divine by revelation, or better still, would be the very science of God and of the Angels. If this be so, it is no doubt by virtue of the idealism, and if I may use the word, of *the angelism* which in general characterizes Cartesian philosophy." Jacques Maritain, *The Dream of Descartes*, trans. Mabelle Anderson (New York: Philosophical Library, 1944) 28.

body and seize upon each other's essences as an act of power. This analogue to the modern scientific project—splitting the atom comes to mind—Tate calls "the angelic imagination."

In "Forms and Citizens," John Crowe Ransom describes a version of this tendency as "predatory," but in his analysis, "[t]he fierce drives of the animals, whether human or otherwise, are only toward a kind of thing, the indifferent instance of a universal, and not some private and irreplaceable thing." Tate sees in Poe a refinement of such drives. Roderick Usher desires the "private and irreplaceable" Madeleine, but in an anti-incarnational sense, as though the essence of the other could only be seized and devoured by circumventing, even debasing (as death debases) the physical body. Poe in this sense anticipates such figures as Michel Foucault, for whom sexual transgression becomes a violent dare that reveals "the limitless reign of the limit," the absence of transcendence. For those no longer capable of finding existence a sign of Existence-in-itself, the body—indeed, the world's body—becomes the means of a metaphysical revenge against the Being who fails to exist but who will nevertheless not allow them to take his place.

When I was about fourteen there were in our house, along with the novels of John Esten Cooke, E. P. Roe, and Augusta Evans, three small volumes of Edgar Allan Poe. That, by my reckoning, was a long time ago. Even then the books were old and worn, whether from use (I suppose not) or from neglect, it did not occur to me to inquire. I remember, or imagine I remember, the binding, which was blue, and the size, which was small, and the paper, which was yellow and very thin. One volume contained the poems, prefaced by Lowell's famous "biography." In this volume I am sure, for I read it more than the others, was the well-known, desperate, and asymmetrical photograph, which I gazed at by the hour and which I hoped that I should some day resemble. Another volume contained most, or at least the most famous, of the tales: "Ligeia," which I liked best (I learned in due time that Poe had, too); "Morella" and "William Wilson," which I now like

best; and "The Fall of the House of Usher," which was a little spoiled
for me even at fourteen by the interjection of the "Mad Tryst of Sir
Launcelot Canning." Perhaps it was in this volume that I admired
"Marginalia," the first "criticism" I remember reading; but I did not
discern either the bogus erudition or the sense of high literature which
Poe was the first American to distinguish from entertainment and self-
improvement through books; the merits as well as the defects went
over my head. "Marginalia" could not at any rate have been in the
third volume, which was given to a single long work: *Eureka—A Prose
Poem*. This astrophilosophical discourse, which the late Paul Valéry
took more seriously than any English or American critic ever did, fell
in with my readings in popular astronomical books. In the backyard I
arranged in a straight line peas, cherries, and oranges, in the proportionate sizes and distances of the sun and planets, and some hundreds
of feet away (an inch perhaps to a thousand light-years) an old volley-
ball of my elder brothers' to represent Alpha Lyrae.

Later, on another occasion, I expect to examine *Eureka* at length,
as I read it now, not as I read it at fourteen; yet before I leave it I
must mention two other circumstances of my boyhood reading and
the feeling that accompanied it. It lives for me as no later experience
of ideas lives, because it was the first I had. The "proposition" that Poe
undertook to demonstrate has come back to me at intervals in the past
thirty-six years with such unpredictable force that now I face it with
mingled resignation and dismay. I can write it without looking it up:

> In the original unity of the first thing lies the secondary cause of all
> things, with the germ of their inevitable annihilation.

This is not the place to try to say what Poe meant by it. I could not, at
fourteen, have guessed what it meant even after I had read the book;
yet it is a fact of my boyhood (which I cannot suppose unique) that
this grandiose formula for cosmic cataclysm became a part of my consciousness through no effort of my own but seemed to come to me like
a dream, and came back later, like a nursery rhyme, or a tag from a
popular song, unbidden.

The other circumstance I am surer of because it was a visible fact, a
signature in faded brown ink on the fly leaf of *Eureka*: It told me years

later that the three volumes had been printed earlier than 1870, the year the man who had owned them died. He was my great-grandfather. My mother had said, often enough, or on some occasion that fixed it in memory, that her grandfather had "known Mr. Poe." (She was of the era when all eminent men, living or recently dead, were "Mr.") I knew as a boy that my great-grandfather had been a "poet," and in 1930 I found some of his poems, which I forbear to discuss. He had for a while been editor of the *Alexandria Gazette* at about the time of Mr. Poe's death. Both were "Virginians," though Virginians of somewhat different schools and points of view. I can see my great-grandfather in Poe's description of a preacher who called upon him in the summer of 1848: "He stood smiling and bowing at the madman Poe."

I have brought together these scattered memories of my first reading of a serious writer because in discussing any writer, or in coming to terms with him, we must avoid the trap of mere abstract evaluation, and try to reproduce the actual conditions of our relation to him. It would be difficult for me to take Poe up, "study" him, and proceed to a critical judgment. One may give these affairs the look of method, and thus deceive almost everybody but oneself. In reading Poe we are not brought up against a large, articulate scheme of experience, such as we see adumbrated in Hawthorne or Melville, which we may partly sever from personal association, both in the writer and in ourselves. Poe surrounds us with Eliot's "wilderness of mirrors," in which we see a subliminal self endlessly repeated, or, turning, a new posture of the same figure. It is not too harsh, I think, to say that it is stupid to suppose that by "evaluating" this forlorn demon in the glass, we dispose of him. For Americans, perhaps for most modern men, he is with us like a dejected cousin: We may "place" him but we may not exclude him from our board. This is the recognition of a relationship, almost of the blood, which we must in honor acknowledge: what destroyed him is potentially destructive of us. Not only this; we must acknowledge another obligation, if, like most men of my generation, we were brought up in houses where the works of Poe took their easy place on the shelf with the family Shakespeare and the early novels of Ellen Glasgow. This is the obligation of loyalty to one's experience: He was in our lives and we cannot pretend that he was not. Not even Poe's great power in Europe is quite so indicative of his peculiar "place" as his unquestioned, if unexamined, acceptance among ordinary gentle people whose literary culture was not highly developed. The horrors of Poe created not a tremor in the bosom of young ladies or a moment's anxiety in the eyes of vigilant mothers. I suppose the gentlemen of the South did not read him much after his time; in his time, they could scarcely have got the full sweep and depth of the horror. Nothing that Mr. Poe wrote, it was said soon after his death, could bring a blush to the cheek of the purest maiden.

But I doubt that maidens read very far in the tales. If they had they would have found nothing to disconcert the image that Miss Susan Ingram recorded from a visit of Poe to her family a few weeks before his death:

> Although I was only a slip of a girl and he what seemed to me then quite an old man, and a great literary one at that, we got on together beautifully. He was one of the most courteous gentlemen I have ever seen, and that gave great charm to his manner. None of his pictures that I have ever seen look like the picture of Poe that I keep in my memory . . . there was something in his face that is in none of them. Perhaps it was in the eyes.

If he was a madman he was also a gentleman. Whether or not we accept Mr. Krutch's theory,[3] we know, as this sensible young lady knew, that she was quite safe with him. A gentleman? Well, his manners were exemplary (when he was not drinking) and to the casual eye at any rate his exalted idealization of Woman (even of some very foolish women) was only a little more humorless, because more intense, than the standard cult of Female Purity in the Old South.

What Mr. Poe on his own had done with the cult it was not possible then to know. A gentleman and a Southerner, he was not quite, perhaps, a Southern gentleman. The lofty intellect of Ligeia, of Madeline, of Berenice, or of Eleanora, had little utility in the social and economic structure of Virginia, which had to be perpetuated through the issue of the female body, while the intellect, which was public and political, remained under the supervision of the gentlemen. Although Morella had a child (Poe's only heroine, I believe, to be so compromised), she

---

3. [Tate] The theory that Poe was sexually impotent.

was scarcely better equipped than Virginia Clemm herself to sustain more than the immaculate half of the vocation of the Southern lady. "But the fires," writes Morella's narrator-husband, "were not of Eros." And we know, at the end of the story, that the daughter is no real daughter but, as Morella's empty "tomb" reveals, Morella herself come back as a vampire to wreak upon her "lover" the vengeance due him. Why is it due him? Because, quite plainly, the lover lacked, as he always lacked with his other heroines, the "fires of Eros." The soul of Morella's husband "burns with fires it had never before known . . . and bitter and tormenting to my spirit was the gradual conviction that I could in no manner define their unusual meaning, or regulate their vague intensity." Perhaps in the soul of John Randolph alone of Virginia gentlemen strange fires burned. The fires that were not of Eros were generally for the land and oratory, and the two fires were predictably regulated.

Poe's strange fire is his leading visual symbol, but there is not space in an essay to list all its appearances. You will see it in the eye of the Raven; in "an eye large, liquid, and luminous beyond comparison," of Roderick Usher; in the burning eye of the old man in "The Tell-Tale Heart"; in "Those eyes! those large, those shining, those divine orbs," of the Lady Ligeia. Poe's heroes and heroines are always burning with a hard, gem-like flame—a bodyless exaltation of spirit that Poe himself seems to have carried into the drawing room, where its limited visibility was sufficient guarantee of gentlemanly behavior. But privately, and thus, for him, publicly, in his stories, he could not "regulate its vague intensity."

I cannot go into this mystery here as fully as I should like; yet I may, I think, ask a question: Why did not Poe use explicitly the universal legend of the vampire? Perhaps some instinct for aesthetic distance made him recoil from it; perhaps the literal, businesslike way the vampire went about making its living revolted the "ideality" of Poe. At any rate D. H. Lawrence was no doubt right in describing as vampires his women characters; the men, soon to join them as "undead," have, by some defect of the moral will, made them so.

The mysterious exaltation of spirit which is invariably the unique distinction of his heroes and heroines is not quite, as I have represented it, bodyless. *It inhabits a human body but that body is dead. The spirits prey upon one another with destructive fire which is at once pure of lust and infernal.* All Poe's characters represent one degree or another in a movement towards an archetypal condition: the survival of the soul in a dead body; but only in "The Facts in the Case of Monsieur Valdemar" is the obsessive subject explicit.

In none of the nineteenth-century comment on "The Fall of the House of Usher" that I have read, and in none of our own period, is there a feeling of shock, or even of surprise, that Roderick Usher is in love with his sister: the relation not being physical, it is "pure." R. H. Stoddard, the least sympathetic of the serious early biographers, disliked Poe's morbidity, but admitted his purity. The American case against Poe, until the first World War, rested upon his moral indifference, or his limited moral range. The range is limited, but there is no indifference; there is rather a compulsive, even a profound, interest in a moral problem of universal concern. His contemporaries could see in the love stories neither the incestuous theme nor what it meant, because it was not represented literally. The theme and its meaning as I see them are unmistakable: The symbolic compulsion that drives through, and beyond, physical incest moves towards the extinction of the beloved's will in complete possession, not of her body, but of her being; there is the reciprocal force, returning upon the lover, of self-destruction. Lawrence shrewdly perceived the significance of Poe's obsession with incestuous love. Two persons of the least dissimilarity offer the least physical resistance to mutual participation in the *fire* of a common being. Poe's most casual reader perceives that his lovers never do anything but contemplate each other, or pore upon the rigmarole of preposterously erudite, ancient books, most of which never existed. They are living in each other's insides, in the hollows of which burns the fire of will and intellect.

The fire is a double symbol; it lights and it burns. It is overtly the "light" of reason but as action it becomes the consuming fire of the abstract intellect, without moral significance, which invades the being of the beloved. It is the fire that, having illuminated, next destroys. Lawrence is again right in singling out for the burden of his insight the epigraph to "Ligeia," which Poe had quoted from Glanvill: "Man does not yield himself to the angels, nor unto death utterly, save through the weakness of his own feeble will." Why do these women of monstrous will and intellect turn into vampires? Because, according to Lawrence, the lovers have not subdued them through the body to the biological level, at which sanity alone is possible, and they retaliate by devouring their men. This view is perhaps only partly right. I suspect that the destruction works both ways, that the typical situation in Poe is more complex than Lawrence's version of it.

If we glance at "The Fall of the House of Usher" we shall be struck by a singular feature of the catastrophe. Bear in mind that Roderick and Madeline are brother and sister, and that the standard hyperaesthesia of the Poe hero acquires in Roderick a sharper reality than in any of the others, except perhaps William Wilson. His naked sensitivity to sound and light is not "regulated" to the forms of the human situation; it is a mechanism operating apart from the moral consciousness. We have here something like a capacity for mere sensation, as distinguished from sensibility, which in Usher is atrophied. In terms of the small distinction that I am offering here, sensibility keeps us in the world; sensation locks us into the self, feeding upon the disintegration of its objects and absorbing them into the void of the ego. The lover, circumventing the body into the secret being of the beloved, tries to convert the spiritual object into an object of sensation: The intellect which knows and the will which possesses are unnaturally turned upon that center of the beloved which should remain inviolate.

As the story of Usher opens, the Lady Madeline is suffering from a strange illness. She dies. Her brother has, of course, possessed her inner being, and killed her; or thinks he has, or at any rate wishes to think that she is dead. This is all a little vague: Perhaps he has deliberately entombed her alive, so that she will die by suffocation—a symbolic action for extinction of being. Why has he committed this monstrous crime? Sister though she is, she is nevertheless not entirely identical with him: She has her own otherness, of however slight degree, resisting his hypertrophied will. He puts her alive, though "cataleptic," into the "tomb." (Poe never uses graves, only tombs, except in "Premature Burial." His corpses, being half dead, are thus only half buried; they rise and walk again.) After some days Madeline breaks out of the tomb and confronts her brother in her bloody cerements. This is the way Poe presents the scene:

. . ."Is she not hurrying to upbraid me for my haste? Have I not heard her footsteps on the stair? Do I not distinguish the heavy and horrible beating of her heart? Madman!"—here he sprang furiously to his feet, and shrieked out his syllables, as if in his effort he were giving up his soul—"Madman! *I tell you that she now stands without the door!*"

As if in the superhuman energy of his utterance there had been found the potency of a spell, the huge antique panels to which the speaker pointed threw slowly back, upon the instant, their ponderous and ebony jaws. It was the work of the rushing gust—, but then without those doors there *did* stand the lofty and enshrouded figure of the Lady Madeline of Usher. There was blood upon her white robes, and the evidence of some bitter struggle upon every portion of her emaciated frame. For a moment she remained trembling to and fro upon the threshold—then, with a low moaning cry, fell heavily inward upon the person of her brother, and in her violent and now final death-agonies, bore him to the floor a corpse, and a victim to the terrors he had anticipated.

Madeline, back from the tomb, neither dead nor alive, is in the middle state of the unquiet spirit of the vampire, whose heart beats are "heavy and horrible." There is no evidence that Poe knew any anthropology; yet in some legends of vampirism the undead has a sluggish pulse, or none at all. In falling prone upon her brother she takes the position of the vampire suffocating its victim in a sexual embrace. By these observations I do not suggest that Poe was conscious of what he was doing; had he been, he might have done it even worse. I am not saying, in other words, that Poe is offering us, in the Lady Madeline, a vampire according to Bram Stoker's specifications. An imagination of any power at all will often project its deepest assumptions about life in symbols that duplicate, without the artist's knowledge, certain meanings, the origins of which are sometimes as old as the race. If a writer ambiguously exalts the "spirit" over the "body," and the spirit must live wholly upon another spirit, some version of the vampire legend is likely to issue as the symbolic situation.

Although the action is reported by a narrator, the fictional point of view is that of Usher: It is all seen through his eyes. But has Madeline herself not also been moving towards the cataclysmic end in the enveloping action outside the frame of the story? Has not her *will to know* done its reciprocal work upon the inner being of her brother? Their very birth had violated their unity of being. They must achieve spiritual identity in mutual destruction. The physical symbolism of the fissured house, of the miasmic air, and of the special order of nature surrounding the House of Usher and conforming to the laws of the spirits inhabiting it—all this supports the central dramatic situation, which moves towards spiritual unity through disintegration.

In the original unity of the first thing lies the secondary cause of all things, with the germ of their inevitable annihilation.

Repeated here, in the context of the recurrent subject of the tales, the thesis of *Eureka* has a sufficient meaning and acquires something of the dignity that Valéry attributed to it. Professor Quinn adduces quotations from mathematical physicists to prove that Poe, in *Eureka*, was a prophet of science. It is a subject on which I am not entitled to an opinion. But even if Professor Quinn is right, the claim is irrelevant, and is only another version of the attempt today to make religion and the arts respectable by showing that they are semi-scientific. Another sort of conjecture seems to me more profitable: that in the history of the moral imagination in the nineteenth century, Poe occupies a special place. No other writer in England or the United States, or, so far as I know, in France, went so far as Poe in his vision of dehumanized man.

His characters are, in the words of William Wilson's double, "dead to the world"; they are machines of sensation and will, with correspondences, in the physical universe, to particles and energy. Poe's engrossing obsession in *Eureka* with the cosmic destiny of man issued in a quasi-cosmology, a more suitable extension of his vision than any mythology, homemade or traditional, could have offered him. The great mythologies are populous worlds, but a cosmology need have nobody in it. In Poe's, the hyperaesthetic egoist has put all other men into his void: He is alone in the world, and thus dead to it. If we place Poe against the complete Christian imagination of Dante, whom he resembles in his insistence upon a cosmic extension of the moral predicament, the limits of his range are apparent, and the extent of his insight within those limits. The quality of Poe's imagination can be located, as I see it, in only two places in Dante's entire scheme of the after-life: Cantos XIII and XXXII of the *Inferno*. In Canto XIII, the Harpies feed upon the living trees enclosing the shades of suicides—those "violent against themselves," who will not resume their bodies at the Resurrection, for "man may not have what he takes from himself." In XXXII, we are in Caïna, the ninth circle, where traitors to their kin lie half buried in ice, up to the pubic shadow—"where the doleful shades were . . . sounding with their teeth like storks." Unmotivated treachery, for the mere intent of injury, and self-violence are Poe's obsessive subjects. He has neither Purgatory nor Heaven; and only two stations in Hell.

Let me turn briefly to the question of Poe's style. He has several styles, and it is not possible to damn them all at once. The critical style, which I shall not be able to examine here, is on occasion the best; he is a lucid and dispassionate expositor, he is capable of clear and rigorous logic (even from mistaken premises, as in "The Rationale of Verse"), when he is not warped by envy or the desire to flatter. He is most judicial with his peers, least with his inferiors, whom he either overestimates or wipes out. As for the fictional style, it, too, varies; it is perhaps at its sustained best, in point of sobriety and restraint, in the tales of deduction. Exceptions to this observation are "Descent into the Maelstrom," *The Narrative of Arthur Gordon Pym*, and perhaps one or two others in a genre which stems from the eighteenth-century "voyage." These fictions demanded a Defoe-like verisimilitude which was apparently beyond his reach when he dealt with his obsessive theme. Again I must make an exception: "William Wilson," one of the serious stories (by serious, I mean an ample treatment of the obsession), is perspicuous in diction and on the whole credible in realistic detail. I quote a paragraph:

> The extensive enclosure was irregular in form, having many capacious recesses. Of these, three or four of the largest constituted the play-ground. It was level, and covered with a hard fine gravel. I well remember it had no trees, nor benches, nor anything similar within it. Of course it was in the rear of the house. In front lay a small parterre, planted with box and other shrubs, but through this sacred division we passed only upon rare occasions indeed—such as a first advent to school or a final departure hence, or perhaps, when a par-

ent or a friend having called upon us, we joyfully took our way home for the Christmas or midsummer holidays.

It is scarcely great prose, but it has an eighteenth-century directness, and even elegance, of which Poe was seldom capable in his stories. I surmise that the playground at Dr. Bransby's school at Stoke-Newington, where, as a child, he was enrolled for five years, recalled one of the few periods of his life which he could detach from the disasters of manhood and face with equanimity. Now a part of the description of the lady Ligeia:

> . . . I examined the contour of the lofty and pale forehead—it was faultless—how cold indeed that word when applied to a majesty so divine!—the skin rivalling the purest ivory, the commanding extent and repose, the gentle prominence of the regions above the temples; and the raven-black, the glossy, the luxuriant, the naturally curling tresses, setting forth the full force of the Homeric epithet, "hyacinthine." I looked at the delicate outline of the nose.

But I refrain. It is easy enough to agree with Aldous Huxley and Yvor Winters, and dismiss this sort of ungrammatical rubbish as too vulgar, or even too idiotic, to reward the time it takes to point it out. But if Poe is worth understanding at all (I assume that he is), we might begin by asking why the writer of the lucid if not very distinguished passage from "William Wilson" repeatedly fell into the bathos of "Ligeia." I confess that Poe's serious style at its typical worst makes the reading of more than one story at a sitting an almost insuperable task. The Gothic glooms, the Venetian interiors, the ancient wine cellars (from which nobody ever enjoys a vintage but always drinks "deep")—all this, done up in a glutinous prose, so fatigues one's attention that with the best will in the world one gives up, unless one gets a clue to the power underlying the flummery.

I have tried in the course of these remarks to point in the direction in which the clue, as I see it, is to be found. I do not see it in the influence of the Gothic novel. This was no doubt there; but no man is going to use so much neo-Gothic, over and over again, unless he means business with it; I think that Poe meant business. If the Gothic influence had not been to hand, he would have invented it, or something equally "unreal" to serve his purpose. His purpose in laying on the thick decor was to simulate sensation. Poe's sensibility, for reasons that I cannot surmise here, was almost completely impoverished. He could feel little but the pressure of his predicament, and his perceptual powers remained undeveloped. Very rarely he gives us a real perception because he is not interested in anything that is alive. Everything in Poe is dead: the houses, the rooms, the furniture, to say nothing of nature and of human beings. He is like a child—all appetite without sensibility; but to be in manhood all appetite, all will, without sensibility, is to be a monster: To feed spiritually upon men without sharing with them a real world is spiritual vampirism. The description of Ligeia's head is that of a dead woman's.

Does it explain anything to say that this is necrophilism? I think not. Poe's prose style, as well as certain qualities of his verse,[4] expresses the kind of "reality" to which he had access: I believe I have indicated that it is a reality sufficiently terrible. In spite of an early classical education and a Christian upbringing, he wrote as if the experience of these traditions had been lost: He was well ahead of his time. He could not relate his special reality to a wider context of insights—a discipline that might have disciplined his prose. From the literary point of view he combined the primitive and the decadent: primitive, because he had neither history nor the historical sense; decadent, because he was the conscious artist of an intensity which lacked moral perspective.

But writers tend to be what they are; I know of no way to make one kind into another. It may have been a condition of Poe's genius that his ignorance should have been what it was. If we read him as formal critics we shall be ready to see that it was another condition of his genius that he should never produce a poem or a story without blemishes, or a critical essay that, despite its acuteness in detail, does not evince provincialism of judgment and lack of knowledge. We must bear in

---

4. [Tate] Poe's verse rhythms are for the metronome, not the human ear. Their real defects are so great that it is not necessary to invent others, as Mr. T. S. Eliot seems to do in *From Poe to Valéry* (New York, 1949). Thus Mr. Eliot (and I cite only one of his observations that seem to me wrong) complains that "the saintly days of yore" could not be an appropriate time for the raven to have lived. Elijah was fed by ravens, a bird which was almost extinct in America in the 1840s. Ravens frequently fed hermits and saints and were in fact a fairly standard feature of saintly equipment.

mind Mr. Eliot's remark that Poe must be viewed as a whole. Even the fiction and the literary journalism that seem without value add to his massive impact upon the reader.

What that impact is today upon other readers I cannot pretend to know. It has been my limited task to set forth here a little of what one reader finds in him, and to acknowledge in his works the presence of an incentive (again, for one man) to self-knowledge. I do not hesitate to say that had Poe not written *Eureka*, I should have been able, a man of this age, myself to formulate a proposition of "inevitable annihilation." I can only invite others to a similar confession. Back of the preceding remarks lies an ambitious assumption, about the period in which we live, which I shall not make explicit. It is enough to say that, if the trappings of Poe's nightmare strike us as tawdry, we had better look to our own. That particular vision in its purity (Poe was very pure) is perhaps not capable of anything better than Mr. Poe's ludicrous decor. Nor have persons eating one another up and calling it spiritual love often achieved a distinguished style either in doing it or in writing about it. It was not Ugolino, it was Dante who wrote about Ugolino with more knowledge than Ugolino had. Mr. Poe tells us in one of his simple poems that from boyhood he had "a demon in my view." Nobody then—my great-grandfather, my mother, three generations—believed him. It is time we did. I confess that his voice is so near that I recoil a little, lest he, Montressor, lead me into the cellar, address me as Fortunato, and wall me up alive. I should join his melancholy troupe of the undead, whose voices are surely as low and harsh as the grating teeth of storks. He is so close to me that I am sometimes tempted to enter the mists of pre-American genealogy to find out whether he may not actually be my cousin.

14

THE SYMBOLIC IMAGINATION

ALLEN TATE

Perhaps his most unforgettable essay—the passage about St. Catherine of Siena remains profoundly shocking after many readings—Allen Tate's "The Symbolic Imagination" might have been called "The Analogical Imagination" or "The Sacramental Imagination." Flannery O'Connor was once taken by some friends to have dinner with the lapsed Catholic Mary McCarthy, who said that she now understood the Eucharist as "a symbol," implying that it was "a pretty good one." As O'Connor wrote to Elizabeth Hester, "I then said, in a very shaky voice, 'Well, if it's a symbol, to hell with it.'"[1]

Tate had his reasons for the term, though, even in an essay about Dante, who was famous for allegory. In 1953, two years after "The Symbolic Imagination" was published, Tate wrote to Donald Davidson about his terza rima poem The Buried Lake, *"What I've been trying for in the past five or six years of practice is an approach to the objective analogical method which dominated poetry up into the Renaissance—in which what looks to us today like metaphor was actually a generally accepted relation between the physical world and the invisible." Acknowledging that no such relation existed today, Tate went on, "All that I can do is to try to tone the language down and to juxtapose objects in such a way as to make them symbolic*

---

1. Flannery O'Connor, *The Habit of Being: Letters of Flannery O'Connor*, Sally Fitzgerald, ed. (New York: Farrar Straus Giroux, 1979), 125.

objects while remaining in the full sense physical objects."[2] The modern world, in other words, can accept "symbolic objects" as it can accept "the symbolic imagination," but Tate's real intention is to bring Dantean analogy back into play. Tate's fascination with Dante, like his attraction to Catholicism, informs his whole career both as a critic and as a poet, and this brilliant essay on Dante's mirrors represents a critical culmination.

THE MIRRORS OF DANTE

It is right even if it is not quite proper to observe, at the beginning of a discourse on Dante, that no writer has held in mind at one time the whole of *The Divine Comedy*: not even Dante, perhaps least of all Dante himself. If Dante and his Dantisti have not been equal to the view of the whole, a view shorter than theirs must be expected of the amateur who, as a writer of verses, vainly seeks absolution from the mortal sin of using poets for what he can get out of them. I expect to look at a single image in the *Paradiso*, and to glance at some of its configurations with other images. I mean the imagery of light, but I mean chiefly its reflections. It was scarcely necessary for Dante to have read, though he did read, the *De Anima*, to learn that sight is the king of the senses and that the human body, which like other organisms lives by *touch*, may be made actual in language only through the imitation of *sight*. And sight in language is imitated not by means of "description"—*ut pictura poesis*—but by doubling the image: Our confidence in its spatial reality is won quite simply by casting the image upon a glass, or otherwise by the insinuation of space between.

I cannot undertake to examine here Dante's double imagery in all its detail, for his light alone could lead us into complexities as rich as life itself. I had almost said richer than life, if by life we mean (as we must mean) what we ourselves are able daily to see, or even what certain writers have seen, with the exception of Shakespeare, and possibly of Sophocles and Henry James. A secondary purpose that I shall have

---

2. Davidson and Tate, *Literary Correspondence*, 369.

in view will be to consider the dramatic implications of the light imagery as they emerge at the resolution of the poem, in canto XXXIII of the *Paradiso*. These implications suggest, to my mind, a radical change in the interpretation of *The Divine Comedy*, and impel me to ask again: What kind of poem is it? In asking this question I shall not be concerned with what we ordinarily consider to be literary criticism; I shall be only incidentally judging, for my main purpose is to describe.

In *Purgatorio* XXX Beatrice appears to Dante first as a voice (what she says need not detain us here), then as light; but not yet the purest light. She is the light of a pair of eyes in which is reflected the image of the gryphon, a symbol of the hypostatic union, of which she herself is a "type." But before Dante perceives this image in her eyes, he says: "A thousand desires hotter than flame held my eyes bound to the shining eyes. . . ."[3] I see no reason to suppose that Dante does not mean what he says. *Mille disiri the fiamma caldi* I take to be the desires, however interfused by this time with courtly and mystical associations, of a man for a woman: the desires that the boy Dante felt for the girl Beatrice in 1274 after he had passed her in a street of Florence. She is the same Beatrice, Dante the same Dante, with differences which do not reject but rather include their sameness. Three dancing girls appear: Dante's allegory, formidable as it is, intensifies rather than impoverishes the reality of the dancers as girls. Their dance is a real dance, their song, in which they make a charming request of Beatrice, is a real song. If Dante expected us to be interested in the dancers only as the Theological Virtues, I see no good reason why he made them girls at all. They are sufficiently convincing as the Three Graces, and I cannot feel in the pun a serious violation of Dante's confidence. The request of the girls is sufficiently remarkable: *Volgi, Beatrice, volgi gli occhi santi*—"Turn, Beatrice, turn those holy eyes." Let Dante see your holy eyes; look into his eyes. Is it extravagant to substitute for the image of the gryphon the image of Dante in Beatrice's eyes? I think not. *He is in her eyes*—as later, in *Paradiso* XXXIII, he will be "in" God. Then a startling second request by the dancers: "Of thy grace do us the favor that thou unveil thy mouth to him"—*disvele / a lui la*

---

3. [Tate] Quotations in English from *The Divine Comedy* are from the translation by Carlyle, Okey, and Wicksteed, in the Temple Classics edition. Here and there I have taken the liberty of neutralizing certain Victorian poeticisms, which were already archaic in that period.

bocca tua—"that he may discern the second beauty which thou hid-est"—*la seconda belleza the to cele*. At this point we get one of the innumerable proofs of Dante's greatness as a poet. We are not shown *la seconda belleza*, the smiling mouth; we are shown, instead, in the first four *terzine* of the next canto, the effect on Dante. For neither Dante nor Homer *describes* his heroine. As Beatrice's mouth is revealed, all Dante's senses but the sense of sight are *tutti spenti;* and sight itself is caught in *l'antica rete*—"the ancient net"—a variation of *l'antica fiamma*—"the ancient flame"—that he had felt again when he had first seen Beatrice in the Earthly Paradise.

What the net is doing here seems now to me plain, after some ten years of obtuseness about it. The general meaning is, as Charles Williams holds, that Dante, having chosen the Way of Affirmation through the physical image, feels her in the Earthly Paradise all that he had *felt* before, along with what he now *knows*. Why did he put the worldly emotion of his youthful life into the figure of the net? It is not demanded by the moment; we should not have the sense missing something if it were not there. If it is a simple metaphor for the obfuscation of sensuality, it is not a power, metaphor; we must remember that Dante uses very few linguistic metaphors, as distinguished from analogical or symbolic objects; when he uses them they are simple and powerful. The net, as I see it, is not simply a metaphor for the "catching" of Dante by Beatrice in 1274, though it is partly *that* ancient net; it is also a net of even more famous antiquity, that in which Venus caught Mars; and it is thus a symbolic object. Moreover, if Beatrice's eyes are univocally divine, why do the three Theological Dancers reproach him with gazing at her "too fixedly"—*troppo fiso*—as if he or anybody else could get too much of the divine light? He is, of course, not yet ready for the full Beatific Vision. But an astonishing feature of the great scene of the divine pageant is that, as a trope, a subjective effect, the smile of Beatrice simultaneously revives his human love (Eros) and directs his will to the anticipation of the Beatific Vision (Agapé): both equally, by means of the action indicated by the blinding effect of both; he is blinded by the net and by the light, not alternately but at one instant.[4]

---

4. [Tate] It seems scarcely necessary to remind the reader that I have followed in the scene of the Earthly Paradise only one thread of an immense number in a vastly complex pattern.

To bring together various meanings at a single moment of action is to exercise what I shall speak of here as the symbolic imagination; but the line of *action* must be unmistakable, we must never be in doubt about what is happening; or at a given stage of his progress the hero does one simple thing, and one only. The symbolic imagination conducts an action through analogy, of the human to the divine, of the natural to the supernatural, of the low to the high, of time to eternity. My literary generation was deeply impressed by Baudelaire's sonnet *Correspondances*, which restated the doctrines of medieval symbolism by way of Swedenborg; we were impressed because we had lost the historical perspective leading back to the original source. But the statement of a doctrine is very different from its possession as experience in poetry. Analogical symbolism need not move towards an act of imagination. It may see in active experience the qualities necessary for static symbolism; for example, the Grave of Jesus, which for the theologian may be a symbol to be expounded in the Illuminative Way, or for the mystic may be an object of contemplation in the Unitive Way. Despite the timeless orders of both rational discourse and intuitive contemplation, it is the business of the symbolic poet to return to the order of temporal sequence—to *action*. His purpose is to show men experiencing whatever they may be capable of, with as much meaning as he may be able to see in it; but the action comes first. Shall we call this the Poetic Way? It is at any rate the way of the poet, who has got to do his work with the body of this world, whatever that body may look like to him, in his time and place—the whirling atoms, the body of a beautiful woman, or a deformed body, or the body of Christ, or even the body of this death. If the poet is able to put into this moving body, or to find in it, a coherent chain of analogies, he will inform an intuitive act with symbolism; his will be in one degree or another the symbolic imagination.

Before I try to illustrate these general reflections, I must make a digression, for my own guidance, which I am not competent to develop as searchingly as my subject demands. The symbolic imagination takes rise from a definite limitation of human rationality which was recognized in the West until the seventeenth century; in this view the intellect cannot have direct knowledge of essences. The only created mind that has this knowledge is the angelic mind.[5] If we do not believe in angels we shall have to invent them in order to explain by parable the remarkable appearance, in Europe, at about the end of the sixteenth century, of a mentality which denied man's commitment to the physical world, and set itself up in quasi-divine independence. This mind has intellect and will without feeling; and it is through feeling alone that we witness the glory of our servitude to the natural world, to St. Thomas's accidents, or, if you will, to Locke's secondary qualities; it is our tie with the world of sense. The angelic mind suffers none of the limitations of sense; it has immediate knowledge of essences; and this knowledge moves through the perfect will to divine love, with which it is at one. Imagination in an angel is thus inconceivable, for the angelic mind transcends the mediation of both image and discourse. I call that human imagination angelic which tries to disintegrate or to circumvent the image in the illusory pursuit of essence. When human beings undertake this ambitious program, divine love becomes so rarefied that it loses its human paradigm, and is dissolved in the worship of intellectual power, the surrogate of divinity that worships itself. It professes to know nature as essence at the same time that it has become alienated from nature in the rejection of its material forms.

> It was, however high the phrases, the common thing from which Dante always started, as it was certainly the greatest and most common to which he came. His images were the natural inevitable images—the girl in the street, the people he knew, the language he learned as a child. In them the great diagrams were perceived; from them the great myths open; by them he understands the final end.[6]

This is the simple secret of Dante, but it is a secret which is not necessarily available to the Christian poet today. The Catholic faith has not changed since Dante's time. But the Catholic sensibility, as we see it in modern Catholic poetry, from Thompson to Lowell, has become angelic, and is not distinguishable (doctrinal differences aside) from poetry by Anglicans, Methodists, Presbyterians, and atheists. I take it

5. [Tate] The difficulties suffered by man as angel were known at least as early as Pascal; but the doctrine of angelism, as a force in the modern mind, has been fully set forth for the first time by Jacques Maritain in *The Dream of Descartes* (New York, 1944).
6. [Tate] Charles Williams, *The Figure of Beatrice* (London, 1943), 44.

that more than doctrine, even if the doctrine be true, is necessary for a great poetry of action. Catholic poets have lost, along with their heretical friends, the power to start with the "common thing": They have lost the gift for concrete experience. The abstraction of the modern mind has obscured their way into the natural order. Nature offers to the symbolic poet clearly denotable objects in depth and in the round, which yield the analogies to the higher syntheses. The modern poet rejects the higher synthesis, or tosses it in a vacuum of abstraction.[7] If he looks at nature he spreads the clear visual image in a complex of metaphor, from one *katachresis* to another through Aristotle's permutations of genus and species. He cannot sustain the prolonged analogy, the second and superior kind of figure that Aristotle doubtless had in mind when he spoke of metaphor as the key to the resemblances of things, and the mark of genius.

That the gift of analogy was not Dante's alone every medievalist knows. The most striking proof of its diffusion, and the most useful example for my purpose that I know, is the letter of St. Catherine of Siena to Brother Raimondo of Capua. A young Sienese, Niccolo Tuldo, had been unjustly convicted of treason and condemned to death. Catherine became his angel of mercy, giving him daily solace—the meaning of the Cross, the healing powers of the Blood; and so reconciled him to the faith that he accepted his last end. Now I have difficulty believing people who say that they live in the Blood of Christ, for I take them to mean that they have the faith and hope some day to live in it. The evidence of the Blood is one's power to produce it, the power to show it as a "common thing" and to make it real, literally, in action. For the report of the Blood is very different from its reality. St. Catherine does not report it; she recreates it, so that its analogical meaning is confirmed again in blood that she has seen. This is how she does it:

> Then [the condemned man] came, like a gentle lamb; and seeing me he began to smile, and wanted me to make the sign of the Cross. When he had received the sign, I said, "Down! To the bridal, my sweetest brother. For soon shalt thou be in the enduring life." He

---

7. [Tate] Another way of putting this is to say that the modern poet, like Valéry or Crane, tries to seize directly the anagogical meaning, without going through the three preparatory stages of letter, allegory, and trope.

prostrated himself with great gentleness, and I stretched out his neck; and bowed me down, and recalled to him the Blood of the Lamb. His lips said naught save Jesus! and Catherine! And so saying, I received his head in my hands, closing my eyes in the divine goodness and saying, "I will."

When he was at rest my soul rested in peace and quiet, and in so great fragrance of blood that I could not bear to remove the blood which had fallen on me from him.

It is deeply shocking, as all proximate incarnations of the Word are shocking, whether in Christ and the saints, or in Dostoevsky, James Joyce, or Henry James. I believe it was T. S. Eliot who made accessible again to an ignorant generation a common Christian insight, when he said that people cannot bear very much reality. I take this to mean that only persons of extraordinary courage, and perhaps even genius, can face the spiritual truth in its physical body. Flaubert said that the artist, the soldier, and the priest face death every day; so do we all; yet it is perhaps nearer to them than to other men; it is their particular responsibility. When St. Catherine "rests in so great fragrance of blood," it is no doubt the Blood of the Offertory which the celebrant offers to God *cum odore suavitatis*, but with the literal odor of the species of wine, not of blood. St. Catherine had the courage of genius which permitted her to *smell* the Blood of Christ in Niccolo Tuldo's blood clotted on her dress: she smelled the two bloods *not alternately but at one instant*, in a single act compounded of spiritual insight and physical perception.

Chekhov said that a gun hanging on the wall at the beginning of a story has got to be fired off before the story ends: Everything in potency awaits its completed purpose in act. If this is a metaphysical principle, it is also the prime necessity of the creative imagination. Is not St. Catherine telling us that the Blood of Christ must be perpetually recreated as a brute fact? If the gun has got to be fired, the Blood has got to be shed, if only because that is the first condition of its appearance; it must move towards the condition of human action, where we may smell it, touch it, and taste it again.

When ecclesiastical censorship of this deep insight in the laity exceeds a just critical prudence, the result is not merely obscurantism in the arts; it is perhaps a covert rejection of the daily renewal of the religious life. Twenty-five years ago the late W. B. Yeats had a contro-versy with the Irish bishops about the famous medieval "Cherry Tree Carol," which the hierarchy wished to suppress as blasphemous. The Blessed Virgin is resting under a cherry tree, too tired to reach up and pluck a cherry. Since Christ lives from the foundations of the world, He is omnipotent in the womb, and He commands the tree to lower a bough for His mother's convenience; which it obligingly does, since it cannot do otherwise. Here again the gun is fired and the Blood is shed. If the modern Church has lost the historic experience of this kind of symbolism, which is more tolerable, I believe, in the Latin countries than with us, it is at least partial evidence that the Church has lost the great culture that it created, and that at intervals has created the life of the Church.

I return from this digression to repeat that Dante was the great master of the symbolism, the meaning of which I have been trying to suggest. But the symbolic "problem" of *The Divine Comedy* we must not suppose Dante to have undertaken analytically; it is our problem, not his. Dr. Flanders Dunbar has stated it with great penetration:

> As with his progress he perceives more and more of ultimate real-ity through the symbol [Beatrice], at the same time the symbol occupies less and less of his attention, until ultimately it takes its place among all created things on a petal of the rose, while he gazes beyond it into the full glory of the sun.[8]

The symbolic problem, then, is: How shall Dante move step by step (literally and allegorically) from the Dark Wood, the negation of light, to the "three circles, of three colors and one magnitude," God Him-self, or pure light, where there are no sensible forms to reflect it? There can be no symbol for God, for that which has itself informed step by step the symbolic progress. Vision, giving us clear visual objects, through physical sight, moving steadily upward towards its anagogi-cal transfiguration, is the first matrix of the vast analogical structure. As Dante sees more he sees less: As he sees more light the nearer he comes to its source, the less he sees of what it had previously lit up. In

---

8. [Tate] H. Flanders Dunbar, *Symbolism in Mediaeval Thought and Its Consummation in The Divine Comedy* (New Haven, 1929), 847.

the Empyrean, at the climax of the Illuminative Way, Beatrice leaves Dante and takes her place in the Rose; St. Bernard now guides him into the Intuitive Way.

For the Illuminative Way is the way to knowledge through the senses, by means of aided reason, but here the "distance" between us and what we see is always the distance between a concept and its object, between the human situation in which the concept arises and the realization of its full meaning. Put otherwise, with the beginning of the *Vita Nuova* in mind, it is the distance between the knowledge of love, which resulted from the earthly love of Dante for Beatrice, and the distant "object," or God, that had made the love in the first place possible: the distance between Beatrice and the light which had made it possible for him to see her. The Kantian synthetic proposition of the entire poem, as we enter it through the symbolism of light, is: Light is Beatrice. Here the eye is still on the human image; it is still on it up to the moment when she takes her place with the other saints in the Rose, where she is only one of many who turn their eyes to the "eternal fountain." Light is Beatrice; light is her *smile;* her final smile, which Dante sees as she enters the Rose, is no longer the mere predicate of a sentence, for there is now no distance between the smile and what had lit it. Although, insofar as it is a smile at all, it is still the smile at the unveiling of the mouth, it is now the smile without the mouth, the smile of light. And thus we arrive at the converse of the proposition: Beatrice is light. Now Dante's eye is on the light itself, but he cannot see it because Beatrice, through whose image he had progressively seen more light, has disappeared; and he can see nothing. There is nothing to *see.* For that which enables sight is not an object of vision. What has been seen is, in what is surely one of the greatest passages of all poetry, "the shadowy prefaces of their truth." Illumination, or intellect guided by divine grace, powerful as it is, halts at the "prefaces." But the Unitive Way leads to the Presence, where both sight and discursive thought cease.

Whether Dante should have tried to give us an image of God, of that which is without image and invisible, is an unanswerable question. Is it possible that we have here a break in the symbolic structure, which up to the end of the poem has been committed to the visible?

At the end we are with Love, whose unpredicated attribute is the entire universe. Has Dante given us, in the "three circles, of three colors and one magnitude," merely the trinitarian and doctrinal equivalent of the ultimate experience, instead of an objective symbol of the experience itself? In the terms of Dante's given structure, such a symbol was perhaps not possible; and strictly speaking it is never possible. If he was going to give us anything he doubtless had to give us just what he gave; he gave it in an act of great artistic heroism. For in the center of the circles he sees the image of man. This is the risk, magnified almost beyond conception, of St. Catherine: the return of the supra-rational and supra-sensible to the "common thing." It is the courage to see again, even in its ultimate cause, the Incarnation.

If we will look closely at the last four lines of the *Paradiso*, and double back on our tracks, I believe that we will see that there is no break in the *dramatic* structure—the structure of the action.[9] For the poem is an action: A man is acting and going somewhere, and things are happening both to him and around him; otherwise the poem would be—what I may have given the impression of its being—a symbolic machine. In the space of an essay I cannot prepare properly the background of the suggestion that I am about to offer. For one thing, we should have to decide who "Dante" is, and where he is in the action that he has depicted—questions that nobody seems to know much about. For what it may be worth, I suggest that the poet has undertaken to involve a fictional character named Dante—at once the poet and not the poet of that name—in a certain action of the greatest possible magnitude, the issue of which is nothing less, perhaps something greater, than life or death. In this action the hero fails. He fails in the sense that he will have to start over again when he steps out of the "poem," as he surely must do if he is going to write it.

Thus I see *The Divine Comedy* as essentially dramatic and, in one of its modes, tragic. Are we to suppose that the hero actually attained to the Beatific Vision? No; for nobody who had would be so foolish as to write a poem about it, if in that spiritual perfection it could even

---

9. [Tate] By "dramatic" I mean something like *practic*, a possible adjective from *praxis*, a general movement of action as potency which it is the purpose of the poem to actualize. In the Thomist sequence, *potentia:actio:actus*, "dramatic" would roughly correspond to the middle term.

occur to him to do so. The poem is a vast paradigm of the possibility of the Beatific Vision. No more than its possibility for the individual person, for "Dante" himself, is here entertained. What shall we make of his failure of memory, the slipping away of the final image, which he calls *tanto oltraggio*—"so great an outrage"? It would be a nice question to decide whether something had slipped away, or whether it had ever been fully there. The vision is imagined, it is *imaged;* its essence is not possessed. I confess that it is not an argument from the poem to say that had Dante claimed its possession, he would have lost that "good of the intellect" which we forfeit when we presume to angelic knowledge; and it was through the good of the intellect that he was able to write the poem. But it is an external argument that I believe cannot be entirely ignored.

The last *terzina* of the last canto tells us: *All' alta fantasia qui mancò possa*—"To the high fantasy here power failed." What power failed? The power to write the poem, or the power to possess as experience the divine essence? Is it a literary or a religious failure? It is obviously and honorably both. It makes no more sense to say Dante achieved his final vision as direct experience than to say that Sophocles married his mother and put out his own eyes; that the experience of the *Oedipus Rex* represents the personal experience of Sophocles. What Dante achieved is an *actual* insight into the great dilemma, eternal life or eternal death, but he has not hedged the dilemma like a bet to warrant himself a favorable issue. As the poem closes, he still faces it, like the rest of us. Like Oedipus, the fictional Dante learns in humility a certain discipline of the will: We may equate up to a point the dark-blindness of Oedipus and the final light-blindness of Dante; both men have succeeded through suffering in blinding themselves to knowledge-through-sense, in the submission of hubris to a higher will.[10] The fictional Dante at the end steps out of the frame and becomes again the historical Dante; Oedipus steps out of his frame, his fictional plot is done, he is back in the world of unformed action, blind and, like Dante, an exile. Shall Oedipus be saved? Shall Dante? We do not know, but to ask the question is to point to a primary consideration in the interpretation of *The Divine Comedy*, particularly if we are dis-

---

10. [Tate] Oedipus does not achieve this until the end of *Oedipus at Colonus*.

posed, as some commentators have been, to believe that Dante the man used his poem arrogantly to predict his own salvation.

If Dante does not wholly succeed in giving us in the "three circles, of three colors and one magnitude," an image of the Godhead, I think we are ready to see that it was not necessary; it was not a part of his purpose. Such an image is not the "final cause" of the poem. The poem is an action; it is an action to the end. For the image that Dante gives us of the Godhead is not an image to be received by the reader as essential knowledge in his own "angelic" intelligence, as an absolute apart from the action. It is a dramatic image; the image is of the action and the action is Dante's. To read Canto XXXIII in any other way would be perhaps to commit the blunder that M. Gilson warns us against: the blunder of thinking that Dante was writing a super-philosophical tract, or a pious embellishment of the doctrines of Thomas Aquinas, instead of a poem. The question, then, is not what is the right anagogical symbol for God; it is rather what symbol for God will serve tropologically (that is, morally and dramatically) for the tragic insight of the poet who knows, through the stages of the Three Ways, that the Beatific Vision is possible but uncertain of realization. Dante sees himself, Man, in the Triune Circles, and he is in the Seraphic Heaven of Love. But at the end desire and will are like a "wheel moving equally"; motion imparted to it at one point turns it as a whole, but it has to be moved, as the wheel of our own desire and will must be moved, by a force outside it. The wheel is Dante's last symbol of the great failure. Since it must be moved, it is not yet at one, not yet in unity, with the divine will; it obeys it, as those other wheels, the sun and stars, moved by love, obey.

I take it that the wheel is the final geometrical projection of the *visual* matrix of analogy; it is what the eye sees, the material form, and what in its anagoge it eventually aspires to become. We must remember that Beatrice's eyes are spheres, no less than the physical universe itself, which is composed of concentric spheres. The first circles that Dante shows us are in Canto III of the *Inferno*, Charon's—"for round his eyes were wheels of flame." The last, the Triune Circles, are the anagoge of the visual circle, and are without extension; they are pure light, the abstraction or sublimation of flame. Flame burning in a circle and light lighting up a circle, and what it encloses, are the prime sensible symbols of the poem. Only Satan, at the geometrical center of the world, occupies a point that cannot be located on any existing arc of the cosmos. This is the spherical (or circular) expression of Satan's absolute privation of light-as-love which in the Empyrean turns the will-wheel of Dante with the cosmic spheres. These are the will of God as love; and if we ignore the dramatic structure, and fail to look closely at the symbolic, we shall conclude that Dante is at one with the purpose of the universe. But, as we have seen, the symbolic structure is complicated by the action, and in the end the action prevails. That is to say, Dante is *still moving*. Everything that moves, says Dante the Thomist in his letter to Can Grande, has some imperfection in it because it is, in the inverse degree of its rate of motion, removed from the Unmoved Mover, the Triune Circles, God. By a twist of this argument, which, of course, as I shall presently indicate, is specious, Satan himself has no imperfection: he too lies immobile—except for the fanning wings that freeze the immobile damned in Giudecca—as the Still Point in the Triune Circles is immobile. If Dante's will is turning like a wheel, he is neither damned nor saved; he is morally active in the universal human predicament. His participation in the love imparted as motion to the universe draws him towards the Triune Circles and to the immobility of peace at the center, as it draws all creatures; but a defection of the will could plunge him into the other "center."

Now Dante is astonished when he sees in the *Primum Mobile* a reversal of the ratio of speed of the spheres as he had observed it on earth, through the senses. "But in the universe of sense," he says to Beatrice, "we may see the circlings more divine as from the center they are more removed." In the spiritual universe the circlings are more divine the nearer they are to the center. It is a matter of perspective; from the earth outward the revolutions of the spheres are increasingly rapid up to the ninth, the *Primum Mobile*, whose speed is just short of infinite; the *Primum Mobile* is trying to achieve with all points of its surface a simultaneous contact with the Still Point of the Empyrean. What he sees in the *Primum Mobile* is this perspective visually reversed; instead of being the outer "crust" of the universe, the *Primum Mobile* is actually next to the central Still Point, whirling with inconceivable speed.

God, the Still Point, is a nonspatial entity which is *everywhere* and *nowhere*. The Ptolemaic cosmos, which had been Christianized by the imposition of the angelic hierarchy of Dionysius, has been, in a way not to be completely visualized, turned inside out. The spheres, which began their career as an astronomical hypothesis, are now no longer necessary; they are replaced in the ultimate reality by nine nonspatial gradations of angelic intelligence, in three triads, the last and ninth circle of "fire" being that of the simple angels, the "farthest" removed in the nonspatial continuum from the Divine Love.

Where then is the earth, with Satan at its exact center? I think we must answer: Where it has always been. But "where" that is we had better not try to say. At any rate neither Satan nor the earth is at the spiritual center. His immobility thus has no perfection. In the full spiritual reality, of which the center of the material universe becomes an outermost "rind," beyond space, Satan does not exist: He exists in the world of sense and in the human will. The darkness of hell, from the point of view of God (if I may be allowed the expression), is not an inner darkness, but an outer. So, in the progress from hell to the Empyrean, Dante has come from the inner darkness of man to the inner light of God; from the outer darkness of God to the outer light of man.

This anagogical conversion of symbol that I have been trying to follow in one of its threads is nowhere by Dante merely *asserted*; it is constantly moving, rendered moment by moment as *action*. Like most good poets, great or minor, Dante wrote better than he had meant to do; for if we took him at his word, in the letter to Can Grande, we should conclude that the *Paradiso* is a work of rhetoric calculated "to remove those living in this life from a state of misery and to guide them to a state of happiness." It seems probable that persons now enrolled among the Blessed got there without being compelled to see on the way all that Dante saw. Were we reading the poem for that kind of instruction, and knew not where else to find it, we might conclude that Dante's *luce intellectual*, with its transformations in the fourfold system of interpretation, is too great a price to pay even for salvation; or, at any rate, for most of us, the wrong price. It would perhaps be a mistake for a man to decide that he has become a Christian at the instance of Dante, unless he is prepared to see all that Dante saw—which is one thing, but always seen in at least two ways.

A clue to two of the ways is the mirror symbol. As we approach it, the kind of warning that Dante at intervals pauses to give us is not out of place. For if the way up to now has been rough, we may expect it from now on to be even rougher. The number of persons, objects, and places in *The Divine Comedy* that are reflections, replicas, or manifestations of things more remote is beyond calculation. The entire natural world is a replica *in reverse* of the supernatural world. That, I believe, we have seen so far only on the dubious authority of my own assertion. But if Dante is a poet (I agree with M. Gilson that he is) he will not be satisfied with assertion as such, even with the authority of the Church to support it. The single authority of poetry is a difficult criterion of actuality that must always remain beyond our reach. And in some sense of this actuality Dante has got to place his vast two-way analogy (heaven like the world, the world like heaven) on the scene of action, and make it move. Let us take the stance of Dante at the beginning of *Paradiso* XXVIII, and try to suggest some of the ways in which he moves it:

> as in the mirror a taper's flame, kindled behind a man, is seen by
> him before it be in his sight or thought,
> as he turns back to see whether the glass speak truth to him, and
> sees that it accords with it as song-words to the music;
> so my memory recalls that I did turn, gazing upon the lovely eyes
> whence love had made the noose to capture me;
> and when I turned, and my own eyes were struck by what appears in
> that orb whenever upon its circling the eye is well fixed,
> a point I saw which rayed forth light so keen that all the vision that
> it flames upon must close because of its sharp point.

(One observes in passing that even in the *Primum Mobile* Beatrice bears the net-noose dimension of meaning.) Beatrice's eyes are a mirror in which is reflected that "sharp point," to which Dante, still at a distance from it, now turns his direct gaze. As he looks at it he sees for the first time what its reflection in Beatrice's eyes could not convey: that it is the sensible world turned inside out. For the sensible world as well as her eyes is only a reflection of the light from the sharp point. Now he is looking at the thing-in-itself. *He has at last turned away from the mirror which is the world.* What happens when we turn away from a mirror to look directly at the object which we saw reflected? I must anticipate Beatrice's famous experiment with one of my own. If you will place upon a table a box open at one end, the open end towards a mirror, and then look into the mirror, you will see the open end. Turn from the mirror and look at the box itself. You still see the open end, and thus you see the object *reversed*. If the box were reproduced, in the sense of being continued or moved *into* the mirror, the actual box would present, when we turn to it, a closed end; for the box and its reflection would show their respectively corresponding sides in congruent projection. Quantitative visualization of the cosmic reversal is not completely possible. But through the mirror analogy Dante performs a stupendous feat of the imagination that in kind has probably not been rivaled by any other poet. And it is an analogy that has been firmly grounded in action.

In conclusion I shall try to point to its literal base; for we have seen it, in *Paradiso* XXVIII, only as a simile; and if we had not had it laid down earlier as a physical fact to which we must assent, a self-contained phenomenon of the natural order, it would no doubt lack at the end that fullness of actuality which we do not wholly understand, but which we require of poetry. The self-contained fact of the natural order is established in canto II of the *Paradiso*, where Beatrice performs a physical experiment. Some scholars have been moved by it to admire Dante for this single ray of positivistic enlightenment feebly glowing in the mind of a medieval poet. So far as I know, our critics have not considered it necessary to be sufficiently unenlightened to see that Beatrice's experiment is merely poetry.

Before I reproduce it I shall exhibit a few more examples of the mirror symbol that appear at intervals in the five last cantos. In Canto XXIX, 25–27, form permeates matter "as in glass . . . a ray so glows that from its coming to its pervading all, there is no interval." Still in XXIX, 142–45, at the end: "See now the height and breadth of the eternal worth, since it has made itself so many mirrors in which it is reflected, remaining in itself one as before." At line 37 of Canto XXX we enter the Empyrean where Dante sees the great River of Light "issuing its living sparks"; it too is a mirror, for Beatrice explains: "The river and the topaz gems that enter and go forth, and the smiling grasses are prefaces of their truth" (i.e., of what they reflect). In Canto XXX, 85–87, Dante bends down to the waves "to make mirrors of my eyes"; and again in XXX he sees the Rose of Paradise, another mirror, in one of his great similes:

> And as a hillside reflects itself in water at its foot, as if to look upon
> its own adornment, when it is rich in grasses and in flowers,
> so, mounting in the light, around, around, casting reflection in
> more than a thousand ranks I saw all that of us have won
> return up yonder.

And finally the climactic reflection, the "telic principle" and the archetype of them all, in Canto XXX, 127–32:

> The circling that in thee [in the Triune God] appeared to be con-
> ceived as a reflected light, by my eyes scanned a little,
> in itself, of its own color, seemed to be painted with our effigy, and
> thereat my sight was all committed to it.

Where have these mirrors, which do their poetic work, the work of making the supra-sensible visible—one of the tasks of all poetry— where have they come from? The remote frame is doubtless the circular or spherical shape of the Ptolemaic cosmos;[11] but if there is glass in the circular frame, it reflects nothing until Virgil has left Dante to Beatrice's guidance in the Earthly Paradise (*Purgatorio* XXXI); where we have already glanced at the unveiling of mouth and eyes. I suggest that Beatrice's eyes in *Purgatorio* XXXI are the first mirror. But the image is not, at this early stage of Beatrice, sufficiently developed to bear all the strain of analogical weight that Dante intends to put upon it. For that purpose the mirror must be established as a literal mirror, a plain mirror, a "common thing."

He not only begins with the common thing; he continues with it, until at the end we come by disarming stages to a scene that no man has ever looked upon before. Every detail of Paradise is a common thing;

---

11. [Tate] The popular "visual" translation of Aristotle's primary Unmoved Mover producing, through being loved, the primary cosmic motion, which is circular. The philosophical source of this idea, Book XII, Chapter 7, of the *Metaphysics*, Dante of course knew.

it is the cumulative combination and recombination of natural objects beyond their "natural" relations, which staggers the imagination. "Not," says Beatrice to Dante, "that such things are in themselves harsh; but on your side is the defect, in that your sight is not yet raised so high."

A mirror is an artifact of the practical intellect, and as such can be explained by natural law: but there is no natural law which explains man as a mirror reflecting the image of God. The great leap is made in the interval between Canto II and Canto XXXIII of the *Paradiso*.

Dante, in Canto II, is baffled by the spots on the moon, supposing them to be due to alternating density and rarity of matter. No, says Beatrice in effect, this would be monism, a materialistic explanation of the diffusion of the divine light. The true explanation is very different: All saved souls are equally saved, and all the heavenly spheres are equally in heaven; but the divine light reaches the remoter spheres and souls according to the spiritual gifts of which they were capable in the natural world. "This is the formal principle," Beatrice says, summing up, "which produces, in conformity to the excellence of the object, the turbid and the clear."

Meanwhile she has asked Dante to consider a physical experiment to illustrate the unequal reception of the divine substance. Take three mirrors, she says, and set two of them side by side, and a third in the middle but farther back. Place a candle behind you, and observe its image reflected in each of the three mirrors. The middle reflection will be smaller but not less bright than the two others: "smaller" stands quantitatively for unequal reception of a quality, spiritual insight; "not less bright" likewise for equality of salvation. But what concerns us is a certain value of the experiment that Dante, I surmise, with the cunning of a great poet, slyly refuses to consider: the dramatic value of the experiment.

There are *three*[12] mirrors each reflecting the one light. In the heart of the Empyrean, as we have seen, Dante says:

> In the profound and shining being of the deep light appeared to me
> *three* circles, of *three* colors and one magnitude.

---

12. [Tate] Only two, placed at unequal distances from the candle, are strictly necessary for the experiment; but three are necessary as pointers towards the anagoge of the Trinity in the Triune Circles.

In the middle is the effigy of man. The physical image of Dante had necessarily been reflected in each of the three mirrors of canto II; but he had not seen it. I suggest that he was not then ready to see it; his dramatic (i.e., tropological) development fell short of the final self-knowledge. Self-knowledge comes to him, as an Aristotelian Recognition and Reversal, when he turns the cosmos inside out by turning away from the "real" mirrors to the one light which has cast the three separate images. For the first time he sees the "one magnitude," the candle itself. And it is all done with the simple apparatus and in conditions laid down in canto II; he achieves the final anagoge and the dramatic recognition by turning around, as if he were still in canto II, and by looking at the candle that has been burning all the time behind his back.

I have described some motions of the symbolic imagination in Dante, and tried to develop a larger motion in one of its narrower aspects. What I have left out of this discussion is very nearly the entire poem. In the long run the light imagery is not the body, it is what permits us to *see* the body, of the poem. The rash suggestion that *The Divine Comedy* has a tragic mode—among other modes—I shall no doubt be made to regret; I cannot defend it further here. Perhaps the symbolic imagination is tragic in sentiment, if not always in form, in the degree of its development. Its every gain beyond the simple realism of experience imposes so great a strain upon any actuality of form as to set the ultimate limit of the gain as a defeat. The high order of the poetic insight that the final insight must elude us, is dramatic in the sense that its fullest image is an action in the shapes of this world: it does not reject, it includes; it sees not only with but through the natural world, to what may lie beyond it. Its humility is witnessed by its modesty. It never begins at the top; it carries the bottom along with it, however high it may climb.

15

SOME READINGS AND MISREADINGS

CAROLINE GORDON

For Caroline Gordon, as for Allen Tate, the debt to Jacques Marit-
ain—the French philosopher who called himself "the peasant of the
Garonne"—was almost incalculable. Commentators on Gordon's
later work, embarrassed by her conversion, thought that she had lost
her bearings, and of course, outside certain Catholic circles, Mari-
tain had no sway. In 1976, Gordon wrote that Maritain himself
was "treated shamefully" by Princeton, where the Tates befriended
the Maritains. "The head of the Philosophy department, 'a Logi-
cal Positivist,' urged him 'not to give the boys so much Plato and
Aristotle but more Bertrand Russell and Whitehead.' He delivered
the lectures which were finally published as Creative Intuition to
a bunch of housewives."[1] But for both Gordon and Tate, despite
their own stormy marriage to each other (twice) and the sadness of
their ultimate divorce, the classical and Catholic tradition remained
central. In "Some Readings and Misreadings," which employs the
insights of Maritain with respect to the novel as Tate had employed
them with Poe, Gordon writes of her discovery in reading the great
novels of the nineteenth century: "On the surface the action seems to
run in one direction while the current, in its depths, runs in quite

---

1. *Letters of Jacques and Raissa Maritain, Allen Tate, and Caroline Gordon*, John M. Dunaway, ed. (Baton Rouge: Louisiana State University Press, 1992), 11.

another." This current in the depths, the true mainstream, she calls "the primal plot: the Christian Scheme of Redemption."

*   Gordon enters the ranks of the Southern Critics very late, long after the Fugitive-Agrarians (all of whom she had known since the 1920s) had made their mark, and her entrance just at the end of the New Criticism marks a broadening and deepening turn toward myth, in which she had been schooled since childhood. This emphasis had been implicit in Southern criticism but rarely explored in the 1930s and 1940s, when poetry was at stake. Thoroughly steeped in the novelistic tradition of Flaubert and James, secretary and long-time friend of Ford Madox Ford, Gordon speaks with authority about fiction. One senses in her fiction and in her criticism a deep awareness of the hidden stream beneath the Southern Renaissance.*

Two passages in Jacques Maritain's *Art and Scholasticism* illuminate the work of certain great nineteenth-century novelists, as well as the work of some of the novelists of our own day. In a discussion of Christian art he says:

> By Christian art I do not mean *ecclesiastical* art, an art specified by an object, an end and definite rules. By Christian art I mean art bearing on the face of it the character of Christianity. Christian art in this sense is not a particular genus of the species art; we do not talk of Christian art as we do of pictorial art or poetic, Gothic, or Byzantine art. A young man does not say to himself: "I am going in for agriculture." There is no school for reaching Christian art. The definition of Christian art is to be found in its subject and its spirit; we talk of Christian art or the art of a Christian as we talk of the art of the bee or the art of man. It is Christianity redeemed.
>
>   . . . wherever art, Egyptian, Greek, or Chinese, has attained a certain degree of grandeur and purity, it is already Christian. . . . Christian in hope, because every spiritual splendour is a promise and a symbol of the divine harmonies of the Gospel.

The novel as we know it today did not exist until the early part of the nineteenth century, when men were given over to industrialism in the social order, materialism in philosophy, and skepticism in religion. Our own century bears the stamp of the century that preceded it; comparatively few men today live consciously by the Christian virtues, to say nothing of Christian philosophy or Christian social order. But the creative imagination—I am speaking particularly of the fiction writer's imagination—does not reckon time in the way in which it is ordinarily reckoned. A novelist's conscious mind may be influenced by what is going on around him, he may announce himself a pragmatist, a skeptic, an atheist while his creative faculties seem to move in and subscribe to a totally different order. Maritain says that after the Renascence "art was so disheartened that it took to living its own life." From this point of view, I have examined some of the great nineteenth century novels. On the surface the action seems to run in one direction while the current, in its depths, runs in quite another. I believe that it could be shown that in the nineteenth century and in our own century as well the fiction writer's imagination often operates within the pattern of Christian symbolism rather than in the patterns of contemporary thought. The peculiarly Christian element of the great nineteenth century novels is their architecture. Many of them are based on the primal plot: the Christian Scheme of Redemption. Madame Bovary, for instance, is strung as tightly as a bow-string on two arcs, which coincide with two visions of Emma. Emma, as she appears on the occasion when Charles is first alone in a room with her, standing tiptoe, her neck on the strain, pouting because she cannot, with her tongue, licks all the sweets from the bottom of her wine-glass, and Emma, who, in the same attitude, except that now she lies prone, takes the chalice of salvation and, dying, presses upon the figure on the crucifix "the fullest kiss of love she has ever given." (The description of the administering of Extreme Unction to Emma is simply a page out of the Paris liturgy put into French, Flaubert wrote Madame Maurice Schlésinger, "but the good folk who watch over the preservation of the liturgy are rather weak in their catechism.")

The Christian Scheme of Redemption is a strange and original plot. Two modern psychologists have commented on its strangeness and originality. In *The Integration of the Personality* Carl Jung conceives of the drama of the human psyche as "a work of redemption." He says:

> The life and death of the God-man . . . a unique sacrifice, bring about the reconciliation of man, who craves redemption, and is lost in materiality, with God . . . man is potentially redeemed at the moment when the eternal Son of God returns to the Father after suffering crucifixion.

In *Totem and Taboo* Sigmund Freud says: "We are much disturbed by the spectacle of a youthful god sacrificing himself," then adds, "but let us pass that over." In the mystery religions of the East, which were so popular in the early days of Christianity and which, in diluted and refined form, are so popular today, the worshipper sacrificed to the god in order to constrain him, to get some of his power, or the god was torn to pieces, as was Dionysos Zagreus, in order that the multitude might feed on him. (In *Totem and Taboo* Freud's imagination is so possessed by this symbolism that parts of the book, if written out of professed faith, might read as an interpretation of the Eucharist.) But pagan gods do not sacrifice themselves. Freud has put his finger on the primary difference between Christianity and other religions.

The primal plot is so deeply rooted in us all that, like Freud, we may apprehend it without realizing what we are doing. This, I think, is the case with Henry James. His father, Henry James, Sr., a follower of Emmanuel Swedenborg, had an antipathy to any kind of orthodoxy. In *Notes of a Son and Brother*, the novelist records himself as "never having been allowed to divine an item of devotional practise," and Graham Greene, in an essay which he has written on "The Altar of the Dead," has commented on James's ignorance of Catholic rites. It would seem that James was ignorant of dogma as well as rites, both Catholic and Protestant. And yet all his novels have one theme: *caritas*, Christian charity.

William Troy, in a provocative essay entitled "The Altar of Henry James," concludes that in all his work James *is* erecting an altar.[2] "And in that case, his altar—what would it be but the sometimes splen-

---

2. [Gordon] The essays by Mr. Troy and Mr. Greene are to be found in the volume *Contemporary Essays*, edited by Sylvia Norman.

did and exultant, sometimes mangled and ignoble body of humanity stretched out in imagination in time and space?" This smacks more of the elder James than the younger. James himself considered "The Ambassadors" the best rounded of all his books. In the crucial interview between Lambert Strether and Madame de Vionnet it is clear that the altar has been erected for a particular sacrifice: the sacrifice of Eros, or pagan love, in order that Agape, Christian love, may be born.

James spares no pains to set his stage for a sacrifice. Madame de Vionnet's drawing-room, ordinarily lamp-lit, is lit tonight by "a pair of clusters of candles that glimmered over the chimney-piece like the tall tapers of an altar."

> The windows were all open, their redundant hangings swaying a little, and he heard once more, from the empty court, the small plash of the fountain. From beyond this, and as from a great distance—beyond the court, beyond the *corps de logis* forming the front—came, as if excited and exciting, the vague voice of Paris.

James tells us that Strether feels that the voice of Paris had come in thus on "the great recorded dates, the days and nights of revolution."

> They were the smell of revolution, the smell of the public temper— or perhaps simply the smell of blood.

Madame de Vionnet is dressed in "simplest, coolest white, of a character so old-fashioned . . . that Madame Roland, on the scaffold, must have worn something like it." She still seems Lambert Strether "the finest and subtlest creature, the happiest apparition it had been given him in all his years to meet," but tonight she seems also "less visibly exempt from the touch of time." She seems to him, indeed, a "vulgarly troubled . . . a maid-servant crying for her young man."

> What was at bottom the matter with her, embroider as she might, and disclaim as she might—what was at bottom the matter with her was simply Chad himself. It was of Chad that she was, after all, renewedly afraid; the very strength of her passion was the very strength of her fear. . . . With the sharpest perception yet, it was like a chill in the air that a creature so fine could be, by mysterious forces, a thing she so exploited. For, at the end of all things,

they *were* mysterious: she had but made Chad what he was—so why could she think she had made him infinite?

James never presents a crucial scene without painstaking preparation. Strether has before this reflected that the trouble with Chad is that he is "*pagan.*" Madame de Vionnet, the high-born lady, is, at bottom, like Emma Bovary, the bourgeois wife: they are both romantics, demanding the infinite of the finite. It is largely through her realization of Chad's limitations—a realization to which she has to be helped by Strether—that Madame de Vionnet arrives at her profession of faith, Christian charity, which she makes that night to him: "The thing is to give, never to take."

It is also possible that the primal plot may operate in a work of art not only without the artist's conscious knowledge but almost against his will. Such a work is James Joyce's *A Portrait of The Artist As a Young Man.* I suspect that this book has been misread by a whole generation. It is not primarily a picture of the artist rebelling against constituted authority. It is rather, the picture of a soul that is being damned for time and eternity caught in the act of foreseeing and foreknowing its damnation. Joyce's story is based on a Greek myth, the story of Dedalus, who created the labyrinth in which King Minos of Crete confined the Minotaur. Stephen Dedalus, Joyce's hero, has for surname the name of the pagan artificer. But his first or Christian name is that of the first martyr, St. Stephen. The Jesuits who have trained him think that he may take orders. The director calls him in one day to question him as to whether he has a vocation. Stephen listens to the director in "reverent silence."

> . . . through the words he heard even more distinctly a voice bidding him approach, offering him secret knowledge and secret power.

But Stephen knows that he will never become a priest:

> The voice of the director urging upon him the proud claims of the church and the mystery and power of the priestly office repeated itself idly in his memory. . . . His soul was not there to hear and greet it . . . a definite and irrevocable act of his threatened to end forever

in time and eternity, his freedom. . . . The snares of the world were its ways of sin. He would fall. He had not yet fallen but he would fall silently, in an instant. Not to fall was too hard, too hard.

When he resists the call to a vocation he knows that it is forever, and as he walks back to his father's house after the conversation with the director he turns his eyes "coldly for an instant towards the faded blue shrine of the Blessed Virgin which stood fowl-wise upon a pole in the ham-shaped encampment of poor cottages. . . . The faint sour stink of rotted cabbages came to him from the gardens on the rising ground above the river. He smiled to think that it was this disorder, the misrule and confusion of his father's house and the stagnation of vegetable life which was to win the day in his soul. . . ."

He enters his father's house by the back door. In the kitchen he finds his younger brothers and sisters still sitting about the table. They have just finished tea and over the small glass jars and jam-pots which do service for tea-cups, among discarded crusts and lumps of sugared bread, turned brown by the tea which has been poured over them, are singing "Oft In the Stilly Night."

Stephen "waited for some moments, listening, before he too took up the air with them. He was listening with pain of spirit to the overtone of weariness behind their frail fresh innocent voices. Even before they set out on life's journey they seemed already weary of the way. . . ." And he is setting out on the same journey, with wings of wax. Stephen, though a believer—he never loses his faith, he denies it—is an anti-Christ and has his precursor, his John the Baptist, to make his way straight for him. He does not love any of his classmates and Cranly is the only one in whom he has confided. He has told Cranly all his sins and his soul-searchings. He asks himself:

> Why was it when he thought of Cranly he could never raise before his mind the entire image of his body but only the image of his head and face? Even now against the grey curtain of the morning he saw it before him like the phantom of a dream, the face of a severed head or death mask, crowned on the brows by its stiff black upright hair as by an iron crown?

At last he has a conversation with Cranly in which the way he is to go is revealed to him:

> —It is a curious thing, do you know—Cranley said dispassion-ately—how your mind is supersaturated with the religion in which you say you disbelieve. Did you believe in it when you were in school? I bet you did.—
>
> —I did—Stephen answered.
>
> —And were you happier then?—Cranly asked softly—happier than you are now, for instance?
>
> —Often happy—Stephen said—and often unhappy. I was some one else then.—
>
> —How some one else? What do you mean by that statement?
>
> —I mean—said Stephen—that I was not myself as I am now, as I had to become.—Not as you are now, not as you had to become—Cranly repeated—Let me ask you a question. Do you love your mother?
>
> Stephen shook his head slowly.
>
> —I don't know what your words mean—he said simply.
>
> —Have you ever loved any one?—Cranly asked.
>
> —Do you mean women?—
>
> —I am not speaking of that—Cranley said in a colder tone.
>
> —I ask you if you ever felt love towards anyone or anything.—
>
> Stephen walked on beside his friend, staring gloomily at the foot-path.
>
> —I tried to love God—he said at length.—It seems now that I failed. It is very difficult. I tried to unite my will with the will of God instant by instant. In that I did not always fail. I could perhaps do that still.

In her *Seraphic Dialogues* St. Catherine of Siena tells us that it is impossible to love God directly; we must love Him through his crea-tures, our fellow-men. Stephen has tried to achieve the impossible. His "disordinate" love will, in the end, bring him to ruin. His sin is the same as Lucifer's; he has said what Lucifer said: "I will not serve."

Stephen's sin, intellectual pride, like all sin, begets in him a terrible restlessness. He is impelled to leave his home and college and seek a new life. His mother, as she puts his *secondhand* clothes in order, prays that in his own life, away from home and friends, he may learn what the heart is and what it feels, but Joyce has given us to understand that this will never happen. Stephen has told Cranly that he is not afraid to make a mistake, "even a great mistake, a lifelong mistake and perhaps for eternity, too."

These two passages throw considerable light on Joyce's intentions. He was a good classicist and had been steeped in Greek mythology. He was also one of the most conscientious literary craftsmen that ever lived. He was not likely to begin his action on a Greek myth without realizing its full implications, nor could he have been guilty of the kind of cheap "modernistic" invention that characterizes Jean-Paul Sartre's play *Les Mouches*. In that play the Eumenides descend to the hero level and after an unconvincing struggle, follow him off the stage like whipped curs. In Joyce Furies remain Furies. The story follows the myth to its unhappy end. Stephen's father, Dedalus, the artificer, is a man of the nineteenth century. His skepticism and materialism have helped to construct the labyrinth from which both he and his son are trying to escape. Mr. Dedalus escapes through this love and of his fellow men. When Stephen goes with his father to his father's college he is amazed at his father's love for his old cronies—there was not one of his set, Simon Dedalus tells his son, who did not have some talent, some merit that lifted him above the ordinary. Stephen, listening, feels that his own heart is as cold as the craters of the moon; the only one of his classmates with whom he is intimate is Cranly and they are intimate only because Cranly feels an almost scientific curiosity about the workings of Stephen's mind. Mr. Dedalus escapes from the trap which his own hands have built, as Dedalus escaped as old. But Dedalus' son, Icarus, flies too near the sun. The wings which his father have made for him are only of wax. They melt under the sun's fierce heat and he falls into the sea and is drowned.

I suspect that Joyce's novel is sounder theologically than a novel by a contemporary novelist which deals with the same situation: a soul choosing damnation. I think that one reason why *The Portrait of The Artist As a Young Man* is superior is that Joyce is convinced that his hero is damned. The other writer, Graham Greene, seems to me to be in some doubt himself as to the outcome of his action, and his book ends in an anticlimax.

Henry Scobie, the hero of Greene's *The Heart of the Matter,* is a major in the British police force of a colonial port—a place where a noise on the tin roof means that a vulture has settled down for the night. Scobie is a long-suffering, much-harassed man who longs only for peace. He sometimes dreams of it. Greene says that

> Once in sleep it had appeared to him as the great glowing shoulder of the moon heaving across his window like an iceberg arctic and destructive in the moment before the world was struck.

We are given to understand that Scobie might have been a different man if his little daughter had lived. But she is dead when the action begins. The only person for whom he now feels any affection is his native servant, Ali, who has been with him for fifteen years, longer than he has been married. He does not love his wife. The only time he is able to endure her is when he feels pity for her. Pity—aside from his attachment to Ali and to his dead daughter—is the only emotion he feels towards any human being, although he is scrupulously consider- ate and just in his dealings with his colleagues and with the natives over whom he has supervision. His wife, who has an annoying habit of hitting the nail on the head, sometimes refers to the fact that he does not love her and says that she would like to go away so he can find the peace of mind of which he is always dreaming. Scobie feels so sorry for her that he goes against his principles and puts himself in the power of a native gangster, Yusef, by borrowing from him the money for her passage to South Africa. She no sooner gets there than she realizes that she should not have left her husband and takes the next boat back.

It is too late. The events which will lead to Scobie's ruin have already been set in train. Yusef has begun to blackmail him and he has become involved in an adulterous love affair. A ship is wrecked off the coast. A young Englishwoman is one of the few persons who survive forty days in open boats. Her name is Helen Rolt and she is brought on the scene half-dead, or, at least, unconscious, one hand clasping a stamp album. At first glance she seems just the girl for Scobie. Her interest in stamp collecting—the album is the only possession she has saved—might make us think that the blood ran calmly in her veins, but as soon as she gets her strength back she is just like every other woman who fails to find love where it has been promised, suspicious, jealous and, finally, given to the same kind of tantrums that Scobie's wife has. Between the two women Scobie's sufferings are so acute that he no longer dreams of peace but actively desires damnation. He has a vision of ultimate happiness: being "alone, with the rain falling, without love or pity."

His wife has come back anxious to devote herself to him and wants to seal what she thinks of as their reconciliation by them taking Communion at the same time. He has sworn to his mistress that he will never desert her and he puts off the ordeal as long as he can, until, driven by what Greene calls "that terrible promiscuous passion which so few experience," pity, he goes with his wife to Mass and, kneeling at the rail, makes one last attempt at prayer, offering up his own damnation for the two women for whom he has never been able to feel any emotion livelier than lust or pity.

I take it that Mr. Greene means us to accept Scobie as a hero, a man who would not only give his life but would risk damnation for his fellow creatures. There have been saints who have told God that they were willing to be damned if their damnation would save their fellow creatures, but they made this prayer out of love, not out of pity. Scobie is a Manichaean hero, engaged from the first in the kind of denial of the natural order that can end only in despair. He admits to himself that he has never loved his wife but he has "taken a terrible private vow to make her happy." He denies the natural order by attempting the impossible; we can only assure people that we love them, we cannot assure their happiness. Greene has a curious paragraph in which he celebrates despair:

> He would still have made the promise even if he could have foreseen all that would come of it. He had always been prepared to accept the responsibility for his actions, and he had always been half aware how far *this* action might carry him. Despair is the price one pays for setting oneself an impossible task. It is, one is told, the unforgiveable sin, but it is a sin the corrupt or evil man never practises. He always has hope. He never reaches the freezing point of know-

ing absolute failure. Only the man of good will carries always in his heart this capacity for damnation.

Joyce's novel ends dramatically on the note of eternal damnation. Joyce does not need to tell us the kind of life Stephen will lead; it is explicit in the action. Greene's action goes on for several chapters after Scobie has committed suicide. The last chapter is an argument between his wife and their priest, Father Rank, as to whether or not he is damned. When Louise Scobie says, "It's no good even praying," Father Rank says: "For goodness' sake, Mrs. Scobie, don't imagine that you—or I—know a thing about God's mercy." When she begins, "The Church says . . ." he replies, "The Church knows all the rules. But it doesn't know what goes on in a human heart. . . . It may seem an odd thing to say when a man's as wrong as he was—but I think, from what I saw of him, that he really loved God." To which the wife replies: "He certainly loved no one else." "And you may be in the right of it there, too," Father Rank says.

The ending is so inconclusive that there has been arguments about whether Scobie was bound for Hell or Purgatory—an argument which Evelyn Waugh once tried to settle by taking a cigar out his mouth long enough to say: "Where is Scobie? In Hell, of course." My own feeling is that in *The Heart of the Matter* Mr. Greene's craftmanship would have been better if reenforced by sounder theology; one should not have to ask oneself exactly how a book ends. The ending should seem the only one possible. Greene's book ends with an anticlimax because Scobie tries to "eat his cake and have it, too" maintaining what we are told is theologically impossible, that he loves God even if he cannot love his fellow men.

In the light of what Maritain has said, I should like to glance at the work of three other novelists. They are: George Bernanos, François Mauriac, and Evelyn Waugh.

Bernanos fills me with more awe than almost any of my contemporaries. No other novelist, except Dostoevesky, has been so bold in exploring the frontiers of the human spirit. The divinity in man seems to be his chief preoccupation, even, when as in *Sous Le Soleil de Satan*, he is writing about the Devil. He tells us the kind of things the saints tell us and in the same authentic accents. As a result, he has a tremendous power, a whole register, so to speak, that is out of the reach of most of his fellow novelists. A writer like Ernest Hemingway seems flat and one-dimensional beside him. Even William Faulkner in his flights, often sounds a note that is strained beside Bernanos's organ tones. And yet I think that Faulkner is, on the whole, a more Christian writer.

Maritain says the novel differs from other forms of literature:

> In having for object not the manufacture of something with its own special beauty in the world of *artefacta* . . . but the conduct of human life itself. . . . It may therefore be understood how honest, universal and authentic the novelist's realism ought to be: only a Christian, nay a mystic, because he has some idea of *what there is in man* can be a complete novelist.

Maritain makes some further remarks about art in general which, I think, apply to the novel as well as any other form of art. Art, he says, must be "gratuitous" and "disinterested" and goes on to explain what he means by these terms:

> In the actual production of the work the virtue of art has only one object, the good of work to be done; to make matter replendent with beauty, to create a thing in accordance with the laws of its being. . . . At the same time its desire is that there shall be nothing in the work eluding its control, that it alone shall regulate the work directly, handle it and shape it.
>
> There are many ways of failing to obtain this "gratuitousness." A man may think, for example, that excellent moral intentions may make up for the deficiencies in the craft of the inspiration, and are sufficient for the construction of the work. Or a man might go so far as to alter the work itself as the rules and the determined way of art require it to be, by the forcible application of alien elements.

Faulkner's *As I Lay Dying* seems to me an example of the kind of work of art Maritain is talking about, a work which is "gratuitous" and "disinterested" and a work which is important in the history of the novel as an art form. With it he takes his place among the writers whom Ezra Pound has called "the innovators," men who have presented "the conduct of human life" in a way in which it has not been

316   🖉 Caroline Gordon

presented before, men who, as it were, have originated a new vehicle for its presentation. In *As I Lay Dying*, Faulkner shows a dramatic grasp as firm and almost as comprehensive as James's and a faithfulness in rendition moment by moment that has been surpassed only by Joyce. Two main currents of fiction meet in this admiral work, which—to change the figure—resembles in its action a football game in which passing, signals, and foot-work are all faultless, each character taking the ball from the character who precedes him and running his required number of yards. The result is action that is as brilliant, as dense and seemingly as credible as life itself, a work that is not only "gratuitous" and "disinterested" but created "in accordance with the laws of its own being."

Bernanos dazzles us by showing us cloud-wrapped heights but he never, for me, at least, achieves the "honest, universal, and authentic realism" in which Faulkner excels.

His novel, *La Joie*, for instance, is the kind of concept that comes only to a first-rate imagination—the life and death of a saint. On the surface, the life of Chantal de Clergerie, like that of any well-brought-up, dutiful young—French!—girl. But the Russian chauffeur, sent to summon her to lunch one day when she has not heard the bell, finds her praying, her eyes wide open, a strange expression on her face, and realizes her secret and when she will not be blackmailed, murders her. This is what we are tempted to do to saints, I suppose, and this is the bold, simple outline of Bernanos's story. A writer this gifted might have had difficulty in persuading us that this young girl was a saint or that a man hated her enough to murder her because she was a saint. But Bernanos makes us believe that Chantal's life and death were as he says they were. What gives us pause is the Abbé Cénabre. The Abbé Cénabre, who appears in another novel of Bernanos's, is a priest who has lost his faith without leaving the Church or relinquishing his priesthood, and has confided his terrible secret to only one person, the Abbé Chévance, Chantal's confessor, and he suspects that when the Abbé Chévance was dying he confided it to Chantal. The spectacle of Chantal's life and martyr's death unhinges his reason and he falls in a fit on the floor beside the body, crying "Pater Noster" in "a superhuman voice," to die later in an asylum for the insane. The action would be more aesthetically satisfying if Bernanos had more regard for his craft, whose first requirement is the contrivance of the illusion of life. It took Lambert Strether several months to find out what kind of woman Madame de Vionnet was. Yet her whole character is revealed—if he had had the wit to read it—when she first comes on the scene:

> . . . dressed in black, but in black that struck him as light and transparent; she was exceedingly fair, and, though she was as markedly slim, her face had a roundness, with eyes far apart and a little strange. Her smile was natural and dim; her hat not extravagant; he had only perhaps a sense of the clink, beneath her fine black sleeves, of more gold bracelets and bangles than he had ever seen a lady wear.

The roundness of her face, her "strange" eyes, the bracelets and bangles that she wears under her "fine, black sleeves," all tell us—after the event, the way life usually tells us—that though conventional by upbringing and inclination, she is, nevertheless, a woman who is capable of having an illicit love affair. But the part the Abbé Cénabre plays in *La Joie* is not prepared for in such painstaking and realistic fashion; his name is not even mentioned until the last part of the book.

If fiction has for its primary concern "the conduct of human life itself" no pains are too great to achieve the desired effect, no pains too small, which is, perhaps, one of the reasons why Maritain says that only a Christian can be "a complete novelist"—even if he be Christian only "in hope." A pagan, attempting to write fiction, is handicapped by the lack of example. Minerva sprang full-grown from the head of Jove, and was not Bacchus taken out of the side of his father's leg? But Christ spent nine months in the Virgin's womb and thirty years in solitude and obscurity. It is the fiction writer's arduous task to imitate, on however lowly a scale, the patience that stooped low enough to lift up a fallen universe. For that patience no detail is too insignificant and no effect will have its full dramatic value unless prepared for. (If Our Lord had begun His ministry with His Transfiguration His Incarnation would doubtless not have been complete. Ford Madox Ford used to say that the worst horror story he knew was the one about the man who was visiting in a country house strange to him and, being wakeful and wanting to smoke in bed, was appalled at having an unseen hand offer him a match. I do not think that there is as wide discrepancy between these two examples as may at first appear. At any rate, I believe that each of them has significance for the writer of fiction.)

François Mauriac has lately been awarded the Nobel prize for imaginative literature. This strikes me as astonishing. Mauriac's novels aroused my admiration long before he was awarded this prize, but the admiration is always mixed with exasperation. Mauriac and Bernanos have opened up to the contemporary novelist who takes his art seriously whole vistas that, in our time at least, remain almost unexplored. Secrets of the human heart seem to have been revealed to each of them that do not seem to have been revealed to writers as great as Balzac or George Eliot. The future of the novel as an art form will be glorious indeed, if any young writer has the strength and daring to follow in their footsteps. But why are they not better artists? Why is Mauriac's art not more like that of the bee—to use Maritain's figure? Everything the bee makes is perfection for the purpose to which it will be put. Art is made by human beings but it should always be approaching perfection. Mauriac's novels are crudely put together; he has little regard for his craft.

In *Le Noeud de Vipères*, he tells his story in the first person. Henry James called this "one of the most barbarous of devices," yet scored one of his greatest triumphs with it in "The Turn of the Screw." The inventions, the devices which serve a novelist best grow, usually, out of his necessity. A writer wants to get something over that he feels nobody else has ever got over, but the conventions of the craft, the very medium itself all seem against him. He stands with his back to the wall, straining at his bonds and, suddenly bursting them asunder, evolves a new device which will serve fiction writers to come for many a year. But he has to feel his bonds constricting him before he can burst them. The great revolutionaries in the arts have been those who take the limitations of their medium seriously. Flaubert was such a writer, James was such a writer. So is William Faulkner. But Mauriac, as far as I can judge, has given little thought to the fundamentals of his craft, the basic problem of viewpoint, for instance. He adopts a viewpoint, uses it long as it suits his convenience, then flings it down to adopt another, seemingly without taking into account the effect such shifts may have on the structure of his novel.

The story of *A Knot of Vipers* is told in the journal in which the old miser, Louis, records his hate of the members of his family. He feels that his revenge will come when they read the journal after his death. But his wife dies first! In the fireplace in her bedroom he finds great masses of charred paper and deciphers enough of what has been written on the paper to discover that she, too, kept a journal. He discovers, too, that his miserliness and his infidelities have caused her all her married life to "be racked by passions that only God can master"—in short that she has longed for his love.

At sixty-eight he feels the "wild delight" that a man might feel at setting out on what promises to be a splendid life. In thinking of his family as *A Knot of Vipers* he has chilled his own life-blood so that, until now, he has hardly lived at all. But his wife is dead. His children and servants—he has as friends—are accustomed to thinking of him as "a monster of solitude and indifference." How can he swim against the stream impose on them the vision of the person he is and always has been? He feels that for this "some especial strength" is needed.

> Yes, but what strength? The aid of some person, of some one in whom we might all have been reunited, of some one who would, in the eyes of my family, have guaranteed the victory which I had won over myself, of some one who would stand my witness, who might relieve me of my hideous burden, and bear it on his own shoulders.

Mauriac's theme is on the grand scale—a dramatization of the redemption of a human soul—but many of his crucial scenes are marred by careless execution. He literally will not give the reader time to take in what is happening. And the whole action is made to turn on coincidence. The husband and wife each reveals his soul through the medium of a journal. It is hardly likely that two people would keep such journals simultaneously. Mauriac fails to convince me that they did.

There is in every artist a still, small and at times intensely disagreeable voice. This monitor has perhaps advised Mauriac that this action is not convincing. He has written an irritable preface to *Le Noeud de Vipères* in which, it seems to me, he shifts the blame to his readers:

> The man here depicted was the enemy of his own flesh and blood. His heart was eaten up by hatred and by avarice. Yet, I would have you, in spite of his baseness, feel pity and be moved by his predicament. All through his dreary life squalid passions stood between him and that radiance which was so close that an occasional ray could still break through to touch and burn him; not only his own passions, but, primarily, those of the luke-warm Christians who spied upon his actions, and whom he himself tormented. . . .
>
> It was not money that this miser really treasured, nor, in his blind fury, was it vengeance that he sought. What is was that he truly loved you may discover who have the strength of mind, and the courage, to follow his story to the end, to that ultimate moment of confession which death cuts short.

Oscar Wilde, who, like King Charles II, uttered words wiser than his acts, says, "He who speaks a word loses faith." He is referring to the risk the imaginative writer runs if he talks about his conception while it is in the process of execution, but the contriver of illusion who yields to the temptation to thrust his head out from behind the curtain and explain to the audience what is going on runs a risk that is almost as great. If he speaks a word he is likely to shatter the audience's faith in his illusion. It takes a great deal more strength and courage to write a novel than to read one. Yet there have been great novelists—Henry James, for example—who could justly complain of never having been properly read. But Mauriac, in explaining in his preface what his story is about, is confessing his own weakness, his own lack of courage, not the reader's. He ought not to have to tell us what his story is about. That ought to be implicit in the action.

Mauriac's work might, I think, be compared with that of another Nobel prize-winner, William Butler Yeats. Yeats was not an avowed Christian. He even dabbled in magic for many years, but his artistic triumphs are still solidly based on the natural order. *In Memory of Major Robert Gregory* shows the poet just moved into the old tower which is to be his new home and thinking of the friends whom he would like to have sup with him. The poem, after he has called them all to mind, turns into an elegy on the friend whom of all men he has ever known he found most naturally good. He defines Robert Gregory's character in terms of *objects* he loved:

> For all things the delighted eye now sees
> Were loved by him; the old storm-broken trees
> That cast their shadows upon road and bridge;
> The ford where drinking cattle make a stir
> Nightly, and started by that sound
> The water-hen must change her ground;
> He might have been your heartiest welcomer.

That kind of patient, passionate portrayal of natural objects is a recognition of the natural order which I can only call Christian, "Christian in hope." Mauriac's loftiest edifices, lacking such a solid foundation, seem always on the verge of toppling. The lurid flames that light up his scenes make them appear less rather than more substantial. He has said that he regrets that he does not find human nature more admirable but that he must portray it as he sees it. One wonders if he would not be a better novelist if he found it more *natural*?

The novelist's foremost concern, certainly, is human nature or, as Maritain puts it, "the conduct of human nature." But Nature in itself is not Art! In this connection I think that the French philosopher has said something else that is of practical value to the novelist:

> In our time the *natural* gift is lightly taken for art itself, especially if it be disguised in clever faking and a voluptuous medley of colours. Now a natural gift is merely a prerequisite condition of art, or again a rough sketch (*inchoatio naturalis*) of the artistic habit. Such an innate disposition is clearly indispensable; but without a culture and a discipline which the Ancients considered should be long, patient and honest; it will never turn into art.

It seems to me that in America the natural gift, the innate predisposition to the writing of fiction has been too much emphasized, and has received too much encouragement. "Flaubert me no Flauberts," Thomas Wolfe, who lived and died an amateur writer, wrote Scott

Fitzgerald when Fitzgerald, overwhelmed with admiration for Wolfe's talent and appalled to reflect how much he had to learn, wrote, offering him advice. There is a feeling in the air that a novelist who admits that he has anything to learn about his craft is that much less of a novelist. As John O'Hara, who considers Ernest Hemingway a better writer than Shakespeare, puts it: "No can do, can teach." (Yeats, attempting to appraise himself as a writer, prophesied that he "would dine at journey's end with Landor and with Donne." Hemingway, attempting the same feat, repudiates the company of fellow writers and defines his own eminence in a figure from the prize-ring. He is not a master, learning what the masters who have gone before him have to teach, but a champion, taking them on, one by one, and defeating all of them except Tolstoi, with whom he has never been matched since they fight in different classes.) The brilliant but unschooled young fiction writer, James Jones, has already received so much praise, so much money for his amateurish efforts that it would seem almost impossible for him to turn into a real novelist. Writers like Somerset Maugham and Louis Bromfield have been so richly rewarded for peddling their natural gifts, "enhanced by clever faking and a voluptuous medley of colours," that neither of them has made a serious effort in years. I think that what I say of America holds true of England, too. Men like Joyce Carey and V. S. Pritchett are bad craftsmen. If there is any British novelist who has mastered any of the great lessons in technique that are to be learned from Henry James I do not know his name or his work.

A trend towards orthodoxy in religion has made itself felt, not only in the world at large by among fiction writers. Among Catholic novelists, Evelyn Waugh is conspicuous for his "honest" and "authentic" realism, but it is hard to consider him a complete novelist." His early novels are brilliant but fragmentary. His characters are not presented in the round but in cinematic flashes. Miss Runcible, sitting up in a hospital bed smiling deliriously, bowing her bandaged head to imaginary visitors:

> Darling . . . how too divine . . . how are you? . . and how are you? .
> . . how angelic of you all to come . . . only you must be careful not
> to fall out at the corners . . . . ooh, just missed it. There goes that

nasty Italian car . . . I wish I knew which thing was which in this car . . . darling do try and drive more straight, my sweet, you were nearly into me then. . . . . Faster.

Miss Runcible, her head cracked in a head-on collision between two automobiles, not knowing "which thing is which," is a brilliant symbol of our times, but she is not a character in fiction in the sense that Emma Bovary or Isabel Archer or Julien Sorel are characters. Mr. Waugh does not explore the consciousness of any one of his characters in these early books. He simply presents them acting in or being acted upon by events which arouse his righteous indignation. You might say that moral indignation is the hero and heroine of all his early novels. It is the only emotion which seems to feel is worth dealing with. As a result, his early novels are like splinters shattered from some marmoreal block whose outlines are so vast that he has not yet taken their measure.

Edmund Wilson, in a review of *Brideshead Revisited*, has complained that Waugh is not as brilliant, not as much fun to read since he "got religion." I think that Mr. Wilson may be right. Waugh is not as sure of himself as he was. He is out after bigger game and goes more cautiously than he used to. The wit which crackled in the early books is gone. Waugh has a new subject, which arouses not moral indignation but awe, a rendering of the mystery of human existence. Lord Marchmain, Lady Marchmain, Sebastian, Julia, Cordelia, Captain Ryder are all more mysterious and hence truer to life than his Ninas or Brendas or Adam Fenwick-Symeses. His realism has always been "honest" and "authentic," even when fragmentary. In *Brideshead Revisited* I think it approaches the universal. In this novel the whole action is permeated by a recognition, a love of the natural order which I do not find in Mauriac, Bernanos, or Greene. I think that he was "Christian in hope" long before he entered the Roman Catholic Church.

16

THE CATHOLIC NOVELIST
IN THE PROTESTANT SOUTH

FLANNERY O'CONNOR

In a letter on Christmas Eve of 1961, Caroline Gordon sent Jacques Maritain "peacock feathers from Flannery O'Connor's peacocks."[1] The gesture in itself seems a fitting introduction to the last essay of this volume. One of O'Connor's pleasures in the long battle with lupus that occupied her entire creative life from 1950 until her death in 1964 was raising peacocks on her mother's farm, Andalusia, outside Milledgeville, Georgia. Who would have thought that the last Agrarian would be a bespectacled Catholic woman, incapable of crossing a room without crutches, who wrote her fierce—and fiercely Southern—stories in a milieu she understood with unsparing insight. To think that feathers from O'Connor's birds made their way to the old philosopher in France, where Allen Tate first had his vision of the French peasants and their long unbroken tradition, moves into circles of gift-giving too graceful for commentary.

Like Gordon, O'Connor was never a literary critic in the way Tate or Ransom were. She did a good deal of eclectic reviewing for the Georgia Bulletin, *a Catholic publication, and she gave occasional talks on the art of fiction, among other things. The pieces collected in* Mystery and Manners *(1969)—the present one from a lecture she gave at Georgetown in 1963—reveal something of what informs her*

---

1. *Exiles and Fugitives*, 79.

consciousness of her craft. In this case, she returns to the advantage of the South for the storyteller, the primary boon being the omnipresence of the scriptures in the Southern imagination: "The Hebrew genius for making the absolute concrete has conditioned the Southerner's way of looking at things. That is one of the reasons why the South is a storytelling section. Our response to life is different if we have been taught only a definition of faith than if we have trembled with Abraham as he held the knife over Isaac." Sally Fitzgerald's publica-tion of O'Connor's letters in The Habit of Being *(1979) introduced O'Connor's wryly comic and highly opinionated personal voice to those who knew her stories—and also gave some sense of how O'Connor dealt with living under Abraham's knife herself. In her introduction, Fitzgerald cites Maritain's* Art and Scholasticism *from the under-lined copy O'Connor had left in her house. Drawing on Maritain's explanation of habitus, she writes that O'Connor not only acquired the "habit of art," but also "a second distinguished habit, which I have called 'the habit of being': an excellence not only of action but of interior disposition and activity that increasingly reflected the object, the being, which specified it, and was itself reflected in what she did and said."[2] Part of what she reflected was the South, whose character she sums up thus: "a distrust of the abstract, a sense of human depen-dence on the grace of God, and a knowledge that evil is not simply a problem to be solved, but a mystery to be endured."*

In the past several years I have gone to speak at a number of Catholic colleges, and I have been pleased to discover that fiction seems to be important to the Catholic student in a way it would not have been twenty, or even ten, years ago. In the past, Catholic imagination in this country has been devoted almost exclusively to practical affairs. Our energies have gone into what has been necessary to sustain exis-tence, and now that our existence is no longer in doubt, we are begin-ning to realize that an impoverishment of the imagination means an impoverishment of the religious life as well.

---

2. O'Connor, *Habit of Being*, xvii.

I am concerned that future Catholics have a literature. I want them to have a literature that will be undeniably theirs, but which will also be understood and cherished by the rest of our countrymen. A literature for ourselves alone is a contradiction in terms. You may ask, why not simply call this literature Christian? Unfortunately, the word Christian is no longer reliable. It has come to mean anyone with a golden heart. And a golden heart would be a positive interference in the writing of fiction.

I am specifically concerned with fiction because that is what I write. There is a certain embarrassment about being a storyteller in these times when stories are considered not quite as satisfying as statements and statements not quite as satisfying as statistics; but in the long run, a people is known, not by its statements or its statistics, but by the stories it tells. Fiction is the most impure and the most modest and the most human of the arts. It is closest to man in his sin and his suffering and his hope, and it is often rejected by Catholics for the very reasons that make it what it is. It escapes any orthodoxy we might set up for it, because its dignity is an imitation of our own, based like our own on free will, a free will that operates even in the teeth of divine displeasure. I won't go far into the subject of whether such a thing as a Catholic novel is possible or not. I feel that this is a bone which has been picked bare without giving anybody any nourishment. I am simply going to assume that novelists who are deeply Catholic will write novels which you may call Catholic if the Catholic aspects of the novel are what interest you. Such a novel may be characterized in any number of other ways, and perhaps the more ways the better.

In American Catholic circles we are long on theories of what Catholic fiction should be, and short on the experience of having any of it. Once when I spoke on this subject at a Catholic university in the South, a gentleman arose and said that the concept *Catholic novel* was a limiting one and that the novelist, like Whitman, should be alien to nothing. All I could say to him was, "Well, I'm alien to a great deal." We are limited human beings, and the novel is a product of our best limitations. We write with the whole personality, and any attempt to circumvent it, whether this be an effort to rise above belief or above background, is going to result in a reduced approach to reality.

But I think that in spite of this spotty and suspect sophistication, which you find here and there among us, the American Catholic feels the same way he has always felt toward the novel: he trusts the fictional imagination about as little as he trusts anything. Before it is well on its feet, he is worrying about how to control it. The young Catholic writer, more than any other, is liable to be smothered at the outset by theory. The Catholic press is constantly broken out in a rash of articles on the failure of the Catholic novelist: the Catholic novelist is failing to reflect the virtue of hope, failing to show the Church's interest in social justice, failing to portray our beliefs in a light that will make them desirable to others. He occasionally writes well, but he always writes wrong.

We have recently gone through a period of self-criticism on the subject of Catholics and scholarship, which for the most part has taken place on a high level. Our scholarship, or lack of it, has been discussed in relation to what scholarship is in itself, and the discussion—when it has been most valuable—has been conducted by those who are scholars and who know from their own experience what the scholar is and does.

But when we talk about the Catholic failure to produce good fiction in this country, we seldom hear from anyone actively engaged in trying to produce it, and the discussion has not yielded any noticeable returns. We hear from editors, schoolteachers, moralists, and housewives; anyone living considers himself an authority on fiction. The novelist, on the other hand, is supposed to be like Mr. Jarrell's pig that didn't know what bacon was. I think, though, that it is occasionally desirable that we look at the novel—even the so-called Catholic novel—from some particular novelist's point of view.

Catholic discussions of novels by Catholics are frequently ridiculous because every given circumstance of the writer is ignored except his Faith. No one taking part in these discussions seems to remember that the eye sees what it has been given to see by concrete circumstances, and the imagination reproduces what, by some related gift, it is able to make live.

I collect articles from the Catholic press on the failures of the Catholic novelist, and recently in one of them I came upon this typical sentence: "Why not a positive novel based on the Church's fight for social justice, or the liturgical revival, or life in a seminary?"

I take it that if seminarians began to write novels about life in the seminary, there would soon be several less seminarians, but we are to assume that anybody who can write at all, and who has the energy to do some research, can give us a novel on this or any needed subject— and can make it positive.

A lot of novels do get written in this way. It is, in fact, the traditional procedure of the hack, and by some accident of God, such a novel might turn out to be a work of art, but the possibility is unlikely.

In this same article, the writer asked this wistful question: "Would it not seem in order now for some of our younger men to explore the possibilities inherent in certain positive factors which make Catholic life and the Catholic position in this country increasingly challenging?"

This attitude, which proceeds from the standpoint of what it would be good to do or have to supply a general need, is totally opposite from the novelist's own approach. No serious novelist "explores possibilities inherent in factors." Conrad wrote that the artist "descends within himself, and in that region of stress and strife, if he be deserving and fortunate, he finds the terms of his appeal."

Where you find the terms of your appeal may have little or nothing to do with what is challenging in the life of the Church at the moment. And this is particularly apparent to the Southern Catholic writer, whose imagination has been molded by life in a region which is traditionally Protestant. The two circumstances that have given character to my own writing have been those of being Southern and being Catholic. This is considered by many to be an unlikely combination, but I have found it to be a most likely one. I think that the South provides the Catholic novelist with some benefits that he usually lacks, and lacks to a conspicuous degree. The Catholic novel can't be categorized by subject matter, but only by what it assumes about human and divine reality. It cannot see man as determined; it cannot see him as totally depraved. It will see him as incomplete in himself, as prone to evil, but as redeemable when his own efforts are assisted by grace. And it will see this grace as working through nature, but as entirely transcending it, so that a door is always open to possibility and the unexpected in the human soul. Its center of meaning will be Christ; its center of destruction will be the devil. No matter how this view of life may be fleshed out, these assumptions form its skeleton.

But you don't write fiction with assumptions. The things we see, hear, smell, and touch affect us long before we believe anything at all, and the South impresses its image on us from the moment we are able to distinguish one sound from another. By the time we are able to use our imaginations for fiction, we find that our senses have responded irrevocably to a certain reality. This discovery of being bound through the senses to a particular society and a particular history, to particular sounds and a particular idiom, is for the writer the beginning of a recognition that first puts his work into real human perspective for him. What the Southern Catholic writer is apt to find, when he descends within his imagination, is not Catholic life but the life of this region in which he is both native and alien. He discovers that the imagination is not free, but bound.

For many young writers, Catholic or other, this is not a pleasant discovery. They feel that the first thing they must do in order to write well is to shake off the clutch of the region. They would like to set their stories in a region whose way of life seems nearer the spirit of what they think they have to say, or better, they would like to eliminate the region altogether and approach the infinite directly. But this is not even a possibility.

The fiction writer finds in time, if not at once, that he cannot proceed at all if he cuts himself off from the sights and sounds that have developed a life of their own in his senses. The novelist is concerned with the mystery of personality, and you cannot say much that is significant about this mystery unless the characters you create exist with the marks of a believable society about them. The larger social context is simply left out of much current fiction, but it cannot be left out by the Southern writer. The image of the South, in all its complexity, is so powerful in us that it is a force which has to be encountered and engaged. The writer must wrestle with it, like Jacob with the angel, until he has extracted a blessing. The writing of any novel worth the effort is a kind of personal encounter, an encounter with the circumstances of the particular writer's imagination, with circumstances which are brought to order only in the actual writing.

The Catholic novel that fails is usually one in which this kind of engagement is absent. It is a novel which doesn't grapple with any particular culture. It may try to make a culture out of the Church, but this is always a mistake because the Church is not a culture. The Catholic novel that fails is a novel in which there is no sense of place, and in which feeling is, by that much, diminished. Its action occurs in an abstracted setting that could be anywhere or nowhere. This reduces its dimensions drastically and cuts down on those tensions that keep fiction from being facile and slick.

The Southern writer's greatest tie with the South is through his ear, which is usually sharp but not too versatile outside his own idiom. With a few exceptions, such as Miss Katherine Anne Porter, he is not too often successfully cosmopolitan in fiction, but the fact is that he doesn't need to be. A distinctive idiom is a powerful instrument for keeping fiction social. When one Southern character speaks, regardless of his station in life, an echo of all Southern life is heard. This helps to keep Southern fiction from being a fiction of purely private experience.

Alienation was once a diagnosis, but in much of the fiction of our time it has become an ideal. The modern hero is the outsider. His experience is rootless. He can go anywhere. He belongs nowhere. Being alien to nothing, he ends up being alienated from any kind of community based on common tastes and interests. The borders of his country are the sides of his skull.

The South is traditionally hostile to outsiders, except on her own terms. She is traditionally against intruders, foreigners from Chicago or New Jersey, all those who come from afar with moral energy that increases in direct proportion to the distance from home. It is difficult to separate the virtues of this quality from the narrowness which accompanies and colors it for the outside world. It is more difficult still to reconcile the South's instinct to preserve her identity with her equal instinct to fall eager victim to every poisonous breath from Hollywood or Madison Avenue. But good and evil appear to be joined in every culture at the spine, and as far as the creation of a body of fiction is concerned, the social is superior to the purely personal. Somewhere is better than anywhere. And traditional manners, however unbalanced, are better than no manners at all.

The writer whose themes are religious particularly needs a region where these themes find a response in the life of the people. The American Catholic is short on places that reflect his particular religious life and his particular problems. This country isn't exactly cut in his image. Where he does have a place—such as the Midwestern parishes, which serve as J. F. Powers' region, or South Boston, which belongs to Edwin O'Connor— these places lack the significant features that result in a high degree of regional self-consciousness. They have no great geographical extent, they have no particularly significant history, certainly no history of defeat; they have no real peasant class, and no cultural unity of the kind you find in the South. So that no matter what the writer brings to them in the way of talents, they don't bring much to him in the way of exploitable benefits. Where Catholics do abound, they usually blend almost imperceptibly into the general materialistic background. If the Catholic faith were central to life in America, Catholic fiction would fare better, but the Church is not central to this society. The things that bind us together as Catholics are known only to ourselves. A secular society understands us less and less. It becomes more and more difficult in America to make belief believable, but in this the Southern writer has the greatest possible advantage. He lives in the Bible Belt.

It was about 1919 that Mencken called the South the Bible Belt and the Sahara of the Bozarts. Today Southern literature is known around the world, and the South is still the Bible Belt. Sam Jones's grandma read the Bible thirty-seven times on her knees. And the rural and small-town South, and even a certain level of the city South, is made up of the descendants of old ladies like her. You don't shake off their influence in even several generations.

To be great storytellers, we need something to measure ourselves against, and this is what we conspicuously lack in this age. Men judge themselves now by what they find themselves doing. The Catholic has the natural law and the teachings of the Church to guide him, but for the writing of fiction, something more is necessary.

For the purposes of fiction, these guides have to exist in a concrete form, known and held sacred by the whole community. They have to exist in the form of stories which affect our image and our judgment of ourselves. Abstractions, formulas, laws will not serve here. We have to have stories in our background. It takes a story to make a story. It takes a story of mythic dimensions, one which belongs to everybody, one in which everybody is able to recognize the hand of God and its descent. In the Protestant South, the Scriptures fill this role.

The Hebrew genius for making the absolute concrete has conditioned the Southerner's way of looking at things. That is one of the reasons why the South is a storytelling section. Our response to life is different if we have been taught only a definition of faith than if we have trembled with Abraham as he held the knife over Isaac. Both of these kinds of knowledge are necessary, but in the last four or five centuries, Catholics have overemphasized the abstract and consequently impoverished their imaginations and their capacity for prophetic insight.

Nothing will insure the future of Catholic fiction so much as the biblical revival that we see signs of now in Catholic life. The Bible is held sacred in the Church, we hear it read at Mass, bits and pieces of it are exposed to us in the liturgy, but because we are not totally dependent on it, it has not penetrated very far into our consciousness nor conditioned our reactions to experience. Unfortunately, where you find Catholics reading the Bible, you find that it is usually a pursuit of the educated, but in the South the Bible is known by the ignorant as well, and it is always that *mythos* which the poor hold in common that is most valuable to the fiction writer. When the poor hold sacred history in common, they have ties to the universal and the holy, which allows the meaning of their every action to be heightened and seen under the aspect of eternity. The writer who views the world in this light will be very thankful if he has been fortunate enough to have the South for his background, because here belief can still be made believable, even if for the modern mind it cannot be made admirable.

Religious enthusiasm is accepted as one of the South's more grotesque features, and it is possible to build upon that acceptance, however little real understanding such acceptance may carry with it. When you write about backwoods prophets, it is very difficult to get across to the modern reader that you take these people seriously, that you are not making fun of them, but that their concerns are your own and, in your judgment, central to human life. It is almost inconceivable to this reader that such could be the case. It is hard enough for him to suspend his disbelief and accept an anagogical level of action at all, harder still for him to accept its action in an obviously grotesque character. He has the mistaken notion that a concern with grace is a concern with exalted human behavior, that it is a pretentious concern. It is, however, simply a concern with the human reaction to that which, instant by instant, gives life to the soul. It is a concern with a realization that breeds charity and with the charity that breeds action. Often the nature of grace can be made plain only by describing its absence.

The Catholic writer may be immersed in the Bible himself, but if his readers and his characters are not, he does not have the instrument to plumb meaning—and specifically Christian meaning—that he would have if the biblical background were known to all. It is what writer, character, and reader share that makes it possible to write fiction at all.

The circumstances of being a Southerner, of living in a non-Catholic but religious society, furnish the Catholic novelist with some very fine antidotes to his own worst tendencies. We too much enjoy indulging ourselves in the logic that kills, in making categories smaller and smaller, in prescribing attitudes and proscribing subjects. For the Catholic, one result of the Counter-Reformation was a practical overemphasis on the legal and logical and a consequent neglect of the Church's broader tradition. The need for this emphasis has now diminished, and the Church is busy encouraging those biblical and liturgical revivals which should restore Catholic life to its proper fullness. Nevertheless the scars of this legalistic approach are still upon us. Those who are long on logic, definitions, abstractions, and formulas are frequently short on a sense of the concrete, and when they find themselves in an environment where their own principles have only a partial application to society, they are forced, not to abandon the principles, but in applying them to a different situation, to come up with fresh reactions.

I often find among Catholics a certain impatience with Southern literature, sometimes a fascinated impatience, but usually a definite feeling that with all the violence and grotesqueries and religious enthusiasm reflected in its fiction, the South—that is, the rural, Protestant, Bible Belt South—is a little beyond the pale of Catholic respect, and that certainly it would be ridiculous to expect the emergence in such soil of anything like a literature inspired by Catholic belief. But for my part, I don't think that this is at all unlikely. There are certain conditions necessary for the emergence of Catholic literature which are found nowhere else in this country in such abundance as in the Protestant South; and I look forward with considerable relish to the day when we are going to have to enlarge our notions about the Catholic novel to include some pretty odd Southern specimens.

It seems to me that the Catholic Southerner's experience of living so intimately with the division of Christendom is an experience that can give much breadth and poignance to the novels he may produce. The Catholic novelist in the South is forced to follow the spirit into strange places and to recognize it in many forms not totally congenial to him. He may feel that the kind of religion that has influenced Southern life has run hand in hand with extreme individualism for so long that there is nothing left of it that he can recognize, but when he penetrates to the human aspiration beneath it, he sees not only what has been lost to the life he observes, but more, the terrible loss to us in the Church of human faith and passion. I think he will feel a good deal more kinship with backwoods prophets and shouting fundamentalists than he will with those politer elements for whom the supernatural is an embarrassment and for whom religion has become a department of sociology or culture or personality development. His interest and sympathy may very well go—as I know my own does—directly to those aspects of Southern life where the religious feeling is most intense and where its outward forms are farthest from the Catholic, and most revealing of a need that only the Church can fill. This is not because, in the felt superiority of orthodoxy, he wishes to subtract one theology from another, but because, descending within himself to find his region, he discovers that it is with these aspects of Southern life that he has a feeling of kinship strong enough to spur him to write.

The result of these underground religious affinities will be a strange and, to many, perverse fiction, one which serves no felt need, which gives us no picture of Catholic life, or the religious experiences that are usual with us, but I believe that it will be Catholic fiction. These people in the invisible Church make discoveries that have meaning for us who are better protected from the vicissitudes of our own natures, and who are often too lazy and satisfied to make any discoveries at all. I believe that the Catholic fiction writer is free to find his subject in the invisible Church and that this will be the vocation of many of us brought up in the South. In a literature that tends naturally to extremes, as Southern literature does, we need something to protect us against the merely extreme, the merely personal, the merely grotesque, and here the Catholic, with his older tradition and his ability to resist the dissolution of belief, can make his contribution to Southern litera-ture, but only if he realizes first that he has as much to learn from it as to give it. The Catholic novelist in the South will bolster the South's best traditions, for they are the same as his own. And the South will perhaps lead him to be less timid as a novelist, more respectful of the concrete, more trustful of the blind imagination.

The opportunities for the potential Catholic writer in the South are so great as to be intimidating. He lives in a region where there is a thriving literary tradition, and this is always an advantage to the writer, who is initially inspired less by life than by the work of his pre-decessors. He lives in a region which is struggling, in both good ways and bad, to preserve its identity, and this is an advantage, for his dra-matic need is to know manners under stress. He lives in the Bible Belt, where belief can be made believable. He has also here a good view of the modern world. A half- hour's ride in this region will take him from places where the life has a distinctly Old Testament flavor to places where the life might be considered post-Christian. Yet all these varied situations can be seen in one glance and heard in one conversation.

I think that Catholic novelists in the future will be able to rein-force the vital strength of Southern literature, for they will know that what has given the South her identity are those beliefs and qualities which she has absorbed from the Scriptures and from her own history of defeat and violation: a distrust of the abstract, a sense of human dependence on the grace of God, and a knowledge that evil is not sim-ply a problem to be solved, but a mystery to be endured.

If all that is missing in this scene is the practical influence of the visible Catholic Church, the writer will find that he has to supply the lack, as best he can, out of himself; and he will do this by the way he uses his eyes. If he uses them in the confidence of his Faith, and according to the needs of what he is making, there will be nothing in life too grotesque, or too "un-Catholic," to supply the materials of his work. Certainly in a secular world, he is in a particular position to appreciate and cherish the Protestant South, to remind us of what we have and what we must keep.

WORKS CITED

Brinkmeyer, Robert H. Jr., *Three Catholic Writers of the Modern South*. Oxford, MS: University of Mississippi Press, 2000.

Brooks, Cleanth, Jr. and Robert Penn Warren. *Understanding Poetry*. New York: Henry Holt and Company, 1938.

Cowan, Louise. "Nature and Grace in Caroline Gordon." In *Studies in Medieval, Renaissance, American Literature: A Festschrift*. Edited by Betsy Colquitt. Fort Worth, TX: Texas Christian University Press, 1971.

———. *The Southern Critics*. Dallas, TX: University of Dallas Press, 1972.

Davidson, Donald. *The Long Street*. Nashville, TN: Vanderbilt University Press, 1961.

———. "The 'Mystery' of the Agrarians." *Saturday Review of Books*, January 23, 1943: 6–7.

Davidson, Donald, and Allen Tate. *The Literary Correspondence of Donald Davidson and Allen Tate*. Edited by John Tyree Fain and Thomas Daniel Young. Athens, GA: University of Georgia Press, 1974.

Donaldson, Susan V. "Introduction." In *I'll Take My Stand*, by Twelve Southerners. Baton Rouge: Louisiana State University Press, 2005.

Genovese, Eugene. *The Southern Tradition: The Achievements and Limitations of an American Conservatism*. Cambridge, MA: Harvard University Press, 1994.

Greenblatt, Stephen. *Learning to Curse: Essays in Early Modern Culture*. New York: Routledge, 1992.

Hofstadter, Richard. *The Age of Reform: From Bryan to FDR*. New York: Vintage, 1955.

Huff, Peter A., *Allen Tate and The Catholic Revival*. Mahwah, NJ: Paulist Press, 1996.

Kirk, Russell. "Introduction." In *The Attack on Leviathan: Regionalism and Nationalism in the United States*, by Donald Davidson. Piscataway, NJ: Transaction Books, 1990.

Krieger, Murray. *The New Apologists for Poetry*. Minneapolis, MN: University of Minnesota Press, 1956.

Kunstler, James Howard. *The Long Emergency: Surviving the Converging Catastrophes of the Twenty-First Century*. New York: Grove Press, 2005.

Lentricchia, Frank. *After the New Criticism*. Chicago: University of Chicago Press, 1980.

Lytle, Andrew, and Allen Tate. *The Lytle-Tate Letters*. Edited by Thomas Daniel Young and Elizabeth Sarcone. Oxford, MS: University of Mississippi Press, 1987.

Maritain, Jacques. *The Dream of Descartes*. Translated by Mabelle Anderson. New York: Philosophical Library, 1944.

Maritain, Jacques, Raissa Maritain, Caroline Gordon, and Allen Tate. *Exiles and Fugitives: The Letters of Jacques and Raissa Maritain, Allen Tate, and Caroline Gordon*. Edited by John M. Dunaway. Baton Rouge: Louisiana State University Press, 1992.

O'Connor, Flannery. *The Habit of Being: Letters of Flannery O'Connor*. Edited by Sally Fitzgerald. New York: Farrar Straus Giroux, 1979.

Ransom, John Crowe. "Poetry: I, The Formal Analysis." In *Selected Essays of John Crowe Ransom*, edited by Thomas Daniel Young and John Hindle. Baton Rouge: Louisiana State University Press, 1984.

———. *Selected Letters of John Crowe Ransom*. Edited by Thomas Daniel Young and George Core. Baton Rouge: Louisiana State University Press, 1985.

———. *The World's Body*. Baton Rouge: Louisiana State University Press, 1968.

Rubin, Louis D. Jr., "A Critic Almost Anonymous: John Crowe Ransom Goes North" in *The New Criticism and After*, ed. Thomas Daniel Young (Charlottesville: University of Virginia Press, 1976), 1–21.

Tate, Allen. "Remarks on the Southern Religion." In *I'll Take My Stand: The South and the Agrarian Tradition*, by Twelve Southerners. Baton Rouge: Louisiana State University Press, 1977.

———. *Essays of Four Decades*. Wilmington, DE: ISI Books, 1999.

———. *Memoirs and Opinions: 1926–1974*. Chicago: The Swallow Press, 1975.

Warren, Robert Penn. *Democracy and Poetry*. Cambridge, MA: Harvard University Press, 1975.

———. *Selected Letters of Robert Penn Warren*. Edited by William Bedford Clark. 4 vols. Baton Rouge: Louisiana State University Press, 2000.

———. *The Legacy of the Civil War*. Lincoln, NE: University of Nebraska Press, 1998.

Wood, Sally. *The Southern Mandarins: Letters of Caroline Gordon to Sally Wood, 1937–1944*. Baton Rouge: Louisiana State University Press, 1984.

INDEX

343